THE
WATCHDOG GUIDE
TO GETTING A BETTER DEAL

David Berry

PENGUIN BOOKS
BBC BOOKS

Acknowledgements

Sorcha Berry-Varley, Shelley Bradley, Nicky Copeland,
Malcolm Stacey, Richard Thomas, Rose Anne Varley,
Geoffrey Woodruffe, the *Watchdog* team.

Published by the Penguin Group and BBC Enterprises Ltd
Penguins Books Ltd, 27 Wrights Lane, London W8 5TZ, England
Penguin Books USA Inc., 375 Hudson Street, New York 10014, USA
Penguin Books Australia Ltd, Ringwood, Victoria, Australia
Penguin Books Canada Ltd, 10 Alcorn Avenue, Toronto, Ontario, Canada
M4V 3B2
Penguin Books (NZ) Ltd, 182 – 190 Wairau Road,
Auckland 10, New Zealand
Penguin Books Ltd, Registered Offices: Harmondsworth,
Middlesex, England
First published by BBC Books, a division of BBC Enterprises Ltd,
and Penguin Books in 1994
0 14 024011 X

PENGUIN BOOKS
BBC BOOKS

THE
WATCHDOG GUIDE
TO GETTING A BETTER DEAL

David Berry has worked as a journalist specializing in social
and consumer affairs for fifteen years. He has written for
the *Guardian*, the *Independent*, the *Observer*,
the *New Statesman* and many other national newspapers
and magazines. He worked for five years as a senior
producer for BBC Radio 4's consumer and investigative
programmes *You and Yours* and *Face the Facts*.
He is currently working as a film director for *Watchdog*.
His last book, *How to Complain*, was published by
BBC Books in 1990.

CONTENTS

INTRODUCTION:
TEN WAYS TO GET
A BETTER DEAL

Did you know that:

▷ most high street shops will give you a discount if you can pluck up the courage to ask for one

▷ eight out of ten people lose money by not claiming compensation when they are hurt or injured

▷ if you buy a £1000 holiday and pay £1 of the cost by credit card and the rest by cheque and the holiday is a complete disaster, you can claim the whole £1000, plus any compensation due, from the credit card company as well as from the travel company

▷ you do not need a receipt to claim your money back if something goes wrong

▷ if a repairman does not turn up for an appointment and you have told him that you are taking a day off work to be there, you can claim back any pay lost from the repairman in compensation.

These are just five of the hundreds of tips you will find in this book to help you save money and get a better deal. The tips come from our experience at BBC Television's *Watchdog* programme during some 15 years of championing people's rights and investigating wrongs. Along the way, we have learned – mostly from our viewers' bitter experiences – about how people get taken advantage of in Britain today, how big the gap is between consumer rights and consumer reality.

On *Watchdog*, we have exposed villains and con men, dubious laws and bizarre trading practices. If the message has often seemed that you cannot really trust anybody, it has been a message that has come out of too many sad stories, too many people we have interviewed whose lives have been shattered, at least for a time, by believing what some salesperson said.

At times, however, it has all felt a little too negative. Our preoccupation as journalists with the big stories, the tales of the unusual, the stories that involve injury, distress and death – the stories, after all, that change laws and business practices – has meant that we have not focused as much on the small points of consumer advice, the tips that make all our lives more pleasurable and fun. This book restores the balance. It is all about the positive steps you can take to make sure you do not get taken for a ride.

A word of warning here. There are no magic secrets, no keys that can unlock closed doors. There are no words you can learn that will ensure you are always served first, that your complaint is always dealt with by the Managing Director, that the item you want to buy is always the best bargain in town. This book cannot tell you these secrets because they do not exist.

What do exist are some crucial maps – maps that describe the world of buying and selling, the tricks of so many different trades. Knowing them will not make you rich, but will save you a few pounds, perhaps more. Each chapter has been written to pass on some of the consumer wisdom and expertise that *Watchdog* has accumulated over the years. As well as informing you of your rights, we tell you how to go about getting them and warn you when it just does not seem worth the trouble.

First, here are ten general tips that are worth remembering in virtually every consumer situation. You may know most of them, but even the ones you do know are very easy to overlook in the heat of a dispute.

TEN WAYS TO GET A BETTER DEAL

Tip 1: know who can help you
It is worth knowing about the range of people who may be able to give you free advice about consumer problems: Citizens Advice Bureaux, local council's Trading Standards or Consumer Protection Department, local library, national consumer organizations, lawyers who offer cheap initial legal advice, trade associations, professional organizations and the many other more specialist sources of help that are mentioned throughout this book.

Tip 2: get and check references
Learn to pick people you can trust and try never to deal with people who do not have a recommendation from someone. If your friends or neighbours cannot help, always ask a tradesman for the names and addresses of a couple of past customers, and make sure that you contact them. Try to check any qualifications or membership of an association as some associations accept anyone as a member if they simply pay an appropriate fee, and some people continue to claim membership when they have left or been thrown out.

Tip 3: always take your time
Good salespeople never hurry you; bad salespeople try to clinch the deal. Resist. Buy things when you are ready. If

any salesperson does not behave completely graciously when you say you would like time to think, take this as an indication that they do not believe that their product is the best and you will come back to buy it.

Tip 4: complaining is fun

When something goes wrong, it is important to complain – not simply for yourself, but for other people as well. A well-founded complaint can make things easier for other people and can often lead to a genuine improvement in a product or service. But there is another reason to complain as well. Complaining can make an everyday experience slightly unusual and much more personal. It can be fun.

It is interesting, too, that when you complain about something that has gone wrong, shop assistants and salespeople change, often revealing their true colours. Fortunately for most British shops and companies these days, these colours are strong, bright, attractive ones. Their staff deal with complaints decently and well and you get glimpses of the personal nature of service on which all good businesses rely and depend. These glimpses often only emerge when there is a problem, so when you complain, you are often left with a much more positive view of the business and its staff than if you had had no problem at all. The most forward-looking companies realize this and have put much thought into their complaints procedures.

However, there are many companies that are still not so enlightened. When you complain to them, they will try to ignore your complaint, and deny your rights. Complaining to these companies can be even more enjoyable *if* you know your consumer rights and you enjoy the challenge of using those rights to get your money back.

Tip 5: learn how to bargain

A price is seldom fixed; it is just an invitation to buy. You can accept the invitation, but decline the price and put in an offer of your own. Whether or not someone accepts your offer is up to them, but, if you bargain quietly and politely and do not ask for too much, you will be surprised by what you can achieve. After all, if a shop makes 10 per cent profit from you instead of 25 per cent, it is better than not having sold the item at all.

Tip 6: cheques have their uses

If someone sends you a cheque in settlement of a dispute, keep it but do not cash it unless you are fully satisfied with the amount. If it is you who is in dispute with someone, send them a cheque for the money you think you owe them with a note on the cheque saying that it is in 'full and final settlement'. If they cash the cheque, you can then claim that they have accepted your offer and that the dispute has been resolved.

Tip 7: always get people's names

If someone will not give you their name, ring back and ask their manager why not. Managers are always very embarrassed by any of their staff behaving in this manner because it sounds like they have something to hide. Sometimes they do.

Tip 8: ask people why

If people will not help you, it is worth just asking them why not?

Tip 9: learn about the small claims court

With all its imperfections, the small claims procedure of the County court or the Scottish sheriff court is the single most important weapon people have in making sure that their rights are enforced. Find out where the nearest court is, learn how to use it and threaten its use when necessary. When you are in dispute with someone, picture yourself in the court explaining the situation to a district judge. Would they believe you or would they believe the other side? What evidence would convince a judge?

Tip 10: be aware of time
Sometimes you have more time than you think. For most common consumer complaints, you have up to six years to take action. However, once you have noticed something is wrong, the longer you leave taking action, the more likely it is that either you will forget about it or someone will argue that you should have acted before.

1

THE HARD SELL ...

Andrew Fitzgerald was one of a number of people taken in by a now defunct telephone car sales company called Autosearch Limited that used to operate from the Brunswick Centre, Liverpool. They rang Mr Fitzgerald after he had put an advertisement in the local paper to try and sell his car. Autosearch promised him that they could get a buyer very quickly indeed by their process of matching buyers and sellers nationwide by computer. Mr Fitzgerald said he would like more details and the company sent them to him, along with an invoice for £70. When Mr Fitzgerald queried this, Autosearch claimed that he had agreed over the phone that they would sell his car, an 'agreement' that was news to him. So, he just ignored the demand. He was then sent a court summons and it took him a year and an appearance in court (Autosearch did not turn up) to clear the matter up.

Anne Edwards is an 87-year-old grandmother who lives in sheltered accommodation in Putney. She suffers terribly from arthritis and has tried all kinds of treatment for the pain. So, she expressed interest when she was introduced to a saleswoman who showed her a thermal pad that, she said, would ease Mrs Edwards' pain. She believed what the saleswoman said and paid £400 for the pad out of money she had saved for her funeral. The saleswoman agreed that Mrs Edwards could have her money back if she was not happy after a month's trial. The pad made no difference to Mrs Edwards' pain, but the saleswoman then went back on her word and refused to give her a refund. Mrs Edwards only got her money back after *Watchdog* pursued the case.

Ella Kolodzeij looks after her four children and her elderly mother by herself. Like many people, she worries about being burgled and so when a salesman called offering a free professional survey of her house, she agreed to it. After several hours of high-pressure sales talk, Mrs Kolodzeij found herself agreeing to the installation of a security alarm system in her house, a security alarm system that she did not need and could not afford. But she had been convinced by the salesman that it was a bargain.

Three different stories, three different salespeople but all with the same result: a customer's trust was abused. Mr Fitzgerald, Mrs Edwards and Mrs Kolodzeij ended up owing money for items that they neither wanted nor needed. They ended up regretting ever getting into conversation with the sellers and determined not to trust any kind of sales talk again.

HOW TO TELL THE REPUTABLE FROM THE CROOKED

There are over a million people in Britain who earn their living by selling. Most of them see their job as one that simply provides people with information and advice about their company's products, but what they do is much more skilful and difficult than that. The most successful salespeople first create and satisfy a need for the product, and then they do more. They persuade their customers that they and their families deserve the product, that their life will be better if they buy it.

What distinguishes the honest salesperson from the crook is not so much the sales techniques involved, nor the salesperson's skill or ability to sell, although some crooks are so good at selling that you wish their talents could be harnessed to do something worthwhile. What marks out the unfair or crooked salesperson is how they deal with customers who change their minds. Good sellers realize that there will always be people who want to go back on a purchase – sometimes for good reasons, sometimes for no apparent reason at all. So, they promise a full refund if people are not satisfied and they *keep* this promise. Bad salespeople or poor shops or businesses do not like giving refunds. They use all kinds of legal and illegal ways to avoid giving any money back, even when a customer is fully entitled to it.

It is by no means easy to recognize the good salesman or woman from the bad. Below are ten pieces of advice written by experienced salespeople for new recruits. Five of them come from a perfectly reputable guide to selling on sale in bookshops, and the other five come from a particularly disreputable guide to selling dodgy timeshare apartments in the Canary Islands, but can you spot which ones come from which? They are surprisingly similar.

1 'Always let the prospective client tell you how he feels. Your mind must be geared to sell to this prospect.' ('Prospects' are potential customers.)
2 'If the order requires his signature, say "Would you kindly OK on this line ..." (Never ask for a signature, just ask the customer to OK it.)'

17

3 'As there is no cooling-off period, anyone found pitching cancellations will be fired immediately.'

4 'You should not always believe the reasons your prospects give you for not wanting to buy. They are often untrue.'

5 'The prospect who says he's not doing anything today is dead scared of doing just that. He knows he's the type that can't resist something good so he tries to put you off guard. Ignore this.'

6 'Eliminate "no" from your sales talk and replace it with two words "yes but ..."'

7 'Do not tell prospects they have to make a decision. No one likes to make decisions. Help them to choose. Making choices is easy.'

8 'It is important to be well-dressed. Dress in the latest fashion but with elegance and restraint.'

9 'The greatest single problem is a prospect saying he will think it over. When someone says this, reduce it to a specific objection and then deal with it.'

10 'Use phrases like "If I could offer you a special deal today ..." and "Is that the only thing stopping you from going ahead?" and "Aside from the money ..." Never say "contract" but say "agreement".'

Tips 1,2,4,6 and 8 are from the reputable sales guide. Tips 3,5,7,9, and 10 are from the dodgy timeshare outfit. The point is that all salespeople use similar tactics to close the sale, tactics that include a mixture of personal friendliness, psychology and strategy. The reputable salespeople say that they avoid pressure selling and that they never engage in the hard sell, but the truth is that it is very difficult to tell skilful persuasion from unfair pressure. Often the hardest sell comes with the sweetest, most considerate voice.

The rational response to all this (and perhaps it is the best response) comes from the cautious consumer. They refuse to buy from any salespeople. Instead, clutching their copy of *Which?*, they ignore any attempt by sales assistants to help them and always come back from shopping with this month's best buy. If their shopping is a little dull, at least they are never ripped off.

Another response people adopt is to consider themselves immune to sales talk. Such people go along to time-share presentations to get the free gift at the end, and chastise other people for being taken in, for being 'so stupid'. This kind of consumer is a keen target for the clever salesperson because anybody can be persuaded to buy virtually anything if the situation is right, as most salespeople know.

For people who are not so fearful of sales talk or are not so arrogant as to think that they will never be taken in, here are some of the most common unfair sales techniques to look out for. See them as warning signals that apply even to the most blue-blooded of salespeople in the best department stores (many of these, after all, are on commission as well). Keep the following phrases in mind, especially when everything seems fine, you feel completely in control and, well, the salesperson is just so nice, so refreshingly different, that they are not really like a salesperson at all, but a friend, and ...

▷ Anybody who takes more than an hour to sell you
   something should not be trusted, however complicated
   their product seems to be. They are either terrible
   salespeople or, more likely, they are deliberately trying
   to wear your resistance down.

▷ Never invite anybody round who has phoned you up out of the blue.

▷ Before agreeing to see any salesperson in your home, find out the costs of rival products.

▷ Never, never sign then and there. All salespeople want you to agree to buy something before they leave and so there will always be promises of discounts, deals and special items for sale that are only available if you buy now. Ignore all of them – these offers will still be there the next morning and any salesperson who says they are not is lying. Insist on time to think.

▷ Beware of anybody who claims they are not really a salesperson, but, instead, is 'doing a survey', conducting some 'market research', or is a manager who 'does not normally make calls like this ...'. These are all tactics to make you think of the salesperson not as a salesperson but as a colleague or as a friend.

▷ Be wary, too, of special offers that are made because of your job or profession or because of where you live. There may indeed be an exclusive offer that is available to you and not to other people, but this does not mean that it is cheaper than other deals on the market that are *not* exclusive but are good value for everybody.

If you do end up buying something from a salesperson that you then regret, you have some protection but only in certain circumstances. If you have bought something in your own home and the salesperson did not have an invitation to call, you have a seven-day cooling-off period in which you can cancel the order and get your money back. This applies even if the item you bought has turned up at your door. If you have invited a salesperson to call, even by simply filling in a coupon, you lose these rights unless you buy the item on credit. Any credit deal arranged for you at home by a salesperson there with you has an automatic five-day cooling-off period. If you decide to cancel the credit, you also have the right to cancel your order.

You generally have no cooling-off rights if you buy something on company property – for example, in a shop, office or salesroom *even if* you pay by credit. So, be wary of any salesperson who wants you to sign an agreement not in your home but in the office or factory.

However, if anything you buy turns out to be faulty, you have the right to claim your money back under the Sale of Goods Act 1979 (see page 44). This applies, too, if the reason you bought something was due to a salesperson's promise that turns out to be far from the truth. The problem is that many of these promises are made verbally and never put in writing and shady companies will dispute that they were ever made. Make a note of any promise a salesperson makes that is important to you (for example, a money-back guarantee) and get them to sign the promise when you sign their piece of paper.

Finally, there is one golden rule about dealing with salespeople. Whatever they say, always keep in mind that their purpose in talking to you – their 'prospect' – is to close the sale with your money or your signature in their pocket. Most of them are far better at doing this than you might think. After all, it is their job.

2

HOW TO SPOT
A CON MAN

SOME TIPS ON HOW TO AVOID BEING TAKEN IN

Kevin Willington was a con man, a con man who dealt in the world of cheap travel. Now in gaol for fraud, what Mr Willington did was to advertise airline tickets that seemed to be a bargain. The tickets were not impossibly cheap, but just slightly cheaper than the best deals available through conventional agents.

He advertised these tickets in national and regional newspapers and magazines, in fact, in any publication that would accept his advertisements without needing money up front. Times were hard for newspaper advertising in the early 1990s and few turned him down.

At *Watchdog,* we first came across Mr Willington one Christmas when one of our viewers from Leicester, a local GP, rang the programme. The GP complained about a business called Travel Systems based in Wakefield. Its boss was someone called Kevin Willington. For £1500, Mr Willington had sold the GP two return tickets to New Zealand for the Christmas holidays. However, the tickets never turned up and when the GP rang the airline, the airline said that the tickets had not been paid for. The GP was furious and felt that Mr Willington had conned him. When we started looking into the affairs of Mr Willington, we thought so, too. Mr Willington had done this before.

A few years ago, he had set up a company called Speedlink UK Ltd that dealt in cheap courier tickets to Europe. Mr Willington sold a large number of tickets and some of his customers did travel, but 200 did not and they lost their money. When the company collapsed in 1988, it owed £250 000.

The Airline Ticket Fraud Squad, based at Heathrow Police Station, investigated Speedlink UK and the affairs of Mr Willington, the only effective director. They arrested him for fraud, but, when he was charged at the magistrates' court, Mr Willington applied for, and was granted, bail. In the year when he was awaiting trial, he caused havoc.

Leaving his base in South London, he moved first to Oxfordshire, then to Manchester and Leeds. Along the way, he set up five new travel businesses, ending up in Wakefield, where he started Travel Systems from a mailing address on the outskirts of town. During this time, he conned another 100 people out of some £100 000 before finally being sentenced at Middlesex Crown Court to 21 years imprisonment. With this kind of business history, how on earth did he get away with it?

Like all good con men, Mr Willington had a number of things going for him. He had, for example, a charming manner. People liked him, at least enough to do business with him. Then, too, he operated in a twilight trade known for its brinkmanship. The best bargains in airline tickets do actually come from small agents – often consisting of just one front person, a secretary and a fax machine. Sometimes there is not even a secretary. Mr Willington's way of doing business, therefore, did not seem that unusual. Finally, Mr Willington always offered his customers some kind of reassurance. He placed advertisements in reputable newspapers. His businesses accepted credit cards. Mr Willington claimed – falsely as it turned out – that he was a member of ABTA and ATOL (see pages 177-178) thus giving the strong impression that his tickets were protected. He had an office, a fax machine and secretaries but they were all part of an answering service he bought for a few pounds per month.

Everything seemed to add up, just as it seemed to do with all the other con men *Watchdog* has investigated over the years. Some people who bought tickets from Mr Willington did eventually receive them, after much persistence, but most never received anything for their money at all.

The worst thing about dealing with con men like Mr Willington is not losing your money, but losing your trust in other people. When you buy something from a shop or a business or an individual, you rely, more often than not, on their word. You trust that they will do their very best to keep their promises. Con men betray this trust, and they leave a very sour taste with their victims, the taste of betrayal.

The problem is not that there are too many fraudsters like Mr Willington around – quite the opposite; there are not enough of them. Con men like Mr Willington are quite rare. If they were more common, they would be far less successful for the simple reason that all of us would be much more on our guard. It would become commonplace not to do deals with anybody without written down promises, guarantees and safeguards.

Guarantees and safeguards like this, of course, do exist already, but most of us usually accept someone's word that they are in place and rarely check up, and most times this is fine. People in business are mostly honest, or at least honest enough not to lie or make promises that they have no intention of keeping. So, the con man prospers on the back of people's faith in human nature.

How can you avoid being taken in? There are no foolproof rules but here are a few suggestions.

▷ If you are dealing with someone new, a new builder or a new garage, for example, always ask for references from three old customers. If you do not get them, just refuse to do business. One villain *Watchdog* investigated tried to get round this by saying that he could not pass such names on because of customer confidentiality and the Data Protection Act. This is nonsense. You can give any customer's name to someone else if you have their permission and satisfied customers are usually delighted to pass their good experience on.

▷ Consider asking for a bank reference and, if you get one, ask your bank manager to interpret it for you. At the very least, you will find out how long the company has banked there and this will give you some idea about how established it is.

▷ Find out where the company office is and ring the office to check what kind of operation it is. Be wary of anybody who has a registered office abroad as they may be out of reach if anything goes wrong. Be wary, too, of anyone whose office is a box number or an answering service. You can find this out simply by asking whomever answers the phone if they are employed by the company or just take messages for them. There *are* reputable firms that trade in this way, but why risk it?

▷ Be wary, too, of phones that are never answered or go dead, constant changes of plans or excuses, endless sales, empty shelves, demands for a large amount of money up front – these are all signs that things are not quite what they seem.

▷ Finally, try to avoid paying for things in advance whenever you are dealing with somebody new to you. If you *do* pay in advance, always pay by credit card so that you can get your money back if things do go wrong.

These suggestions should help you spot the more obvious villains at least, but spotting the clever confidence trickster depends more on instinct than anything else.

One London company *Watchdog* investigated had a perfectly respectable office in a smart part of town. Their bank reference seemed fine. They even provided the name and address of a satisfied customer (the only one, as it turned out). However, after discovering dozens of complaints about the company, we decided to do a report about them. When we were filming outside their offices, their landlord came out and asked what we were doing. He said he did not know of any complaints, but he was sure that they were crooks. He did not have any evidence and they always paid their bills in time, but it was their style. Despite being charming, nobody who worked for them seemed particularly nice.

Someone's style can, in the end, be the tell-tale sign. Many estate agents lost money to Mr Willington, mentioned earlier, but one agent in South London did not. Everything Mr Willington told the agent checked out, but there was something about him that the agent distrusted. When he asked other people in his office, it turned out that nobody had liked Mr Willington when they had met him. So, the agent decided not to grant Mr Willington any credit and to insist that all money owing had to be paid well in advance. Unlike the other estate agents, this agent lost no money to Mr Willington.

NEW KINDS OF CON TRICKS

Con men will always be with us. Every trade, business and profession has its villains who use what often turn out to be quite remarkable levels of ingenuity and guile to get something for nothing.

Some businesses, however, seem to attract more con men than others. These are often businesses that exist on the margins of their trade, new business opportunities that usually involve some kind of direct selling of a product yet to be found in the shops. All this provides ample opportunity for someone to spread a web of unsubstantiated claims and promises, claims that are almost impossible to disprove and promises that may indeed turn out to be true.

Twenty years ago, con men flourished in the motor trade and in the building industry, particularly in the new home improvements trades. The names have become clichés: the used-car salesman, the cowboy builder, the dodgy double-glazing salesman, the roofer who knocks on your door and says you have some slates missing that he will replace very cheaply.

In the last decade, other trades and products have contributed more than their fair share of villains. The cowboy builder has been supplanted in popular mythology by the timeshare tout. Dodgy double-glazing salesmen seem less common these days than salespeople pushing dubious water purifiers, energy efficiency products and home security systems.

In the last few years, some new kinds of frauds have emerged that seem likely to offer continued opportunities for fraudsters to make easy money.

▷ *The Euro-con:* Catherine Kew invested her life savings of £45 000 in gemstones sold to her by a company of gem brokers in Holland that called itself the Royal Antwerp Group. The gemstones turned out to be worth a mere £2600, but Mrs Kew, like many other people, had been taken in by grand claims and keen salesmanship. Somehow, the claims seemed much more plausible coming, as they did, from the capital of the international jewel trade.

▷ *The franchise caper:* Eric Williams had a very good job in London, but he was desperate to move back to Liverpool where his family lived. So, he was attracted by an advertisement in a national newspaper placed by a company that claimed he could earn £60 000 a year in any part of the country. When Mr Williams phoned up, it turned out to be a franchise operation. For £6000, he could buy the rights to market the business in five areas of Liverpool with an expected turnover of over £61 000. The figures seemed impressive and Mr Williams paid up, but it proved impossible to make the franchise work. Like many poor franchise deals, it was not tried and tested. It was simply a good idea in theory that turned out to be a very poor idea in practice and Mr Williams paid the price. There are plenty of opportunities to make your fortune with a franchise, but also plenty of opportunities for rogues to exploit people's natural optimism and belief that they can make a go of a venture that never stands any chance of success.

▷ *The new miracle cures:* When the National Health Service (NHS) was established in 1948, it seemed that the age of magic potions and miracle cures promoted by quacks and charlatans had finally come to an end. Unfortunately, this faith was misplaced, particularly in three areas where it became clear that the NHS could do little: being overweight, chronic pain and psychological distress. Into these areas have come the new quacks and they have brought with them tales of new wonder foods, new kinds of apparatus that cure the pains modern drugs cannot reach, new mental techniques that banish misery and depression. People are desperate and so they get taken in. Their doctors, after all, can offer them very little.

HOW TO INVESTIGATE A VILLAIN

If you have been a victim of a con man or fraudster, one way you can get your own back is to investigate their activities. You may be able to uncover evidence of fraud or other offences. Trading standards officers and the police often do not have the time to follow up complaints unless there is some kind of systematic pattern, and you may be able to provide that pattern. Also, consumer programmes like *Watchdog* will be much more interested in your story if there is evidence that your complaint is not an isolated one.

Investigating people is certainly not as difficult as it

may seem and it can be great fun. It is a little like playing the private detective. Most con men are too arrogant to hide their tracks, so any dirt that is around usually rises to the surface. Where there is one complaint, there are likely to be others. First, however, an important word of warning: most con men are not violent themselves but some surround themselves with minders, usually local yobbos who can turn *very* nasty indeed, so *take very great care* and always *tell family or friends what you are doing.*

To find out any solid evidence of wrongdoing – or to trace someone who has vanished – will usually require some dogged detection. Like private detectives, you can pick up information from a wide variety of sources, but your success depends upon how persuasive you are in getting people to talk to you. Here are some leads.

TRADING STANDARDS DEPARTMENTS

Trading standards officers investigate consumer complaints, and their investigations are confidential. However, they can tell you if someone has been charged with a consumer offence or been found guilty in court. You may find that some officers are willing to share 'off the record' their concerns with you about someone on their patch who seems to have attracted a large number of complaints. The trading standards department most likely to be able to help you is the one located closest to the villain's address or headquarters.

COMPANIES HOUSE

If the business you have been dealing with is a limited company (it will say Ltd or plc after its name), you can find out some very useful information by contacting one of the search rooms of Companies House. There are search rooms in London, Cardiff, Edinburgh, Glasgow, Manchester, Birmingham and Leeds. If you go in person, you can look up any limited company on their computer for £2, but you will need their *company* name, not any trading name they might use. The computer will tell you the company number and address, whether it has been liquidated or not and the names and addresses of the directors.

For £2.50, you can also look up any individual and find out what directorships they may have. This search will also tell you if someone is a disqualified director. For £3, you can receive a microfilm copy of a company's full record, which will include its annual accounts. You can also order a copy of any document about a company over the phone: it will cost you £7 (they accept payment by credit card). The document you will want is a copy of the latest returns and accounts. The phone numbers of the search rooms can be found under Companies House in the phone book. Although the information can be invaluable, for smaller companies the financial information provided is limited and sometimes it is out-of-date or non-existent.

If Companies House has no information on a company, you have either got the wrong name or the business is not a limited company but a partnership or a sole trader. This means that the people behind the business are fully responsible for any debts the business has incurred, even if the business has ceased trading. (If a limited company is liquidated, there is very little chance of anybody getting any money they are owed back.)

COUNTY COURT JUDGMENTS

You can find out if a company or an individual has any County court judgments against them by writing to the Registry of County Court Judgments (send them the name plus a fee of £4.50 for judgments for England and Wales or £4.50 for judgments made in the sheriff courts of Scotland). You must be sure of the *full* name of an individual or a company and their address, otherwise they will be difficult to locate in the index.

BANKRUPTCY AND LIQUIDATION

Individuals and sole traders who cannot pay their debts become bankrupt. You can find out if an individual is bankrupt by writing to the Bankruptcy Search Room at the Insolvency Service in Birmingham. Again, you must have precise names as the search is done by computer, but there is no charge. If an individual is bankrupt, they are not allowed, by law, to be in effective charge of a company. Most bankrupts are discharged after three years.

If a limited company is insolvent and the directors know, it should usually cease trading. What happens after this varies. One option is that a creditor who has a debenture on the company's assets (usually a bank) can appoint an administrative receiver to run the company. The company continues to trade under the receiver's direction until it gets enough money to pay off its debts.

Another option is that the company can appoint a liquidator and go into voluntary liquidation. The liquidator, who must be a member of a professionally recognized body, is there simply to wind up the company. The liquidator collects any money available, cashes in any assets and pays the creditors in a strict order. Taxes are paid first, then employees, then secured creditors and, finally, unsecured creditors (most customers are likely to be unsecured and so unlikely to get any money when a company is liquidated as they will be a long way down the queue to receive what remains). The liquidator should send a report about the company to the Insolvency Service and can also report the company to the Crown Prosecution Service if there is evidence of fraud or other criminal activities.

Finally, the creditors of a company can petition a court to have the company wound up. If the petition is granted, the court appoints an official receiver and the company goes into receivership. The receiver's pay is paid by the court and a report on each director is sent automatically to the Insolvency Service, which can apply to a court to have any director banned from holding directorships for up to 15 years. You should be able to find out if a company has been liquidated or a director banned by contacting Companies House.

All these procedures would seem to make the running down of a business a strictly controlled affair, but, unfortunately, there are numerous problems. For a start, the chances of a rogue director escaping a banning order are quite high. A 1993 report by the National Audit Office concluded that only one in every ten directors whom receivers felt were unfit to run a company were actually banned. The rest were allowed to carry on in business.

Many directors who do end up with a ban simply ignore their banning order because they know their chances of detection are small. According to the National Audit Office, only 50 per cent of banned directors are listed on public records. Finally, although banned directors are not allowed to make any important business decisions in any new company, there is nothing stopping them being employed as 'consultants'.

If you are able to discover any major irregularities, you should let the Companies Investigation Branch know. They have the power to conduct a confidential investigation into a company's affairs, although they use this power rarely. They will not tell you if they are investigating any company you are concerned about, although the odds are against it as they only investigate a handful of companies every year.

Finally, people who lose money as a result of a company that goes bust are often disturbed by the ease with which the company's directors can start again with a new business and no debts. Most of the time, this is perfectly legal, although the Insolvency Act 1986 forbids directors of a liquidated company from setting up a new company with a similar sounding name. This law is, however, widely ignored and so-called 'phoenix' companies (firms that emerge from the ashes of the old) still flourish.

OTHER SOURCES OF INFORMATION

Unlike government or council officials or the police, local *journalists* will usually be quite happy to share information with you – especially if it will lead to a story in their paper. Most will have access to a cuttings library that could turn up other stories of rogue companies or what individuals have done in the past, for example, court appearances.

Another useful source is your local *reference library*, which may have issues of the local or regional paper indexed so you can check names.

TRACKING PEOPLE DOWN

Often the problem is not one of discovering more evidence of villainy, but simply that of tracking down someone who has fled. You should not ignore the more obvious places – telephone directories, electoral roll (available at your local reference library), chambers of commerce, professional or trade associations – but you are far more likely to pick up information informally by what private detectives call 'leg work'.

Call at any address you have and talk to anybody you can find, there or next door. People will generally tell you things if you approach them in the right way, especially if they have their own suspicions about the company or the individuals or if they are owed money themselves. Neighbours are useful sources of information, as are business competitors.

In the end, you are limited only by your imagination and guile. You *can* track down most con men if you can simply spare the time to do so, but do take care.

3

SHOPPING

BARGAIN HUNTING

Gary Woffinden, Andy Peake and Cathy Ives are all bargain hunters. Whenever they go shopping, they are looking for that extra pound off and they are not afraid to ask for it – not just in street markets but in well-known high street shops as well. They see a price tag merely as an opening bid that is certain to be reduced in the end. So Cathy Ives has negotiated deals on children's clothing, carpets and a three-piece suite. Andy Peake has bought clothes and sports equipment for virtually half-price. Gary Woffinden has managed 20 per cent discounts on a microwave, radio cassette, a portable TV and kitchen cutlery. How do they do it?

Over the years, they have all developed their own bargaining techniques. They have learned what to bargain for, when to bargain for it and how to clinch the deal. Some of these techniques – and more besides – are listed below, but the most important thing these three bargain hunters have going for them is not any particular technique, but an attitude. They are simply unafraid to ask for money off. They do not find it embarrassing and they are not bothered about someone turning them down because they can always shop elsewhere, although most of the time there is no need.

If you want a real bargain, you have to be prepared to negotiate and this means being prepared for the occasional shop assistant looking down their nose at you and saying that their shop does not give discounts, even for cash. Some people find that they enjoy bargaining and take such set-backs in good spirit; for other people, it takes the pleasure out of shopping – just try it and see.

SOME HANDY BARGAINING TIPS

▷ Shops give discounts by reducing their profit margins. The profit margins vary for different goods – from 10 per cent or less on everyday items to 100 per cent or more on some luxury goods. A good general rule for bargaining is to try for 25 per cent off and settle for between 10 and 15 per cent.

▷ If you feel embarrassed about asking for a discount, an easy way to start is to ask if there is any reduction 'for cash'.

▷ Know when to buy. August, for example, is a bad time to bargain for a new car; try December instead. September is a good time to bargain for electrical goods, but Christmas is not. Some managers say that the end of the week or the end of the month is best because that is when sales targets have to be met and so any sale is welcome. Most bargain hunters, however, prefer Mondays or Tuesdays when shops are quiet and managers can give discounts without other customers realizing what is going on.

▷ Make clear to the sales assistant that you intend to buy something. The assistant must realize that if they do not get the sale, you will not be coming back and are likely to buy the item you want from the competition. (Useful words to use are 'today' and 'now' – for example, 'I would like to buy this hi-fi today.')

▷ Have a target price in your mind, but do not reveal it straight away. Let the sales assistant make the running, by saying that you need some 'help' with the price or by asking directly what kind of discount they are able to offer.

▷ An alternative strategy is to say simply that all you can afford for an item priced £350 is £275. Sometimes this can be very effective indeed.

▷ Allow the sales assistant a 'get out' so that he or she can pretend that they are not really giving you a discount. The classic word is 'cash' – often this can act as a trigger to discounts of 15 per cent or more even though it is unclear if the shop is gaining any real advantage by accepting cash rather than credit. Other useful phrases to use are 'end-of-line deals', or items that have been 'on display'. Again, this gives the shop an excuse to offer you money off (if the item you buy is really shop-soiled, though, make sure the discount you negotiate is substantial).

▷ Check out the extras that are available, the things that the shop can throw in with the item you want to buy. You will always (well, virtually always) be offered free batteries, accessories and delivery – but only if you ask for them. Be more ambitious by asking, for example, for free CDs with a CD player or free cushions with a settee.

▷ Do not just walk away when the shop assistant refuses any deal. It is still quite unusual for high street shops to be asked for a discount, so allow them some thinking time. Hang around the shop for a while or suggest they think about it while you go for a cup of coffee.

▷ Finally, try and *enjoy* the experience. If you are always pleasant, polite and see it all as a bit of a game, shop assistants will enjoy it, too, and they will be more likely to give you a discount as a tribute to your bargaining abilities.

WHEN A BARGAIN IS NOT A BARGAIN

While many shops do their best to pretend that they never give discounts, very few of them can resist enticing customers with bargains of their own. So there are new year sales, summer sales, special reductions, blue cross days, clearance sales and countless others. There are special offers and promotions with free holidays as a prize – or, at least, it seems that they are free until you read the small print. If all else fails, many shops now fall back on the traditional price promise: if you can buy the product cheaper elsewhere, the shop will refund the difference.

Sometimes these sales and special offers *do* produce a bargain, but, most times, things turn out to be a disappointment. Sometimes the offers are completely misleading. (There is a useful, if somewhat obvious, tip when shopping at sales – it is always to look at the sale price of an item, not at its reduction because even at £50 off, some things can still be overpriced and poor value.)

Consumers do have some protection against misleading offers. The Consumer Protection Act 1987 made it a criminal offence to give a 'misleading price indication' and this Act applies to *all* prices, including those in sales. With the 1987 Act, there came a code of practice that spelled out what a misleading price indication might mean. So, for example, VAT must always be included in the price if the majority of customers are not trade. Words like 'worth' and 'value' should not be used to compare prices. Reductions must not be made without quoting the higher price, and the item should have been available at the higher price for at least 28 days. Products for which there are introductory offers must be offered at a higher price after the offer period ends. Free offers must state the conditions of the offer.

It is worth knowing all this and then being aware that the code does not have the full force of law. Shops do not have to follow it as long as they can show, if challenged, that their prices are not misleading. They are rarely challenged to do so.

The effect of all this is that there are a number of techniques used by shops, sometimes quite well-known shops, which are certainly very close to being misleading, but, at the moment are perfectly lawful. Here are a few:

▷ *The closing down sale:* Peter Allingham bought a carpet in a closing down sale from a shop in London's West End. Two years later, he was in the same London street and he noticed that the shop was still there and that it still had a closing down sale. There is nothing illegal about this because shops can have as many closing down sales as they want, as long as the prices are genuine reductions.

▷ *The price promise:* Geoff Howes bought an answering machine from a major electrical store. He was reassured by the shop's price promise, which stated that it would refund the difference if a customer could buy something cheaper in any shop nearby. Two days later, Mr Howes spotted the same answering machine

£5 cheaper in another shop, but, when he went back to the original shop, they refused to give him back the £5 because the other shop was one and a half miles away and not, in their terms, 'nearby'.

▷ *The special finance deal:* Be wary of any offer that applies not to the actual *price* of an item, but to the *credit* you can use to pay for it. Terms like 0 per cent interest may *seem* generous, but they often disguise the fact that the items to which they apply may be cheaper elsewhere. If anything is on offer at a very low interest rate, try asking for a discount instead.

Another problem is that most finance deals are often not quite what they seem. Always check the APR (see page 231) and ask the shop for a written quotation for the total amount you will have to pay. You may be surprised.

▷ *The free gift:* In the autumn of 1992, Hoover introduced a new promotion to boost sales of its appliances. The promotion seemed simple enough. Buy any Hoover appliance over £100 and you would get two free flights to America or Europe. Thousands of people took up the offer, far more than Hoover ever anticipated. Inevitably, the promotion fell apart, but, instead of trying to sort the mess out, the travel agents Hoover appointed tried to make it difficult for people to claim their flights. They then tried to ensure people bought accommodation, insurance or car hire through them before they got the flights they wanted. Hundreds of people were left without the flights they had been promised and so many of them had to cancel arranged family visits, holidays and even honeymoons booked on the basis of Hoover's special offer.

Other companies have made sure that their special offers are not so oversubscribed. Their strategy is quite simple. They make any offer *look* more enticing than it actually *is*. Customers discover the drawbacks only after they have bought the product and read the terms and conditions of the offer in the small print. So, for example, 'two flights for the price of one' has a condition in the small print that requires you to pay for one full standard fare on a flight for which most other passengers have received a discount. 'Free hotel accommodation' comes with a condition that you have to buy several expensive hotel meals. 'Free five-year insurance' just guarantees *parts* that go wrong, not the *labour* needed to effect the repair. 'Free travel' involves staying at particular hotels at a rate much higher than other tourists can negotiate. (When you see the word 'free', always ask yourself 'Why?')

QUALITY AND VALUE

Getting a good deal when shopping is not simply about finding the best bargains but about discovering the items that seem to be the best value – items that last longer, perform better or give more pleasure. It is about buying things that are of a good quality for the price. Serious shoppers develop a talent for recognizing quality, for sniffing out the best buy. The rest of us read *Which?* magazine.

Which?, the magazine of the Consumers Association, did not invent product testing and 'best buys'. Both ideas were American and were first developed by an economist called Stuart Chase and a mechanical engineer called F. J.

Schlink. They wrote a book in 1927 entitled *Your Money's Worth*. It revealed to the American public the detailed research done by the American Government in order to make sure that it obtained the best deal from its commercial suppliers. Their book led both to the formation of the Consumers Union in the USA and, in 1937, to the American magazine *Consumer Reports* – the magazine that started regular product testing.

The British magazine, *Which?*, came later. It was set up with the help of two Americans in the late 1950s but it has certainly made up for any lost time. *Which?* provides the accurate independent research that people need to be able to find items that offer the highest quality and the best value. Virtually every women's magazine and colour supplement now has a best buy section – almost all of them inspired by *Which?* It is probably the best magazine of its kind in the world.

Its only drawbacks are its expense (the annual subscription costs about £50) and, something more difficult to define, a kind of super-rationality. Reading *Which?* leaves you with little sense of the psychological reality of shopping where intangibles like colour, name and status of a product, along with the pleasure of buying from one shop rather than another, all matter – sometimes a great deal. In its efforts to make shopping a *science*, where value can be measured and quantified, *Which?* sometimes ignores shopping as an *art* and a pastime where the pleasure may well wholly come from buying something that certainly is *not* a best buy.

There are other indications of quality and value apart from *Which?* and its various competitors. The British Standards Institution's Kitemarks indicate that a product has been independently tested and meets standards of safety, quality or performance. Another quality mark used is the Gold Award, given by the Furniture Industry Research Association to items that have met a wide range of standards concerning durability and design. Other safety marks are described on page 73.

WHEN THINGS GO WRONG:
THE SALE OF GOODS ACT 1979

Even with the best deals from the best shops, something will go wrong at some time or another. When it does, there is one extremely useful law that gives considerable protection to consumers: the Sale of Goods Act 1979. This law states that all goods sold by any trader must meet three reasonably simple conditions. The goods must be:

▷ of merchantable quality
▷ as described
▷ fit for purpose.

If they do *not* meet all these conditions, then you are entitled to your money back. As, on average, one in ten people who buy things from shops find something that is not right, it is worth having these three phrases at your fingertips. What do they mean?

Merchantable quality means that an item must meet the standard you would reasonably expect it to meet given its price. An expensive washing machine should work to a higher standard than a cheaper one, but *both* should wash clothes. In practice, if an item is not of merchantable quality, it is usually because it is faulty.

As described means that anything you buy must match any description given to you of it. This could be an advertisement, a catalogue or even a sales assistant's promise.

Fit for purpose means that anything you buy must do any job either a sales assistant told you it would or any job you said to an assistant you wanted it for.

As long as you act swiftly to reject any item you buy from a trader that does not meet one of these three conditions, you are entitled to your money back. This is not all. You may also be entitled to:

▷ *compensation* for any damage the item caused when it was in your possession
▷ *the cost* of hiring a replacement
▷ *postage* or travel costs incurred in bringing the item back to the trader.

The only conditions are that these costs are reasonable and that you do not try to profit from your complaint.

These three conditions in the Sale of Goods Act apply not only to conventional shops, but to market stalls, mail-order companies – in fact, anybody who can be classified as a trader. The Act also applies to items bought in a sale, to items bought as part of a bargaining deal and to second-hand goods, although, obviously, the standard expected of these goods is lower than that expected of those bought new.

HOW TO COMPLAIN
ABOUT FAULTY GOODS

The most difficult thing about complaining about faulty goods is making sure you actually do it. Many people who have good cause to complain never seem to get around to it; they just forget or simply cannot be bothered. This is a shame because the act of complaining is pretty straightforward and may well benefit others as well as yourself. Here is how to do it.

▷ *Contact* the shop as soon as you can and ask to speak to the manager. If you cannot get back to the shop quickly, drop them a note explaining what has happened and tell them you will be calling in soon to sort the matter out.

▷ *Explain* what the problem is and say to the shop what you would like them to do about it.

▷ If what is wrong is a *minor* fault, it is usually best to allow the shop time to repair it or put it right.

▷ If what is wrong is *major*, think about whether you would prefer your money back or a repair. If you accept a repair, get the shop to sign a note written on your receipt saying that you are reserving your right to your money back if the repair turns out to be unsatisfactory.

▷ If the repair is going to take some time, make sure the shop supplies – or pays for – a temporary replacement.

▷ Claim any *expenses* and compensation that have arisen as a direct result of the faulty item.

With most shops – certainly most well-known shops – this will be the end of the matter. They will be annoyed and embarrassed that something they have sold has caused problems and they will arrange to give your money back or repair the item. Occasionally, however, things turn out to be a little more difficult. The shop may dispute either the fault or that you are entitled to your money back. Here are some things that might be said.

▷ *They say you must have a receipt:* To claim your money back from a trader, you have to show proof of purchase. This does not, however, have to be a receipt. You could provide a credit card slip or a cheque stub or, indeed, just the word of someone you were shopping with at the time. You could also see if the sales assistant who sold you the item remembers the sale. If you have none of these, it is still worth just giving your word to the manager that you bought the item recently in their shop. Few shops will dispute this.

▷ *They say the fault was not there when you bought it:* What you need to establish is that the fault is an inherent defect and not one caused by your misuse. So, you should suggest that the item is tested either by the shop or by another specialist trader. Make clear to the shop that you will be claiming back any money you will have to pay for the testing if the item does turn out to have inherent defects. (Sometimes testing can determine the nature of a fault. Sometimes, however, this proves impossible. If the testing produces an ambiguous result, there is little you can do, apart from appealing to the trader's good nature. It is up to you to prove an item was faulty when you bought it, not up to the trader to prove that it was not.)

Another argument occasionally put forward by shops is that you did not follow the instructions properly. What you have to show then is either that the instructions are unreasonable or that you *did* follow them and the fault still occurred. If the instructions are incorrect, it will be in both the shop's and the manufacturer's interests to sort the matter out.

▷ *They say the fault was pointed out to you:* If this is true, then you are not entitled to your money back as you were well aware of the condition of the item before you paid your money. The shop could also argue that the faults were so obvious that you should have noticed them when you bought the item. You would have to show the opposite.

▷ *They say you have to take it up with the manufacturer:* Under the Sale of Goods Act 1979, your contract is with the shop, not with the manufacturer. You should remind them gently about this and tell them that *they* are responsible for dealing with the problem, not the manufacturer. If the shop then suggests that you should claim back under the manufacturer's guarantee, decline the offer and say that you would like the shop to deal with it instead.

Unfortunately, many sales assistants in even the most reputable department stores confuse their shop's legal obligations with manufacturers' guarantees. So, you may have to spend ten minutes or so establishing this difference in the sales assistant's mind while they increasingly come to regard you as an awkward customer. (For more on manufacturers and guarantees see page 51.)

▷ *They offer you a credit note but not your money back:* It is best not to accept the offer of a credit note unless you are very sure that you want to spend the money in that shop. Once you have accepted a credit note, your rights to a cash refund are cancelled.

▷ *The shop still does not budge:* If a shop still refuses to give you your money back, ask them to whom you should address a letter of complaint. Then go home and produce as professional a letter as you can muster. In your letter, go over your story again and say what you would like the shop to do. Try to make the letter as brief as you can, check there are no spelling mistakes and make sure that you have the right address. Quote the Sale of Goods Act 1979 and say that you will take them to the small claims court if they do not deal with the matter within 14 days. Send your letter recorded delivery, remind them that court action will cost them more money and ask them to whom the summons should be addressed.

If the shop still does nothing, go along to your County court (find their address in the phone book under 'Courts') and take out a summons against them (see page 270 for how to do this). When they receive a summons, most traders will accept defeat, if you have a good case, and pay up. It is always worth persisting with a complaint to the point of court action as some traders will only give refunds when they realize that you are determined not to give up.

There is one situation, however, when it is *not* advisable to push all the way to the doors of the County court for a refund. Shops do not quote it very often, but, when they do, they reveal the one major flaw in the Sale of Goods Act 1979 for consumers – the problem of 'acceptance' and time.

▷ *When you have accepted an item:* Leslie Bernstein from London bought a Datsun from a garage in Golders Green called Pampsons Motors. Four weeks and two short trips later, he heard a noise coming from the Datsun's engine when he was out driving. He pulled over to the hard shoulder and turned the engine off. When he tried to restart, the ignition was jammed.

The car, it turned out, had a seized camshaft. Mr Bernstein wanted to hand the car back to the garage and get his money back, but the garage refused. They were only prepared to repair the car, not give a refund. Encouraged by his daughter, who was a barrister, Mr Bernstein took the company to court, but he lost.

The Sale of Goods Act 1979 gives people a 'reasonable time' to discover any faults in something they have bought. In court, the Judge ruled that the four weeks Mr Bernstein had owned the Datsun *did* constitute a reasonable time under the Act and so he was deemed to have 'accepted' the car and lost his right to reject the Datsun and claim a refund. All he was entitled to under the Act was compensation and damages for the trouble the car had cost him. The compensation covered the cost of the repair.

The Bernstein case has become a famous one in consumer law. It is important because it says that people have quite a short amount of time to discover any fault in something they buy. They then lose their right to a refund even if they only become aware of the fault later. What this 'amount of time' is, nobody knows. It is not laid down in the Act and there have been very few cases in court to establish how long this might be. Presumably it will be different for a car, a clock or a washing machine.

The best rule of thumb is this: you can argue quite strongly for a refund during the first few weeks after you have bought a faulty item. You will probably get away with asking for one for the first few months, perhaps the first year, but, after that, you will have to settle for compensation.

CLAIMING COMPENSATION

When you claim compensation under the Sale of Goods Act, what you are claiming is the difference in value between the faulty item and the value it would have had if it had not been faulty. In practice, this adds up to a free repair. Here is what to do:

▷ contact the shop, explain the problem and ask them to repair your item free of charge

▷ if they ask you if it is under guarantee, tell them you are not claiming under the guarantee, but claiming compensation under the Sale of Goods Act 1979

▷ if they are not prepared to give you a free repair (and a replacement while they are doing the repair), tell them you will be claiming from them the difference in price between what the item is worth now and what it should be worth.

There are no time-limits for claiming compensation but you have to be reasonable. If a new kettle went wrong after six months, it seems perfectly reasonable to insist on compensation from the shop, which will usually mean they will repair the item free of charge. But if the kettle went wrong after a year or two, your right to compensation may well have been lost since kettles are often not expected to last much longer than this, especially if they have been heavily used.

MANUFACTURERS' GUARANTEES

'Guarantee', has echoes of both promise and safety net, and few people today will make any major purchase without making sure it has one. Guarantees or manufacturer's warranties are a big selling point, yet, all they offer is a free repair for a limited period of time – usually a year, occasionally two – and sometimes even this promise is hedged with conditions. The customer may have to pay postage or delivery charges and few guarantees will offer a replacement while the item is being repaired. In most cases, people are better off claiming a refund or compensation from the shop under the Sale of Goods Act. A manufacturer's guarantee or warranty can never take away these rights. It just gives another option that, most of the time, it is best to ignore. There is, however, one situation when a manufacturer's guarantee might prove useful and that is when a shop has gone out of business.

PRIVATE SELLERS

When you buy an item from a shop, it must be 'of merchantable quality', 'fit for purpose' and 'as described', but, when you buy something from a private seller – a friend, perhaps, or through a small ad in the newspaper – the item must only be 'as described'. If it turns out to be faulty, you cannot obtain a refund unless the seller told you it was in 'full working order'.

So, what you should do when you buy, say, a second-hand car (see also pages 170 to 172) privately is ask the seller about the item. Get them to describe it to you, preferably in front of a witness. If the seller turns out to be a trader in disguise, all your rights under the Sale of Goods Act 1979 apply. You should, by the way, always be very careful when buying any item from a private seller which could cause harm if it goes wrong, for example, car seats or electrical equipment. You have no guarantee that these meet the required safety standards, even if they are reputable makes, since they may well have been misused or worn out.

ALTERNATIVES TO COURT

Paying by credit card

If a shop refuses to give you a refund, there is an extremely useful alternative to court action. It only applies, however, to items costing more than £100 that are paid for in whole or in part by credit card. The Consumer Credit Act 1974 makes a credit card company jointly liable with a trader for a faulty item. This means that you can claim your money back from either the credit card company or the shop.

This part of the Consumer Credit Act always seems rather extraordinary. The credit card company almost certainly knew nothing about the item you bought, yet they are expected to take joint liability for any problems that emerge. Also you do not have to pay all or, indeed, most of the price of the item by credit card, as long as the *total* price is over £100 (there is a maximum limit of £30 000 per item and a limit of £15 000 paid by credit). Even if you paid just £1 of a £1000 item by credit card and paid the rest in cash, you can still claim the *whole* £1000 from the credit card company if the item turns out to be faulty, *plus* any damages or expenses incurred.

If you have paid less than £100 for goods by credit card, try and claim your money back from the credit card company if your goods never arrived. The companies are under no legal obligation to refund your money, but often they will under complicated 'chargeback' rules.

All this applies to personal (not business) credit cards and store-cards. It does not apply to charge cards like American Express and Diners Cards although they will often give refunds to their card-holders in these circumstances. The Consumer Credit Act also does not apply to debit cards like Connect and Switch.

Claiming from a credit card company is usually more complicated than claiming from a shop. The credit card company will usually insist that you claim your money back first from the shop. Legally, this is up to you and not the credit company as 'joint liability' makes the credit card company and the shop equally responsible. In practice, it is usually easier to try the shop first. If this is not convenient – for example, if a shop is a long distance away or the trader has gone bust or disappeared – persevere with your claim against the credit card company and remind them of their legal obligations. You will eventually get your money back or, at least, you will in most circumstances.

Catherine Whitehorn was one of the unlucky ones. She bought a camera from a specialist shop when she was on holiday in America and she paid for it with her Barclaycard. Soon after she arrived home, the camera started going wrong. After weeks of fruitless correspondence with the shop, she tried to claim her money back from Barclaycard, but Barclaycard turned her down. They said that in their opinion joint liability under the Consumer Credit Act did not apply abroad – a fact that is disputed by consumer organizations. Mrs Whitehorn decided to take Barclaycard to the small claims court.

However, in court, Barclaycard changed their defence. They argued that although Mrs Whitehorn was a signature on the card, she was not the main cardholder. The main cardholder was her husband. So, Barclaycard said they had no contract with her, only with her husband. The Judge agreed and Mrs Whitehorn lost her case.

All this seems rather mean as Mr Whitehorn could quite easily have bought the item and signed the credit card slip instead. To confuse matters even further, Barclays say that, in practice, they *do* accept equal liability for anyone who is a signature on their cards, main card-holder or not. The reason they refused to pay Mrs Whitehorn was because she bought the item abroad, but Barclays' lawyers simply used the fact that she was not the main cardholder as an easy way to win the case.

Arbitration

Traders selling certain kinds of products – most notably photographic equipment, shoes, cars and motorcycles – may offer you the option of taking a dispute with them to arbitration rather than to the small claims court. This arbitration is usually independent but arranged through an appropriate trade association. Some arbitration schemes are approved by the Office of Fair Trading. They cost about the same as going to the small claims court.

You can only use arbitration if both you and the trader agree to it and you will almost certainly lose your right to go to court if you are not satisfied with the arbitrator's decision. Unless you have had a bad experience with your local small claims court or you cannot face going to court at all, only consider arbitration if you want to claim back more than the small claims limit – currently £1000 in England and Wales, £500 in Northern Ireland and £750 in Scotland (for more on arbitration, see page 293).

BRINGING SOMETHING BACK
THAT IS NOT FAULTY

The Sale of Goods Act 1979 only gives you a right to a

refund if something you buy is faulty. If you do not like it or it is the wrong size or wrong colour, then you have no rights by law. Most shops, however, will allow you to exchange an item if you bring it back straight away. Some shops will allow their store cardholders to be credited with no questions asked and other shops go further and promise a refund if you bring back an item you do not want as long as it is in a resaleable condition. If any trader promises you a refund if you are not happy with a purchase, either in writing or verbally, they have to honour it, by law. The difficulty with shady traders is that they make promises like this verbally. The promises are then denied when someone brings something back. Try to get any such promise in writing.

FALSE DESCRIPTIONS

The Sale of Goods Act 1979 is a *civil* law. If a shop breaks the law, the only remedy is to take them to the civil courts. If there was no intention to deceive, no criminal offence has been committed and the shop cannot be prosecuted.

The shop can be prosecuted, however, if it breaks the Trade Descriptions Act 1968, a *criminal* law. This Act, described as a 'consumers' charter' when it was first introduced, makes it an offence for a trader to describe falsely something they have for sale. So, describing a synthetic garment as wool or saying that a toy made in China was made in Italy or showing a misleading picture or illustration are all offences under this Act.

The Act applies to any description a trader might make. It could be in an advertisement or on a sign or label, in a shop window or just a verbal description from a sales assistant. If you think a trader has broken the Act, contact your local trading standards office. They will investigate and may well prosecute if there is evidence that the trader knew the description was false or did not bother to check whether or not the description was true.

ADVERTISEMENTS

Advertising works by influencing the decisions we make about what to buy. It usually does this by associating the product with some view of ourselves, often some dream or some image we would like to come true. We buy the product because we are attracted by the dream.

Some consumer advisers contrast the lack of reliable information provided in advertisements with the carefully sifted objective analysis in a *Which?* report or that of its competitors. Their conclusion is that advertisements are of little help in making the best choice about what to buy.

Of course, there is some truth in this. Finding out about what is available and what is recommended by experts is the only way to make sure you get a good deal for expensive purchases like washing machines and cars, but, for everyday items, advertisements, particularly television advertisements, can be very useful indeed. This is partly because they tell you about new products that you may not have seen before and may not have tried and partly because of something else.

If you go into a small shop, a corner supermarket, for example, or a small hardware store, you are confronted by a number of different and some quite obscure brands.

Which one do you choose? The advantage of choosing the most heavily advertised brand is that at least you can be reasonably sure that the product is safe and hygienic. Companies that advertise heavily usually have some kind of quality control, if only to protect their name.

If you are unhappy with an advertisement, there are three organizations that can look into complaints: the Advertising Standards Authority (for ads in newspapers, magazines, brochures, cinemas and on billboards), the Independent Television Commission (for ads on television) and the Radio Authority (for ads on radio). These three organizations insist that advertisements have to be honest, legal, decent and truthful. They also lay down particular requirements, for example, about being careful not to play on people's distress or on how testimonials are used.

The Independent Television Commission and the Radio Authority can ban advertisements that break their codes. The Advertising Standards Authority can refer a company to the Office of Fair Trading if an offending ad is not withdrawn. Most are.

SHOPS HAVE RIGHTS, TOO

The law gives protection to traders as well as to shoppers. The most important right traders have is that they are under no obligation to sell you or anybody else anything at all. Just because a shop is in a main shopping street and is open during regular shopping hours does not mean to say that it must serve you. Any shop, market stall, mail-order company or, indeed, any restaurant, pub, cinema or nightclub, can refuse your custom and they do not have to give any reason for their refusal. (If, however, you could prove that the only reason you were refused service was because of your colour, the shop could face action under the Race Relations Act 1976.)

Shops can also ban you from their premises even if you have been a regular customer and done nothing wrong. Harold Pearson was banned from his local Gateway and Sue King was banned from her local branch of Tesco. In Mr Pearson's case, it was because the shop thought he had not paid for a bunch of bananas. In fact, he had bought the bananas in a shop across the road from Gateway and was able to prove this quite easily, but, instead of an apology, the supermarket chain banned him from their store.

Tesco banned Miss King because they did not like the way she shopped. When her solicitor pressed them for an explanation, the store replied that she had behaved in the manner of someone who was going to steal. Tesco said that when she had noticed store detectives, she had put products back on the shelf. This completely baffled Miss King. The only occasion she could recall remotely like the one the shop described was one time when she had put a couple of items back on the wrong shelf.

When *Watchdog* intervened on her behalf, Tesco apologized and lifted her ban, but they were under no obligation to and, while she or, indeed, Mr Pearson could have sued for libel, in practice, this was not really a realistic option for either of them.

DEPOSITS

Shops have another important right as well. They can keep a deposit if you change your mind about a purchase. They can also claim compensation if they can prove that they ordered the item especially for you. One way around this is to ask the shop to write on the receipt the words 'fully refundable'. You can then claim that you paid the deposit as a gesture of goodwill and so you are entitled to the deposit back if you change your mind.

DELIVERY PROBLEMS

Dennis Ratcliffe suffers from severe arthritis. He spent a year searching for the right furniture that would help ease the pain of his condition. Eventually he found two sofas that suited him in a local furniture shop. He put down £1000 deposit, but he had to wait five months because, the shop said, the manufacturers had moved their factory. After one call from *Watchdog*, the sofas were delivered promptly.

Unfortunately, *Watchdog* does not have the time or resources to take up all consumer problems like Mr Ratcliffe's (his was one entry in a *Watchdog* competition to find the 'longest wait'), but there are things you can do instead.

The key phrase to remember is to 'make time of the essence'. What this phrase means is to make the delivery time an important part of your contract with the shop. When you buy something that is going to be delivered later, write on your receipt and on the shop's order form the date by which you want the item delivered. If the item does not arrive, you will then be entitled to cancel the contract and get your money back.

Of course, in practice, most people just take a shop assistant's word and accept that something may take a 'few weeks' to be delivered. Most times it does, but, occasionally, these few weeks turn into a few months and then you need to act.

Write to the shop and tell them that you are 'making time of the essence'. Set them a deadline for the delivery and tell them that you will claim your money back if the deadline is not met.

Another problem is when a shop promises it will deliver an item at a particular time. You take the time off work to be there to take delivery, but the item never arrives. It is possible to claim compensation, although you will have to show that you lost money as a result and that could be difficult if you are on PAYE. You will also have to show that the failure to deliver was not due to circumstances beyond the shop's control.

Sometimes, too, an item is delivered that turns out to be faulty or broken. Often this only becomes apparent long after the delivery men have left. It is always worth writing on the delivery form 'received uninspected' to cover these situations.

SHOPPING BY MAIL

You have exactly the same rights when you buy something through the post as when you buy something from a shop. If an item bought by mail order is faulty or if it does not match any description or promise made about it in an advertisement or catalogue, you can send it back and claim a refund, plus postage costs and any other expenses.

Most reputable mail-order companies go further than this and abide by the British Codes of Advertising Practice and Sales Promotion that are administered by the Advertising Standards Authority. These allow customers to return any item within seven days and claim a refund even if the only problem was that they did not like it. The Codes also state that goods should normally arrive within 28 days. If they do not, the supplier should write and tell you and give you the chance to cancel.

The major problem with shopping by mail is not faulty goods, but companies going out of business. If you sent money to a company through the post as a result of an advertisement in a newspaper or magazine and the company goes bust, you may be able to get your money back from the Mail Order Protection Service (MOPS). Not every newspaper and magazine, however, is a member of the scheme and not every kind of advertisement is covered.

Tom, a 13-year-old, noticed an advertisement in a magazine from a company running a video games swapping business. Tom sent off his old game plus £3.50, but he got nothing back. The owner of the company claimed subsequently that Tom's game had been stolen. Tom tried to claim back compensation from MOPS, but, even though the magazine was a member of the scheme, Tom was turned down. The reason was because the MOPS scheme covers goods, but not services. The video games swapping business was counted as a service.

The scheme also does not cover classified advertisements, and it does not cover you, for some reason, if you send away for a leaflet first and then decide to buy the item advertised.

SHOPPING BY TELEPHONE

Keith Hancock, a retired toolmaker from Oxford, was rung up one morning by a company he had never heard of called Preferred Products. They told Mr Hancock that he had won one of five prizes, all of which were worth at least £1000. All he had to do was to buy £399-worth of cleaning products.

Mr Hancock declined, but the company was persistent. They rung him up another five times and he eventually agreed to the deal and gave the company his credit card number. His prize turned out to be a bracelet worth, at best, £50 pounds.

Mr Hancock was furious and tried to cancel, but the company refused. They were under no legal obligation to give him a refund as there is no cooling-off period for this kind of selling by phone. If Mr Hancock could *prove* he bought the cleaning products as a result of false promises, he might be able to claim a refund, but the promises that all the prizes were worth £1000 were made over the phone.

Mark Tenner, the Managing Director of Preferred Products, defended his company's telemarketing approach strongly when he appeared on *Watchdog*. He admitted that sometimes his sales staff made promises that they should not have done. He confirmed, too, that people who are rung up do not have to buy anything to win a prize (it would be an offence under gaming law if they had to make a purchase). He also agreed that most of the prizes given out were bracelets that were worth nothing like £1000. However, according to Mr Tenner, all this should not detract from the one most important thing. This kind of selling, he argued, is going to be the shopping of the future. With the spread of cable and satellite television, Britain will take to shopping by telephone in the way Americans have done in the last decade – at least, that is what Mr Tenner, who is American, thinks.

It is unlikely to happen here in quite the same way, however. The Americans have a long tradition of buying by mail, but, in Britain, mail order has been restricted largely to the top or the bottom of the market. There is little doubt, however, that telemarketing and shopping by cable television will increase in the next few years. There is already a channel on satellite television devoted to shopping and Mr Tenner alone has ambitions to ring hundreds of thousands of people across the UK. (These ambitions seem unlikely to be realized as shortly after *Watchdog* broadcast the item about Preferred Products, the company ceased trading and Mr Tenner went back to the United States.)

If you do receive a cold telesales call from someone promising a prize, here are two tips on how to handle it:

▷ ask the salesperson if they can spare a few moments to hear you talk about bringing God into their life
▷ ask the salesperson for their home phone number and address (they have yours, after all) because you are sure you may 'need it sometime'.

MAILING LISTS

Mailing lists are compiled from freely available information (for example, the electoral register) or from buying the response lists from other companies. These response lists are often quite valuable as they enable a company to target particular audiences that may well be interested in their product. Men who buy shirts from specialist mail-order shirtmakers are, so mail-order companies believe, more likely than not to be interested in fine wines. So, the shirtmaking company will sell its customer list to a wine merchant and vice versa. Of course, most of the shirtmakers' customers will throw the wine catalogue away, but the beauty of mail order, at least from a company's point of view, is that they only need a small percentage of customers, perhaps as little as 2 per cent, to respond for them to make money. Once you have given your name to any kind of commercial organization (and some non-commercial ones), offers will start pouring through your letterbox.

You cannot stop any company putting your name on their list, although, if a company is going to put you on a computerized list and then sell the list to another company, it must state this on its literature. You can, however, find out if your name is on any computerized list by using the Data Protection Act 1984. Any organization that holds any computerized information about you – even if it is just your name and address – must tell you if you ask them, although they can charge a £10 fee for this. Anything that is incorrect in your file must be changed. If it is not changed, contact the Data Protection Registrar. You can also find out information about any credit rating file kept on you for just £1 (see page 237).

DOORSTEP SELLING

While it is true that unscrupulous hard sell techniques are used as much in shops as they are door-to-door, there is no doubt that these techniques are more effective in the hands of a skilled doorstep seller. This is partly due to the particular skills of the salesperson (and some are very skilful indeed) but the main reason is more straightforward: people behave differently in their own homes. Defences come down and natural courtesy and friendliness emerge. The result is that the customer is off-guard and is less likely to recognize a poor deal. Some customers can be manipulated into buying things they do not need or even want.

The great advantage of buying in a shop is that people are in a shopping frame of mind. They have chosen to spend the time examining a range of products and comparing them with others. They can ignore any salesperson's advice and stay in the shop for as long or as short a time as they want to. In most shops, there is little pressure to buy and little confusion about the customer's relationship with the shop assistants. At home with a salesperson, the relationship can become very confused, often to the salesperson's advantage, and there is no opportunity to compare the product on offer with its rivals.

There are tips on how to deal with doorstep sellers, but the best tip is the simplest one: just tell them to go away.

AUCTIONS

Most auctions now welcome anybody who wants to buy, members of the public as well as trade. They are often good places to pick up a bargain, but only if you know what you are doing. The four classic rules for buying at auctions are:

▷ not to buy the first time you go
▷ always look at something before you buy
▷ have a set limit you do not go above
▷ never bid first. The auctioneer might well lower his price if nobody bids.

People often associate auctions with the well-known London auction houses like Sotheby's and Christie's, but the real bargains are found in the less prestigious, suburban auctions, where household goods, overstocks and antiques are often jumbled up, and also at government auctions, which tend to concentrate on liquidated and bankrupt stock.

Auctions can be tracked down in the Yellow Pages or in local papers. It is worth telephoning an auction house in advance to see if the auction is open to the public and to find out how you can get hold of a catalogue. Ask them if there is any viewing in advance, what methods of payment are used and if you have to pay an extra buyer's premium and VAT on top of the bidding price. The best time for a bargain is usually in the summer when most people are away on holiday.

Of course, one reason items are so cheap in an auction is that customers usually have no right to a refund if something they buy turns out to be faulty. This is because auctioneers are agents and are allowed to set their own conditions of sale. These conditions usually cancel any rights the customer may have against the auction house. However, the descriptions in auction catalogues must not be intentionally misleading as the Trade Descriptions Act 1968 still applies.

Other sales not to be confused with auctions are 'mock auctions', one-off sales, usually held in a hotel or pub and advertised by fly sheets that promise ridiculous bargains like televisions for £50. There are bargains at these sales, but they never go to members of the public. The crowd is whipped up to think that everything on sale is a bargain and they then pay over the odds for poor-quality products. There is a law against mock auctions – the Mock Auction Act 1961 – but it is virtually unenforceable.

STOLEN GOODS

If you buy something that turns out to be stolen, you have no right to keep it. You will have to give it back if the owner claims it and can prove it belongs to them. This rule applies even if you had no idea that the item was stolen, but there is one rather curious exception. If you buy something in 'good faith' between the hours of sunrise and sunset at a 'market overt', you *can* keep it.

Not every market is a market overt. Such a market has to have been trading since time immemorial and in the kind of goods then that they sell now. For example, Portobello Market in West London is a market overt, but only for fruit and veg, not for antiques. The most famous market overt is the Friday antiques market in Bermondsey in South London. If something is much cheaper there than it should be, you may well have a bargain, but you will have to live with the nagging feeling that you have purchased cheaply someone else's property that was stolen.

BUYING ABROAD

Sometimes it is well worth buying an item abroad. Sometimes it is even worth making a special trip. You can save thousands of pounds buying certain new cars in Belgium, Holland or France, for example, even after paying duty (see page 167). In America and the Far East, most computer, photographic and electrical equipment is considerably cheaper than it is in the UK. France, of course, offers good value for beer and some but not all kinds of wine. What happens, though, if you buy something abroad that turns out to be faulty?

Most developed countries give consumers similar rights to those extended to consumers in Britain if things go wrong. Indeed, some countries, like Germany and the United States, offer more ways in which to get your money back due to legally enforceable guarantees or tough 'lemon' laws (you can return an item and get your money back if it turns out to be a 'lemon'). The problem is that you can only enforce these rights in the country concerned and, for many people who buy things abroad, faults only emerge when they get home.

Some major manufacturers will offer an international guarantee that allows customers to return any faulty item bought abroad to a British agent. This guarantee will usually promise only a repair, not a replacement or a refund. It is, of course, better than nothing. You should ask about this before you buy, but, whether or not you will get a trustworthy answer is debatable.

Another obvious thing to check – although it is surprising how many people do not – is if something you buy abroad will actually work in Britain. Television sets and videos bought in America, for example, are useless here because the television system there is different.

One thing worth doing when you pay for items abroad is to use a credit card. Although it is not clear if the credit card companies are bound by law to refund you if an item you buy abroad on credit turns out to be faulty, some credit card companies will deal sympathetically with complaints, especially if fraud is involved.

FRANCHISES

The high streets of Britain – or, more accurately, the shopping malls – look increasingly alike. In every major town or city, there are branches of the same well-known household chains, but, some chain shops are not quite what they seem. Unlike other shops, they are not owned by one company, but are franchises.

The idea behind franchising is quite simple. The parent company sells know-how, help, training and back-up to independent operators who pay a signing on fee and a percentage of turnover. Many high-street franchises are very successful – a good example is Benetton.

Teenager Lee Begley bought a Benetton sweatshirt for his mother for her birthday, but, unfortunately, it was the wrong size. So, his mother took it back to the shop, only to find that the Benetton branch had closed down. She tried another branch, but she was then refused a refund. The reason for this was that Benetton is a franchise operation, so all the shops are independent businesses and decisions about exchanges are left to the discretion of individual shops. Other franchise shops *do* allow customers to change goods in their shops even when they were not purchased in that particular one, but there is no law saying that they have to.

However, all these well-known franchises do have good quality control and their businesses work. There are many other franchise operations that have neither, and one reason is that franchising offers an easy opportunity for con men (see page 28). It is difficult, however, in the early stages to tell which new franchise idea will eventually turn into a success. Most will not, but one or two will.

If you are interested in buying a franchise, here are some tips:

▷ always ask to speak to at least three people who have already taken out a franchise with the company
▷ get a solicitor who has dealt with franchises before to scrutinize the contract
▷ get all promises of income, training and advertising in writing
▷ never invest all your life's savings in the idea until you have tested it out (no idea is that good).

UNSAFE PRODUCTS

The main emphasis in this chapter – indeed, the main emphasis throughout this book – is on how to get value for money, how to get a good deal. This has always been a major concern of consumer organizations and consumer programmes like *Watchdog*, but, side-by-side with this has been another concern, that of safety – particularly the safety of products and the consequent responsibilities of retailers, manufacturers and the Government for ensuring

71

that all products meet the best safety standards.

There is not the space here to chart the battles that have gone on (and still go on) about product design, appropriate safety standards and gaps in systems and procedures that become clear only when a tragedy has occurred. Simply to record some of *Watchdog*'s own investigations would take up another book. However, one short story sums up much of the frustration those involved in the programme have often experienced. It is the problem of hot oven doors.

In 1984, *Watchdog* reported on the case of Andrew West, a toddler who had just learned to walk. For a split second, he put his hand on the door of his family's oven and he suffered burns so severe that his hand has never fully recovered. Since Andrew's injury, 5000 other children have been injured in this way.

The problem is that the temperature of the outside of some oven doors can go up to 115°C, a temperature that is considerably hotter than a pan of boiling water, but few people realize this until there is an accident. Since the initial *Watchdog* report, some manufacturers have come up with cooler ovens, but they are not compelled to do so by law and, until they are, children every year will suffer as Andrew has.

Hot oven doors is just one story of unsafe appliances, but it is fair to say that some things have changed for the better. At least some manufacturers are more willing these days to issue a speedy recall when a dangerous fault has been reported although few use the most effective method – television advertising. Trading standards officers – the officials responsible for investigating unsafe goods – have developed systems to ensure that unsafe products identified in one part of the country do not flourish unnoticed in another. There is also the Consumer Protection Act 1987. This Act imposes a general duty on all suppliers of goods – wholesalers as well as manufacturers and retailers – to ensure that their products are safe. Breach of this duty is normally a criminal offence and could lead to prosecution.

The Act also allows people to claim compensation for any injury or damage to property over £275, but legal claims involving injury and death are always complicated, so never start an action like this without specialist legal advice. The manufacturer of a product may claim that you used the product without care or attention and you will need a good solicitor to prove the contrary.

Another obstacle, particularly for claims against drug-manufacturers, is what has become known as the 'development risks defence'. This allows manufacturers and suppliers to claim that they could not be expected to know the harmful effects of their products because the appropriate scientific or technological knowledge was not available to them at that time.

SAFETY MARKS

Some goods are covered by specific safety regulations. Examples are foam-filled furniture (after a long battle and many unnecessary deaths) and motorcycle helmets. These regulations insist that all goods sold have to meet standards drawn up by the British Standards Institution. Most British Standards are, however, voluntary. A BSI Kitemark or Safety Mark on a product tells you that it has been tested independently, but if a product only states that it *conforms* to a British Standard, you have no such guarantee as this will be only the manufacturer's opinion. Other safety marks you may come across are the CE mark, the Lion symbol for toys and the BEAB mark for electrical items.

FOOD

Like all goods sold by traders, all food must meet the three conditions of the Sale of Goods Act 1979 (see page 44). If it does not, you are entitled to your money back. All food on sale must also meet the requirements of the Food Act 1984. This makes it a criminal offence for food to be sold that is unfit for consumption or harmful to health.

If you discover anything wrong with the food you buy, take it back not to the shop, but to your local council's environmental health department. The shop is likely to confiscate the evidence, take the food away and just give you a refund. But the council will test the food independently and keep it as evidence for any prosecution of a shop or a manufacturer. If they do prosecute and the shop is found guilty, you can use the decision to claim compensation for any loss you have suffered.

Environmental health officers also enforce the Food Safety Act 1990, which imposes quite stringent controls on the preparation of food for public sale. However, concerns and complaints about food labelling, food quality and weights and measures are dealt with by trading standards officers.

4

SERVICES

GENERAL ADVICE FOR PRACTICAL SERVICES

It was when sewerage started spilling out of a manhole in the garden that Robin Verden decided he needed an emergency plumber. He looked in the Yellow Pages and chose a local plumbing company whose advertisement said that no call out fees were charged, yet one of the first things the plumber did when he arrived at Mr Verden's house was to take down his credit card number and then ring his office to check the number out. Mr Verden was a little suspicious about this, but the plumber seemed to know what he was doing.

The first action the plumber took was to pour acid down the drain. He next tried to use rods, but the only effect was to jet up dark liquid into Mr Verden's shower room. The plumber then decided to call in a colleague who brought a special video camera with him to take pictures of any blockages in the drain. So it went on. Hours later, they located the blockage in a neighbour's garden, which another firm eventually dealt with. For all this detective work, the plumber's company deducted £1051 from Mr Verden's credit card account.

The same company charged single parent Jenny Graham £336 for just two hours work unblocking her toilet. They claimed they had used some £70-worth of chemicals for a job the total cost of which they had indicated originally would not be more than £50.

75

Ex-employees testified that they were encouraged to spin out jobs so that the labour costs at the end were high. One of the easiest jobs for this kind of sharp practice is a blocked drain because most customers usually have no idea how severe a blockage is.

This company was offering a service. It was not a very good one as it turned out, but it was a service none the less. What they share with estate agents and lawyers, dating agencies and architects is the simple fact that they hire out their skills and labour for reward. Most people who offer services are hardworking – they have to be. Some are incompetent. A few are crooks.

However, there are some differences between practical services, which are learned usually 'on the job', and professional services, which require training and qualifications. This chapter looks at the practical services provided by tradesmen, shops and the basic utilities, water, gas, electricity, post and phones. The next chapter looks at services provided by professionals. As yesterday's tradesman often becomes tomorrow's professional, the division is, to some extent, somewhat arbitrary.

Before all this, however, it is worth looking at some general principles that apply to *all* services, both trade and professional.

THE SUPPLY OF GOODS AND SERVICES ACT 1982

This law states that all service contracts must be carried out with reasonable care and skill, within a reasonable time, if no specific time was agreed, and at a reasonable price, if no specific price was agreed. It also says that all materials used must meet similar conditions to those laid down in the Sale of Goods Act 1979, that is, they must be 'of merchantable quality', 'as described' and 'fit for purpose' (see page 44).

The law does not apply to services provided free, nor to services rendered by family or friends. It also does not apply in Scotland, although you have similar rights there under Scottish common law. Apart from these exceptions, this is a very useful law indeed, although, as it is a civil law, you will have to settle any dispute yourself, if necessary through the civil courts.

What the law means is that if a plumber comes out to unblock a drain or an electrician to fix some faulty wiring or a lawyer advises you about a will, none of them can charge what they want, or, to be accurate, they can *try* and charge what they want, but you can refuse to pay it and only pay what is 'reasonable'. The question, of course, is what is reasonable?

In practice, the test of 'reasonableness' is what amount a County court judge will decide is reasonable. Judges will be influenced by other firms' prices, independent expert reports, witnesses and written documents like advertisements, quotations and estimates (*quotations* are firm prices for a job, while *estimates* mean that the final price can turn out to be more, but it should not be all that much more, unless something unforeseen has occurred).

Under the Supply of Goods and Services Act 1982, the burden of proof is on the customer, which means that it will be up to you to show that the bill is unreasonable, not up to the tradesman or professional to show that it is reasonable. If the bill really is unreasonable, though, it should not be difficult to prove.

CHALLENGING A BILL

▷ Ask for a detailed breakdown of the number of hours worked, the cost per hour, the work done in this time and the cost of the materials used.

▷ Compare this with your memory of how many hours the tradesmen actually worked. Have you any proof of this?

▷ Get two quotes from other businesses in the area for the same job (you may have to pay for these).

▷ Write to the company and dispute the bill. Send them a cheque for the amount you think is reasonable, based on the quotes you have received. Mark on the cheque that it is in 'full and final settlement'.

▷ If the company continues to demand the whole amount, suggest it takes you to the County court for the remainder of its bill. Tell them you will be counterclaiming for your expenses resisting their claim.

In most cases, this will be the end of the matter. Sometimes, however, you may get taken to court – or at least threatened repeatedly with court action. If you think you have a good case, respond to any summons, keep a note of all your expenses and look forward to your day in court (see Chapter 9 for much more about the small claims court).

CHALLENGING SHODDY WORK

To move from Cornwall to Wiltshire, Graham and Helen Ash-Porter looked out for a cheap removal company. They thought they had found just the man in Bernard Heffernan, who ran a business called Pick Security from a farm near Plymouth. In fact, Mr Heffernan was so cheap that the Ash-Porters even queried his quote. They thought he could not possibly move all their possessions for a mere £500, and it was true, he could not.

On the day of the removal, his men turned up in one proper van plus a horsebox. Many of the Ash-Porters' possessions had to be left behind. Some of them were stored by Mr Heffernan, who demanded more money before he would release them. Many things were damaged and Graham Ash-Porter sent Mr Heffernan a bill for £3000. Mr Heffernan disputed the bill and said he had done a good job for the price. The dispute dragged on for several months and the Ash-Porters prepared to take Mr Heffernan to court. Unfortunately, Mr Heffernan then closed down Pick Security and disappeared.

The Ash-Porters had an extremely good case. Although Mr Heffernan was cheap, he was obliged to do the job to a reasonable standard. Clearly, moving people's possessions in a horsebox and causing considerable damage to their furniture did not constitute a reasonable standard and Graham Ash-Porter was entitled to compensation.

You cannot expect the Mr Heffernans of this world to deliver the kind of service provided by the up-market firms. What you can expect is that they do a job competently and well. If they do not, you should give them the opportunity to try again. If they still seem incapable of providing a reasonable standard of work, you should then get estimates from other firms to finish the work properly. The amount they charge can be deducted from the money you owe the original firm. If you have paid the firm already, threaten them with legal action under the Supply of Goods and Services Act 1982, unless they pay you back.

CHALLENGING TIME

Often the problem with people who provide a service is not their fees nor their workmanship, but the time they take. If you have not agreed a time limit for the job, the 1982 Act says that they must finish it within a reasonable amount of time, the time you would normally expect someone suitably trained to do the job. You are entitled to compensation if you have incurred expenses because the tradesman took longer than was reasonable, but what you need to be careful about is whether or not you were warned that there might be any hold-ups.

Try to remember if any time was estimated for the job and then ring around and get estimates for the time it would take other firms. Then, put in writing a reasonable deadline for the job to be finished, along with a warning that you will be claiming compensation if the deadline is not met.

UNFAIR TERMS AND THE SMALL PRINT

Many tradesmen, retailers and professionals who sell a service to the public use a standard contract and this will have a number of standard terms and conditions. Sometimes, the consumer is not even aware of these conditions. For example, most travellers who buy a railway ticket have only the vaguest idea of what the railway's conditions of carriage are. Most of the time, however, the conditions of the contract are written down in what has become known as the 'small print'. One of the most important parts of this small print, at least from the point of view of business, is the restrictions on their liability should anything go wrong. A standard condition in most removal company contracts, for example, is one that restricts liability for damage to any one item to £10 or £20. Equally, in most car parks there are signs that state that the company is not liable for any damage caused there.

The Unfair Contract Terms Act 1977 gives some protection to consumers against these conditions, which are known as *exclusion clauses*, most of which are only noticed when something goes wrong. The Act allows an individual to challenge any exclusion or exemption clause in a contract on the basis that it is unfair. However, most people assume that if something is in writing, it cannot be challenged and so few consumers have ever used the Act to resolve a dispute. There is also the worry that challenging a contract term in court could prove very costly indeed with no guarantee of winning. Help, though, is on its way.

From January 1995, the EC Directive on Unfair Terms in Consumer Contracts must become British law. This Directive insists that all standard terms and conditions in contracts, whether in writing or not, must not be unfair, unless a term has been negotiated individually. The Directive also allows consumer organizations to challenge particular standard terms and conditions to establish whether or not they are reasonable.

FINDING THE BEST SUPPLIER

It is much easier, of course, to make sure that you deal with honest, reliable tradesmen, professionals and retailers in the first place than it is to deal with the situation that results when you have *not* dealt with such people. In this and the following chapter, you will find some specific ideas on how to find the best builder, the best doctor and so on, but here are some general tips.

▷ Do not rely on the Yellow Pages or its competitors – anybody can advertise in these directories and the claims made in the advertisements are not checked. The size of an ad is no indication that it comes from a trustworthy firm.

▷ Always ask for and check references. If you cannot find, for example, a builder who has been personally recommended to you, ask him for the names and addresses of two satisfied customers. Do not deal with anybody who cannot provide these.

▷ Check that they have the necessary insurance so that you have some kind of guarantee that you will get your money back if things go wrong. Insurances to look out for are *indemnity insurance* if your property or possessions are damaged; and a *warranty guarantee* backed by insurance cover (an ordinary 20-year tradesman's guarantee is no good as the tradesman may well go out of business before then). Make sure you see the insurance policy before you sign up.

▷ Check qualifications and membership of a *trade* or *professional association*. Avoid any professional who is not a member of an appropriate body, but be more flexible towards tradesmen as some of the best tradesmen have despaired of the various trade associations that exist. If someone is not a member of an association, ask them why not and see how convinced you are by their explanation.

▷ Finally, try to avoid paying anybody in advance, either in cash or by giving your credit card number. This will make it easier for you if you end up in a dispute because it will be up to them to take you to court, rather than the reverse.

TRADE ASSOCIATIONS

In every trade, there are one and often two or three trade associations that compete with each other for members. Some of these associations have very few members indeed. They are simply grandiose names for collaborations between a few firms.

One problem with trade associations is that there is nothing stopping anybody setting up a British Association of ... well, of anything. The British Association of Consumer Journalists has just two members, both on the *Watchdog* team, but the name sounds impressive. The two of us who are members are certain that if we put stickers on particular products saying 'as recommended by the British Association of Consumer Journalists', people would buy the product on the basis of this recommendation. Not, of course, that we would dream of doing such a thing, but it would be perfectly legal.

It is worth remembering, too, a truism that is often forgotten. Trade associations exist not for the general public, but for their members. Sometimes the interests of the public and the interests of a trade are the same, but sometimes they conflict.

To be fair, most trade associations see making sure that customers are happy with their trade as an important part of the job. They are usually more aware than their members of how important it is to deal fairly and sympathetically with complaints. At least some of them know about the idea that sorting out a complaint can turn an unhappy customer into one who will recommend the firm to neighbours and friends.

Most trade associations will offer some or all of the following services to the public.

▷ A *list* of their members in your area. They will also check any claim of membership.
▷ A *code of practice* that sets down minimum standards for members. Check if the code is compulsory and whether or not it is approved by the Office of Fair Trading. Ask them to send you a copy.
▷ A *complaints procedure*. This could be a simple conciliation service or it could be a full *arbitration* service, which can be used as an alternative to court action if a dispute cannot be resolved (see page 293).
▷ A *warranty guarantee scheme* that guarantees the work of their members if they go out of business. Check that the scheme is backed by insurance and ask to see a copy of the insurance policy.

Few trade associations, however, police their trade. They rarely check members' work and usually accept what their members say. Trade associations, too, have few sanctions that they can use if any member misbehaves. They can expel people, but this can mean little, with some people who have been expelled still continuing to claim membership long after they have been thrown out. In any case, expulsion in most trade associations is extremely rare.

Another problem is that a code of practice sounds more impressive than it actually is. Most codes are laudable attempts to put in writing the acceptable behaviour of people in the trade, but the codes have no legal power and what happens is that good firms know about the code and try to put it into practice while bad firms just ignore it.

84

THE BUILDING TRADE

The cowboy builder – the builder who does a completely botched job and runs off with your money – is actually quite rare. Far more common are builders who do not manage to do the job you expected either because they overreach themselves or because some of the subcontractors they use are better than others. In building, more than any other trade, the temptation to cut corners, sometimes literally, is overwhelming.

To avoid this happening, it is worth drawing up a contract with a builder after you have checked them out first. Any contract should specify exactly what work you want done, the cost of the work (you should always ask for a written quotation, not a verbal estimate), the materials to be used, cancellation rights and guarantees, the start and completion time and who will clear up the mess. The contract can simply consist of all these points typed out, copied and signed by both you and the builder.

Some builders will refuse to put anything in writing, a sign that they are not the kind of people with whom you want to do business. Other builders will insist that you sign *their* contract, which will usually be some kind of 'Form of Contract for Building Works'. Make sure the contract includes all the points above and does not include any term you feel unhappy with, for example, a term that limits their liability if they destroy your house. You can always add terms to and subtract terms from a contract as long as both parties agree to it. If the builder objects to you doing this, think again about whether you want to do business with them on their terms or yours.

If you have some kind of contract worked out in

advance, all you need do when things go wrong is draw the builder's attention to it. You can then:

▷ refuse to pay some or all of the bill
▷ insist that work not done properly is done again
▷ if the builder keeps putting off completing a job, tell them that you will get another company to do the work and that you will knock the resulting cost off their bill.

You have these rights under the Supply of Goods and Services Act 1982 even if you have *not* drawn up anything in writing beforehand, but it is much easier to enforce your rights if it is clear that a written agreement has been broken.

As things can go wrong so easily with building work, you should try to pay only for *materials* in advance, paying the remainder of the bill only when *all* the work has been completed and checked. If a builder cannot afford to work like this, find someone else.

Try to make sure that each stage is completely finished before you pay for it, although, in law, anybody is entitled to be paid if a contract has been 'substantially performed', even if everything agreed in advance has not been done. If you have paid the agreed fee and the builder is slow finishing off the work, threaten them with the small claims court. This will usually work.

One trade association, the Chartered Institute of Building, insists that potential members sit examinations and publishes a list of approved building firms and individual builders who are members.

Finally, it is worth emphasizing how important it is to take your time to find the kind of builder you trust. Builders have the potential not simply to rip you off, but to destroy your home and make your life completely miserable. Make sure you see several builders and compare them with each other before making the final decision.

New homes

When you buy a newly built house, you should make sure that it is protected by a structural warranty. If you are buying the house on a mortgage, the finance company or building society will insist that the house has one.

There are two organizations that provide these warranties for new houses: the long-established National House Building Council (NHBC) and the insurance company-owned Foundation 15 (Zurich Municipal). New house builders register with either company and they are checked out before being taken on. Their houses are then inspected to make sure that they reach the standards required. The builder pays a premium and the house is given a 10-year structural warranty.

During the first two years, the houseowner is protected against most technical defects as long as they were the result of the builder's work. The builder pledges to put the defects right. If there is a disagreement between the builder and the houseowner, NHBC or Zurich Municipal will send an inspector down. Either party can appeal against the inspector's ruling and if that happens, it will then go to arbitration.

During the eight final years after this, the warranty becomes an insurance policy. The houseowner claims direct from NHBC or Zurich Municipal for major damage to the house that has come about as a result of structural defects.

The NHBC's warranty scheme is more common than its competitor's and, while many houseowners have been pleased with the scheme, it has caused some headaches. One problem is that some things are just not covered. If a builder has promised to put in a jacuzzi and has then left it out, the NHBC warranty scheme will not help. The same applies to boundary disputes. These kinds of disputes will have to be sorted out with the builders themselves.

Second, there is a grey area concerning defects that are decorative rather than structural. The NHBC says that, at least in the first two years, houseowners can claim for these defects as long as they can show that they were caused by the builder, but some houseowners have found that NHBC inspectors agree with the builder when they claim that you cannot expect a house to be free of all defects. Also, after two years, the NHBC warranty only covers major structural damage.

PLUMBERS

People ring plumbers in an emergency. They need someone fast and they look for a plumber in the Yellow Pages or some other local directory. There is no guarantee that you will avoid cowboys this way. Instead, you could try the Institute of Plumbing, which can supply you with a list of registered plumbers in your area. The Institute does not, however, offer any guarantee scheme, but it will look into complaints about any of its 10 000 members.

If the problem is a blocked drain, it is worth contacting your local council's environmental services department. Someone there should be able to tell you whose responsibility the drain is – most likely it will be yours. Some local authorities offer a service for unblocking drains and, although you will have to pay for it, it is likely to be a trustworthy service.

HOME IMPROVEMENTS

Most builders offer home improvement services, such as double glazing, extensions, fitted kitchens and conservatories. However, there are many firms that specialize in one of these areas and they often offer a complete package of design, units and installation. Along with the package, however, there comes a negative image, exemplified by the dodgy double-glazing salesperson or the cheap and cheerful conservatory that lets water in the first time it rains, or the company that seemed to be trustworthy and then went bankrupt leaving hundreds of half-completed kitchens.

There is a trade association in the industry: the Glass and Glazing Federation. It does not guarantee members' work, but it does offer a deposit indemnity fund and it will try and conciliate if things go wrong.

The Federation also offers an independent arbitration service that is worth knowing about because often the sums of money involved are over the small claims court limit. In a survey of three arbitration schemes carried out by the National Consumers Council, it came out top: two out of three people who used it were satisfied. Some, but not all, of the Federation's members offer an insurance-backed warranty of their work.

REPAIRS SERVICES

When things go wrong with major household appliances, like dishwashers, cookers, washing machines and freezers, the repair bill can often turn out to be more than the machine is worth. So, before calling out someone, make sure the problem is not something as straightforward as a blown fuse.

It is worth considering, too, whether or not you will have to pay the bill for any repair. Most manufacturers and some retailers guarantee items for up to two years, and you have rights under the Sale of Goods Act for six years after you have bought an item, if you can show that the fault was inherent and not due to your misuse.

Always ask a repair company what the call out charge will be and if it will be added to the bill. Check, too, that it is familiar with the machine and has access to parts. It is worth obtaining a quote before agreeing to substantive work and a second opinion if the quote seems high. Make sure VAT and labour are included.

One way to avoid the cost of repairs is to take out an *extended warranty* when you buy a new appliance. These are offered by manufacturers and some retailers, but they may be a bad deal: regular research by *Which?* magazine has shown that they are often not worth the money.

For items that you can take back to have repaired, smaller electrical items, for example, or your car, motorcycle or bike, it is useful to know that the repairer can take what is called a *lien* out on your property if you fail to pay their bill. This means that they can keep hold of it lawfully. To get your property back, you will have to pay the bill or get a court order.

If you bring an item in for repair and forget about it, the Torts (Interference with Goods) Act 1977 gives you some protection. It says that the shop must contact you in writing about your property before they get rid of it. They must tell you how much money you owe and warn you that they will dispose of your goods unless you pay up (this law does not apply in Scotland).

Another law, the law of *bailment*, allows you to claim compensation if an item of yours is damaged while being repaired. This law imposes a duty on a repairer to look after your property with all due care.

REMOVALS

Jenny Mowatt is used to giving people advice. She works as an adviser at a Citizens Advice Bureau in Kent. One thing she always tells people is to go for a quality firm, not just for the firm that provides the cheapest quote. So, when she needed to put her house contents in storage for a few months when she moved house, she chose Pickfords – a name she thought she could trust.

Pickfords stored Mrs Mowatt's furniture in their warehouse in Watford and, one night in March 1990, the warehouse caught fire and everything was destroyed. Mrs Mowatt was one of some 200 people who lost everything – all her furniture, precious possessions, family photographs and mementos.

Mrs Mowatt had taken out fire insurance but she was underinsured. She was only insured for £8000 of the £24 000 her belongings were worth because she never dreamed that everything would be destroyed by a fire. It emerged afterwards that there was no fire alarm in the warehouse, no sprinkler system and no internal walls – all measures that could have limited the damage done by the fire. Pickfords denied liability for the fire and would not pay Mrs Mowatt a penny in compensation. Their contract with her excluded liability for damage caused by fire.

The exclusion clauses buried in the small print of removals company contracts – and in the contracts of their insurance companies – cast a shadow over an industry that, by and large, does a good job. Other conditions to look out for are the seven-day limit for putting in a claim, the limit of £10 to £20 per item if something is broken or lost and a clause that states that you must go to arbitration in any dispute (this last, though, is nonsense – the Consumer Arbitration Agreements Act 1988 made such clauses unenforceable).

One solution is to ignore any insurance on offer by a removals company and, instead, contact your house contents insurers. For a small extra payment, they will cover any damage to your property during your removal or storage.

Another solution is to challenge the small print clauses in court by using the Unfair Contract Terms Act 1977 (see page 81). This could work, although it could prove risky if the amount you are claiming is over the small claims court limit and your case ends up in the full County or sheriff court.

The best advice to follow when you want to find a trustworthy removals firm is to rely on the personal recommendations of other people. There is a trade association, the British Association of Removers, which does vet members and offers a conciliation and arbitration service if things go wrong. They will send you a list of their members in your area.

DRY-CLEANERS

People often have problems with dry-cleaners – or, at least, with some dry-cleaners. Clothes come back with holes in them or the colours have faded. The dry-cleaner claims that it is not their fault and points to a notice that says all clothes are cleaned at the owner's risk. What can you do?

The first thing is to ignore the notice. If a dry-cleaner has damaged your clothes due to negligence, they are liable for the damage. However, you may have to show that the damage done was due to the dry-cleaning and for this you will need independent testing. The trade association, the Textile Services Association, will provide a list of independent laboratories that will test clothes at a cost of £40 to £90. The Association's code of practice states that their members must pay the testing fee if the customer turns out to be right.

Sometimes clothes are damaged not because of the dry-cleaning system itself, but because the method used was inappropriate. This could be due to lack of care by staff, but they may claim that they followed the instructions on the label. You would then have to claim compensation from the manufacturer.

FILM PROCESSING

Millions of films are sent by customers through the post each year to be developed. Most come back safely, but, occasionally, things go wrong.

Richard and Fiona Dakin took dozens of photos of their first child, Laura. They sent the film to Trueprint, but the Dakins' photos were lost. Trueprint gave them vouchers and the Dakins thought nothing more about it. After all, these things happen. They took more pictures of Laura and then sent off three more reels to Trueprint. Unfortunately, the company lost two of these three films as well and the Dakins now have no pictures of the first four months of Laura's life.

If a photoprocessing company loses your photos, their usual response is to send you a free film and vouchers. The companies say that customers are warned to take out insurance if a film is of special value, but, when *Watchdog* investigated, we could find no such insurance on the market.

If you do lose a film of special significance to you, ask the company for compensation. You will need evidence both of posting and that the photos were of an event that is 'unrepeatable', but it is possible to negotiate compensation of £50 to £200 per film.

DATING AGENCIES AND TICKET AGENCIES

Iris Bass from New York paid £150 to a dating agency called English Rose for some introductions to suitable men, but she was disappointed by the information she was sent and she complained. English Rose were, however, quite unapologetic.

They said that it was all Miss Bass' fault because the photos she had sent them of herself showed that she had 'made no effort with her appearance' and that her hair appeared 'greasy and uncombed'. Worse was to follow. Miss Bass then received another offer from English Rose which suggested she went on their 'élite portfolio' for an extra £40. When the company was contacted about this, they conceded that attempting to include Miss Bass in the élite portfolio was a mistake. She is not sure if this was a compliment or not.

She was entitled to her money back, but only if the company were unable to make amends. With a dating agency – or, indeed, with any similar kind of business – you pay for a service over a period of time. A company has time to deliver its promises and it cannot be expected to provide everything straight away.

Ticket agencies are rather different. They act as agents for other companies and they claim not to be liable if things go wrong. This is nonsense: if you lose money as a result of their incompetence or lack of care, you can sue them for compensation.

Many of the deals some ticket agents offer are poor ones. Margaret Stone and a group of friends from Nottingham bought tickets for a performance of *Les Misérables* in London. They paid £1000 in November to a London agent for 42 seats for a performance the following April, which worked out at more than £20 a ticket. The tickets did not arrive until a few days before the performance and when Mrs Stone opened the letter, she realized why. The face value of the tickets was only £5.50 and

£7.50 each – the cheapest seats in the house.

Unfortunately, all this is completely legal (at least as this book goes to print). Ticket agencies can charge what they like, so it is always best to check with the theatre first to see if you can buy tickets direct. If the theatre is sold out, make sure you ask any agent how much the face value of the ticket is before parting with any money (they will soon *have* to tell you if proposed government regulations become law).

RESTAURANTS AND PUBS

When a meal you have ordered turns out to be not as you expected, here is what to do.

▷ If the standard of the food is poor, complain at once – not after you have eaten the meal. If you do not complain straight away, the restaurant may claim that you are just trying to avoid payment.

▷ If you have complained throughout the meal and the food has not improved, make this clear to the manager and offer to pay what you think is a reasonable amount instead of the bill. Give the manager your name and address.

▷ If the manager threatens to call the police, tell them it is a civil matter and that the police will not be interested.

▷ If the police are called, stay in the restaurant until they come. Then explain to them that you are not trying to avoid payment, but that you have complained during the meal about the food and that you are exercising your rights under civil law to deduct money from the bill. As long as you are not committing any breach of the peace, the police have no power to intervene.

▷ If the restaurant tries to threaten you or detain you until you pay the full bill, tell them that you are going to call the police.

If you are persistent and calm, you will usually win your case. Most restaurant managers will accept defeat and not bother to sue you for the amount you have deducted. You can, of course, pay the full amount and then take the restaurant to the small claims court for the difference between the bill and what you think the meal was worth. The chances are, though, that after you get home you will never do it.

If the food was fine, but the *service* was poor, you can deduct some or all of any service charge made, even if the charge was added automatically to your bill and is stated clearly on the menu.

A GUIDE TO THE BASIC SERVICES – THE UTILITIES

With the exception, at least at present, of The Post Office, all the other basic utilities – gas, electricity, water and telephones – are run by private companies. Laws such as the Supply of Goods and Services Act 1982 and the Unfair Contract Terms Act 1977 still apply, but the British Telecoms and the British Gases of this world are in a quite different league from small tradesmen.

The problem is not one of how to avoid being ripped off – cowboys and crooks do not tend to work for such companies as London Electricity or North West Water –

the problem is how to deal with the bureaucracy of a monopoly supplier where customer choice can turn out to be no choice at all.

Two things can help. Each service, with the exception of The Post Office, has an official *regulator*. Two of their important tasks are to approve price increases and to monitor customer complaints. The regulators have also encouraged 'customers' charters', backed up by guaranteed standards schemes. These schemes lay down the standard of service to which the company aspires and they state the kind of compensation a company will pay if the standards are not met. If you have not received one of these with your bill over the last year, ring the company up and ask them to send one to you. They are useful to have handy if there is a problem.

The regulators have made a difference: customers have far more rights now than they did ten, even five years ago. The question is, are they effective enough? The National Association of Citizens Advice Bureaux concluded recently that the regulators had failed adequately to safeguard poorer consumers against the commercial interests of the new privatized companies. Certainly the style of the regulators has varied between the combative approach taken towards the gas and telephone companies by OFGAS and OFTEL, and the more conciliatory approach towards the electricity and the water companies taken by OFFER and OFWAT.

This may be down to personalities. Much depends on how the Director-General of the particular regulator interprets their role, and the first regulators of the gas and telephone industries were keen to make their role felt. On the other hand, both OFGAS and OFTEL have been dealing, in the main, with one, large, national company over a number of years. OFFER and OFWAT have had to cope with monitoring a dozen or more regional companies in a much shorter space of time.

The usefulness of the various consumer initiatives is debatable. They all fit quite neatly into the Government's Citizens' Charter initiative and, indeed, were early models for it, but, an opinion poll conducted on behalf of the Government in 1993 concluded that most people thought that public services had not improved or had actually deteriorated since the initiative had been established. The services asked about included water, electricity and gas.

What has been noticeable, however, has been a change of attitude towards dealing with complaints. There is a perception, signified by British Gas's commissioned research into their complaints procedures, that how a company deals with dissatisfied customers is as important as attracting new business. This perception may not as yet be one that is held at Board level, but it is at least a hopeful sign for the future.

GAS

Gas, at the moment, means British Gas – the monopoly supplier of mains gas for virtually all domestic households in Great Britain. But in 1996, this monopoly will end and there will be full competition, at least according to the Government, by 1998. Until then, there is just British Gas and the industry regulator, OFGAS.

OFGAS will deal with complaints, but only as a last resort. The first approach should be to British Gas itself, which has its own complaints procedure. If the complaint cannot be resolved, contact the Gas Consumers Council, an independent body. The Council can force British Gas to respond and justify their decision, but not change it – only OFGAS is able to do this.

British Gas's customer initiative is called 'Commitment to Customers'. It promises, for example, to pay £20 per day if the gas supply is interrupted for more than a day, and £10 if an appointment is missed or cancelled less than 24 hours in advance. About 18 000 people have received money since Commitment to Customers was introduced.

Meters, bills and disconnection

If you suspect that your meter is at fault, British Gas will test it for you. If you are not satisfied, you can ask them to arrange an independent examination. Then an examiner will take the meter away and test it, but you will have to pay about £30 for this to be done. This will be refunded if the meter turns out to be faulty.

Like the other utilities, British Gas has a code of practice concerning disconnections. The idea is to try to separate people who *cannot* pay from people who *will not* pay. Only the latter should be disconnected, at least in theory.

If you have problems paying the bill, get in touch with British Gas immediately or ask your local Citizens Advice Bureau to liaise on your behalf. If you are disputing a bill, pay the part of it you do not dispute and make sure British Gas know about the dispute – they should not cut you off while the dispute is being sorted out.

Right of supply

You have a right to be connected to mains gas if you are within 22.8 metres (25 yards) of the supply. British Gas has standard connection fees and may well charge you a deposit, although you could challenge this by providing a banker's reference. If you are further than 22.8 metres (25 yards) away, British Gas may quote you a price, but are under no obligation to do the work. Contact the Gas Consumers Council if you have any problems.

Gas services and repairs

British Gas is, at present, the only supplier of mains gas to almost all consumers, but it is by no means the only company that repairs and services gas appliances. There are some 50 000 gas fitters and they range from British Gas's national operation to one-man outfits. However, every gas fitter must be registered by law with CORGI, an independent body that carries out regular checks on fitters. You should always make sure that any people working with gas in the home (including people who repair central heating systems if they run on gas) are registered.

One problem with registration is that CORGI only registers *firms,* not *individuals*. So, you cannot be sure that the actual fitter doing your work is competent. When *Watchdog* asked six gas fitters chosen at random from Birmingham's Yellow Pages to check up on a gas boiler known to be unsafe, only two spotted all the hazards. All of them were registered with CORGI. As some 40 people die every year from carbon monoxide poisoning caused by unsafe gas appliances, this matters a great deal.

There is no foolproof way to spot a good gas fitter. On balance, it is probably safest to opt for British Gas as their fitters are more likely to be aware of all the gas safety regulations and to have been trained in all the things that can go wrong.

Another hazard in the gas repair business is that of

being charged for unnecessary work. The only way to avoid this is always to get another quote, especially when the first quote specifies some major work that needs to be done, like the replacement of a boiler.

If you come across any gas fitter who fails to spot an unsafe appliance or who repairs an appliance in an unsafe way, report them to CORGI and they will take action. CORGI, however, cannot deal with complaints about overcharging or charging for unnecessary work. For this you will have to use the Supply of Goods and Services Act 1982 and threaten or use the small claims court.

ELECTRICITY

Unlike gas, the 14 private electricity supply companies in Great Britain are regional and not national monopolies. The regulator of the industry in Great Britain is the Director-General of Electricity Supply and head of OFFER (Northern Ireland Electricity is regulated by OFFER Northern Ireland).

There is no equivalent of the Gas Consumers Council for electricity, but each region has its own consumer committee that is based at regional OFFER offices. These committees deal with customer complaints, although customers are expected to go through the electricity company's complaints procedure first.

Each electricity company has its own customers' charter although the charters are all very similar to each other. Each charter has to meet minimum guaranteed standards of service that have been agreed with OFFER. These guarantees promise, for example, that the company will pay

£20 if they do not respond to a complaint about billing within 10 working days and £20 if they miss an appointment. Some companies go further than this minimum and have earned the Government's Charter Mark for improvements to the service they provide.

Right of supply

Unlike gas, the electricity companies have a legal obligation to connect you unless your circumstances are exceptional. They can charge you the full cost of connection, but there is no charge if you are just taking over a supply. However, if you are a new customer or live in a rough area, the company may well charge you a hefty deposit – perhaps £200 or more.

Meters and bills

Like gas, you are responsible for the electricity on your side of the meter. The electricity company will test your meter for you but they can charge up to £20 to do this, although you will be refunded if the meter is faulty. If you are not satisfied with this test, you can ask OFFER to test the meter as well. One in ten meters OFFER check turn out to be faulty, although most faults are minor.

Disconnection

Before they disconnect you, electricity companies have to offer you a payments plan that must take your circumstances into account. They can only disconnect you if they have offered you alternative ways of paying your bill, for example, a pre-payment meter, and you have turned these down. If they do disconnect you, they must give you two working days' notice. Get immediate help, if you are unable to pay a bill, from your local Citizens Advice Bureau.

Electricians

You can ask your electricity company to check your wiring, although you may, of course, be charged for this. It may be better to choose an independent electrician instead. Some electricity companies send around independent sales-people when they get a request from a customer for a routine check. These salespeople are unlikely to be quali-fied electricians, so ask anybody who turns up from an elec-tricity company if they are qualified.

Because of the potential danger involved – dozens of people are killed every year because plugs have been wired up wrongly – you should always make sure an electrician is trained and qualified. There is no equivalent of the compulsory gas registration system run by CORGI, but the National Inspection Council for Electrical Inspection Contracting (NICEIC) checks out electricians in a similar way, as does the Electrical Contractors Association. You would be silly to use any electrician to do work in your house who is not approved by one of these two organiza-tions. Always check.

WATER

Like electricity, the water companies are regional mono-polies. There are 10 large companies that supply both drinking water and collect sewerage, and another 20 smaller companies that supply just drinking water. If you are in one of the smaller water company areas, your sewer-age services will come from a larger water company, even though you will only be billed by the smaller company. It can be confusing.

What can be confusing, too, is that there are not one but three different water watchdogs. The regulator of the water industry is the Director-General of Water Services who is the head of OFWAT. This person is concerned with the price and supply of drinking water and sewerage services in England and Wales (in Scotland and Northern Ireland, water is provided, for the moment at least, by local government).

The Drinking Water Inspectorate monitors the quality of water that comes out of the tap. The National Rivers Authority watches over the state of lakes and rivers.

Most customer complaints about water are dealt with by OFWAT or by the 10 customer service committees. The committees expect you to complain to the water company first. Each committee can recommend action if they think a complaint is justified, but, if the water company refuses to take any action, the committee must refer the matter to the Director-General of Water Services. The Director-General can order a water company to comply, although this power is rarely used.

In conjunction with OFWAT, each water company has drawn up guaranteed standards of service. These schemes entitle customers to compensation, for example, if a water company breaks an appointment without 24 hours' notice or does not respond to a complaint within 20 days. The compensation is usually £10 and paid automatically, but the schemes do not cover everything that can go wrong, as some residents of the pretty Lancashire village of Helmshore found out.

They had suffered a dirty water supply for 15 years. Every so often, a kind of brown gunge came out of their taps. The water company responsible, North West Water, say that it is due to an old treatment works and to old pipes that cannot be replaced until 1995. Until then, the Helmshore residents will have to put up with it, and pay the same bill as everyone else. Despite the guaranteed standards scheme, they were not entitled to any compensation because this kind of problem is not covered by the scheme.

Just 50 miles away, Tony McMahon runs a hairdressing shop in New Brighton in the Wirral. He has had to install his own emergency system because, in the summer, the water supply in New Brighton occasionally dries up. Residents are often without water for hours at a time, but they are not entitled to compensation because the standards scheme only pays out when the supply is cut off for 24 hours or more, and then only if it is the water company's fault.

Prices and meters

Since the privatization of water in England and Wales, water bills have risen dramatically. The water companies claim that this is because more money is needed to rebuild and replace centuries-old pipes and reservoirs and to build new ones. Another reason put forward is the new customer demand for ever cleaner water, a demand that has been reinforced by new EC regulations. This has led to increased investment and new spending on purification equipment. The Director-General of Water Services has accepted these arguments, but many consumers remain to be convinced.

Most water bills at the moment are based on the old rateable values. In the next few years, this will change as each water company decides how it is going to charge for water (they have up until 1999 to do this). Some companies, like Welsh Water, have elected for a flat fee charging system. Other companies intend to develop a system similar to that used for the Council Tax. Another option is water metering, which is particularly attractive to water companies in the South because they do not have unlimited supplies of water. Anglian Water has already opted for universal water metering.

It is possible to obtain a meter from any water company. The meter is usually free, although you will have to pay for installation and this can cost from £60 to £200 depending on whether or not your water company encourages metering. It may also be possible to get a water meter installed privately. If you have a meter, you are responsible for all the water consumed your side of the meter, so it is important to make sure that there are no unnoticed leaks.

Connection
Like electricity companies, the water companies must connect you to the water supply unless they can show exceptional circumstances.

However, as well as a connection charge, water companies can make another charge as well: an infrastructure charge. This is a perfectly legal charge, although it is extremely unfair.

The Netherthall playgroup in Yorkshire started life in the classroom of a local school, but the school needed their classroom back, so the playgroup got permission to put up their own building in the school field. The playgroup raised £15 000 and, as the building was being completed, they asked for quotes from the phone, electricity and water companies to connect their services to the building. The quotes came back: phone, £180; electricity, £270; water, £2000. It seemed ridiculous.

Yorkshire Water were charging the playgroup a £750 connection charge and a £1300 infrastructure charge. The playgroup appealed to the company and to OFWAT. Yorkshire Water turned them down and while OFWAT sympathized, they could do nothing about it. Fortunately, a charity heard about their situation and paid the huge water bill. Otherwise the playgroup would have had to close down completely.

Pressure and discoloration

Apart from connection charges, most complaints about water involve low pressure and discoloration. As the examples of Helmshore and Mr McMahon show, it can be difficult to get compensation under the guaranteed standards scheme, but it is certainly worth trying as companies can make discretionary payments if you have a good case.

One thing to find out is what the water company's diagnosis of the problem is and what their proposed solution is. If the solution seems to you too long term, pressure through local papers, councillors and MPs can make the water company reconsider its priorities.

Water companies usually insist that discoloured water is perfectly safe to drink, if hardly palatable. If you suspect that any drinking water is unsafe, contact the Drinking Water Inspectorate which will investigate the water.

Disconnection

Each water company has a disconnection procedure, agreed with OFWAT. The procedure is meant to give people who cannot pay their bill time to sort the matter out. It does not mean that people will *not* be cut off: 18 000 people were disconnected in England and Wales in 1992 (in Scotland, you cannot be cut off for not paying your water bill). Most people who were cut off, however, were reconnected within a few days. You can usually avoid disconnection if you contact your local Citizens Advice Bureau. The water companies need a court order to disconnect and they have to give you 14 days' notice.

Burst pipes

All pipes your side of the stopcock are your responsibility. It is usually situated near the front boundary of your property. If your pipes burst, it is up to you to get them repaired, not the water company (see page 88).

TELEPHONE

Despite ten years of privatization, most domestic customers still hire telephone services from British Telecom (BT). In the next few years, this could well change. BT's established competitor, Mercury, has expanded into the domestic market and offers cheap deals on overseas calls. However, the big challenge to BT is likely to come from cable companies, which are beginning to offer phone services as well. For most people, this option is still a few years away, although for some it is already a reality.

BT and the other companies (including Kingston Communications in Hull) are regulated by the Director-General of Telecommunications and Head of OFTEL. OFTEL also deals with complaints, although you can also obtain advice from your local telecommunications advisory committee. It can refer the complaint to one of the four advisory committees on telecommunications which work closely with OFTEL. You can find their addresses in the phone book or by ringing OFTEL in London.

OFTEL monitors British Telecom's Customer Guarantee Scheme. This scheme offers compensation if the company misses targets such as not repairing a fault on the line by the end of the next day after it has been reported. The compensation is, however, quite small. It is possible to claim up to £1000 if you have been deprived of the use of a telephone by BT, but you will have to show actual financial loss and you must have tried to minimize your losses. Any claim must be made within two months.

Meters and bills

If you think you have been overcharged, you can ask BT to check your meter. This meter, by the way, is not in your home, but at the exchange. The best way to make sure your bill is correct is to ask BT for an itemized bill. This service is free and is available in most places in the country. You can then see at once if there are any phantom calls.

Phantom calls often turn out to be 0898 calls that the owner of the line denies ever making. BT take the view that it is usually someone in the household who is making these calls. At issue is whether or not it is possible for someone to tap into your phone line and use it to make calls. An OFTEL investigation concluded that it is possible for this to happen, but that the problem is not widespread.

BT have now agreed with OFTEL that they will not charge for phantom calls if a customer can show that their phone could not have been used during the period in question. However, any claim may have to go through BT's arbitration procedure.

If you do dispute calls, what you should do is pay the

part of the bill that you do not dispute, and tell BT that you are disputing the rest of the bill. Otherwise, you may be cut off.

To buy or to rent?
Apart from the few people left with a hard-wire connection rather than a socket one, there is no obligation for anyone to use a BT phone. If you do rent a BT phone, you should consider buying your own as it works out much cheaper. If you do buy a phone, buy one with a Mercury button that will allow you to choose between BT and Mercury, unless your exchange allows you to tap into the Mercury system without the special button.

If you do not rent a phone from BT and there is a fault on your line, BT will charge you a call out fee if the fault turns out to be due to your equipment. So, it is a good idea before calling BT out to check if it is the phone itself by trying another phone on the line. If your phone is at fault, you have the same rights to a refund as you have with any other purchase (see page 44).

Connection and disconnection
BT have a legal obligation to provide telephone services, subject to satisfactory credit references. For a brand-new telephone line, the current charge is £116. Most new customers take over an existing line and there is generally no charge for this if the handover is within 24 hours and BT have been given seven days' notice. If not, the current charge is £36.78.

BT are entitled to disconnect people who do not pay their bill as long as they give seven days' notice.

0898 calls
0898 calls are the generic term for the telephone services

for which customers pay a premium rate. 0898 was merely the first code used by BT and is now given over mainly to what are known as the 'sexy Sue' services. BT also own 0891 numbers. Mercury own 0839, 0660 and 0881; Vodaphone 0831, 0836, 0336 and 0338. There are sure to be others by the time this book is published.

'Owning' is, in fact, a slightly misleading term as 90 per cent of these lines are rented out to other companies that are called 'service providers'. They, in turn, rent these lines to smaller companies and so it goes on. There are now some 17 000 lines and they offer a wide variety of services, from the conventional to the pornographic to the fraudulent. Some of the services provide extremely useful information, but many of them try and ensure that the people simply stay on the line as long as possible.

Peter Taylor from Essex had been unemployed for two years when he saw an advertisement from a record company that said they were looking for warehouse staff. The advertised pay was £6 an hour, and all Mr Taylor had to do was call an 0898 number. However, when he did, the recorded message lasted some 10 minutes before it asked Mr Taylor for his name and address. This 10-minute call cost him £5. Mr Taylor receive an application form, which he completed and sent back, but he heard nothing more. The record company that placed the 0898 advertisement admitted eventually that there were no jobs available.

This 0898 was banned by ICSTIS, the independent body that watches over 0898 lines and is financed by the telephone industry. It deals with complaints and has a code of practice that lays down guidelines for the various services on offer. For example, if you are using an 0898 number to advertise jobs, you have to provide evidence that there are genuine jobs on offer. All 0898 services must say the full cost of the service either on their advertisements or at the start of the message. The problem is that these lines come and go at an amazing speed. By the time ICSTIS starts looking at one line, it could have easily changed hands.

POST

The postal services are the only basic service still run by the State rather than by a privatized company, at least at present. This does not seem to have done them any harm at all, at least in the public's eyes. The postal services usually do better than the other services in opinion polls and in the handling of complaints.

The post is, in fact, three different businesses: the Royal Mail, which deals with letters; Parcelforce; and Counter Services, which looks after the 1000 crown post offices and the 20 000 sub-post offices. Each of these businesses has a code of practice and there is also a Post Office customers' charter.

If you have problems with your post, you should first complain to the manager or sub-postmaster. If the problem is not resolved, ask your local post office for the address of the appropriate district and write to their customer care department. If there are still problems, contact your local post office advisory committee (the customer care department will give you their address). If necessary, they can refer the complaint to one of the four national Post Office Users National Councils (POUNC), the postal services' consumer watchdog. You can also

113

contact your national POUNC direct. POUNC can deal with problems like mail which does not arrive. It can also press The Post Office to revise and change the local mail delivery system.

If your mail or parcel is lost, The Post Office has limited the compensation it will pay to £24, unless you have taken out extra insurance or sent it registered. You must get claims in within one month. It is possible to fight for higher compensation, if necessary, by using The Post Office's arbitration service.

Stop Press

At the time this book was going to press, the Government announced its intention to privatize the Royal Mail and Parcelforce, though not Counter Services.

5

THE PROFESSIONALS

DEALING WITH PROFESSIONALS

When Marjorie Poulten first started vomiting and losing weight, her GP told her not to worry as she probably only had a touch of food poisoning. Two weeks and two more visits later, the condition of Mrs Poulten, aged 67, had deteriorated. The doctor, however, still thought a visit to a specialist was unnecessary. It was 19 December 1989.

Two days later, Mrs Poulten was rushed into hospital where she underwent an emergency operation for a burst ulcer. She had lost so much weight that the surgeon was not even sure that she would survive the anaesthetic.

Mrs Poulten did survive, but only just. Her daughter-in-law Anita Poulten wanted to know how it had all been allowed to happen, how the GP seemed to have got it so wrong.

After trying, unsuccessfully, to get answers from the doctor, Anita Poulten made a formal complaint to the local Family Health Services Authority (FHSA). She won her case: the doctor was eventually found to be in breach of his terms of service. However, the complaint took 15 months to sort out and involved an immense amount of work. Anita Poulten found the hearing intimidating. 'I think a lot of people do give up even when they've got a very good case,' she says now, 'They get worn down.'

As Mrs Poulten's experience shows, it is just as easy to be let down badly by a professional as by any other person who provides a service. Just because someone has a few letters after their name does not mean to say that their bill is always correct or their time is always recorded accurately or the service they perform is adequate. The problem, as Mrs Poulten found out, is that when things go wrong with a professional, it can prove difficult to sort the matter out. When a dry-cleaner ruins your clothes or a builder ruins your house, it is usually straightforward to work out what exactly has gone wrong. When your health is ruined by a doctor's negligence or when you lose thousands of pounds due to a lawyer's incompetence, your troubles are often only just beginning.

SOME GENERAL ADVICE

Just like any tradesman, professionals hire out their services for money, so, the advice given on pages 76 to 84 is relevant here, too. The Supply of Goods and Services Act 1982 applies as much to an architect as to a plumber: they must do the work in a reasonable amount of time, to a reasonable standard and at a reasonable price if no price was agreed beforehand.

Professionals also have a *duty of care* towards you and your property. They can be held responsible if an injury or damage happens as a result of their advice or under their supervision, unless they can show that it was due to something or someone outside their control.

However, the essential difference between professionals and other people who provide services is that, before they can practise, professionals need to have gained qualifications and be members of professional organizations, while most tradesmen learn their trade on the job and many never join any trade association in their lives.

PROFESSIONAL ORGANIZATIONS

Most professional organizations have rules of conduct that their members must follow. If any member is found guilty of breaking the code, they can be expelled. In some professions, where the professional organization has regulatory power – for example, in law and medicine – expelled members can no longer practise.

At first sight, this seems to serve as an extremely useful guarantee to the customer – just check, for example, that a solicitor has a practising certificate from the Law Society and you are   assured you will be treated fairly, but, as the 17 000 complaints made to the Solicitors Complaints Bureau every year testify, this is far from the case.

For one thing, permanent expulsion from a professional organization is rare. As expulsion can mean depriving someone of their livelihood, most professional bodies only use this power in extremely serious cases of bringing the profession into disrepute. Few disputes between a professional and a customer tend to qualify, even though the effect on the customer can be quite devastating. Few professional organizations have any power to offer compensation to people who have had a bad deal from one of their members. You still have to go to court to get this, just as you would have to in the case of a cowboy builder.

What is true, however, is that most professional organizations offer advice and help if you run into problems with one of its members. Many investigate complaints from the public and some offer an arbitration service as an alternative to going to court. If a professional organization does expel or suspend someone as a result of your complaint, this will provide useful evidence for damages or compensation claims.

HOW TO GET A GOOD DEAL
FROM A PROFESSIONAL

▷ *Always check people:* You should make sure that people are who they say they are. Check their qualifications and their membership of a professional organization. Make sure, too, that they have professional indemnity insurance as this will ensure that if you sue a professional for damages and win, your claim will be paid.

▷ *Find someone you are happy with before you start:* The two best ways of finding a professional are personal recommendation and by asking a professional organization to send you a list of their members who work near you.

  If you can, it is worth talking on the phone to two or three different professionals before choosing one. You need to find out if they have particular experience in the kind of work you want done and you also need to know if you feel comfortable dealing with them. The best professionals can explain things clearly without using jargon. If they cannot give you clear answers, the likelihood is that they probably do not understand what they are talking about themselves.

▷ *Be clear about how much it will cost:* You need to find out three important figures before you agree to any work: an estimate or quotation for the total cost, the charge made per hour, and any other additional costs that may be added to your bill, like VAT or other expenses. Any professional who is reticent about talking about money is behaving very unprofessionally; drop them and find someone else.

118

▷ *See if you can do some of the routine work yourself:*
Professionals charge from £50 per hour upwards. It is
silly to pay this money for routine work that could be
done by yourself or by family or friends. Many routine
tasks are, in fact, done not by the professionals
themselves but by members of their staff, although you
will usually be charged the full hourly cost. So, discuss
with the professional whether or not there are any jobs
you can do to keep the bill down.

▷ *Keep records of the work:* You will usually be charged by
the hour and, as the hourly charge is quite high, it
makes sense to keep a note of how much time a
professional takes. Keep a note of the time you spend
talking to them on the phone, and the time the
professional spends with you at their office or in your
home. Often some of this time feels like 'social' time,
especially when you are getting on well together and a
friendship develops. You may feel differently about it
when you are charged for this social time as well as for
the time spent actually doing the work.

▷ *Keep track of the bill:* Although you may have an
estimate of the total cost at the start of the job, the
work done may turn out to be totally different. The
final bill is unlikely to be less than the estimate and can
often turn out to be much more. One useful thing to
agree is that you should be notified if your bill goes
over a certain amount, say £500 or £1000. This will
enable you to keep track of the bill and, if necessary,
call a halt before the bill expands beyond your means.

ARCHITECTS

The title 'architect' is protected by law. *All* architects must be registered with the Architects Registration Council of the United Kingdom (ARCUK). ARCUK will deal with complaints about disgraceful misconduct. The professional association, the Royal Institute of British Architects (RIBA) (or its equivalent in Northern Ireland and Scotland) will look into breaches of professional standards. They can also help you find another architect if things go wrong. Neither organization, however, can help you gain compensation or even help you challenge an architects' bill. You will have to initiate your own legal action to do this, although RIBA does offer arbitration as an alternative to going to court.

SURVEYORS AND STRUCTURAL ENGINEERS

Anybody can call themselves a surveyor or a structural engineer. Unlike an architect, they do not have to be registered with any professional body, so it is important to check their qualifications.

Surveyors can have a number of different qualifications. The most common is membership of the Royal Institution of Chartered Surveyors. Structural engineers are usually members of the Institute of Structural Engineers. Check an individual's membership and do not employ someone who is not a member.

All things being equal, it is better to employ a surveyor or a structural engineer who has local knowledge because such a person will know about houses like yours and about the peculiarities of the land on which it has been built. It should also mean that they are aware not only of planning permissions and council plans, but of suggestions and rumours of development.

Structural engineers and surveyors often end up supervising building work, particularly major work involved in cases of subsidence, for example. They are then responsible for checking and approving that all the work has been done, although you will probably pay the builder separately. Thus, if anything does go wrong with the work, you should claim against the surveyor or structural engineer, so make sure they have the appropriate professional indemnity insurance before employing them. This particularly applies to 'weekenders', people who have a full-time job working for a company or a local council and do private work in their spare time.

Weekenders can offer a good deal, particularly when it comes to price, but the disadvantage is that when things go wrong, they are often not around or cannot get to the site quickly. There are also problems if they are ill. If you employ a weekender, check what cover there is if something unforeseen happens.

The most important thing to do before employing a surveyor is to make sure that they are experienced in the kind of work you want them to do. This is particularly important if you are commissioning a homebuying report or a full building (structural) survey before you buy a house. If you do decide that a full survey is worth the extra money, make sure that the surveyor has permission to take up floorboards, otherwise the report may not be worth a great deal.

If your surveyor does not point out something that later

turns out to be a significant problem, you can sue them. You will have to show, however, that the surveyor could have been reasonably expected to spot the fault and that you have lost money as a result.

If you want to complain about a surveyor, the key thing is to move fast. Get another surveyor to provide you with a report that says that the fault should have been noticed and was within the scope of the original survey. You then have a choice between going to court or, if the surveyor is a member of the Royal Institution of Chartered Surveyors, opting for its arbitration service. The surveyor must agree to arbitration as well.

If you go to court, you can only claim the difference in value between what you paid for a house and what you would have paid if you had known about the problem. This could well be less than the cost of a repair.

While the Royal Institution of Chartered Surveyors and the other professional organizations cannot deal with complaints about negligence or, indeed, with any claims for compensation, they will look into complaints about professional misconduct, for example, unnecessary delays or failure to disclose a conflict of interest.

ESTATE AGENTS

Chris Nichols from Andover in Hampshire was desperate to sell his house, but the housing market was completely static. Even advertisements that he had placed himself in the national papers had no effect. Indeed, the only response he received from these advertisements was a telephone call from an international estate agent that was called London Investment Property Services Limited. What the agent told Mr Nichols seemed to make sense.

They talked about the market there was for English property in Hong Kong, a market that consisted of ex-patriates and of Hong Kong Chinese people who wanted a bolt-hole before Hong Kong was handed back to mainland China. London Investment Property Services would include Mr Nichols' house in their 'international showcase advertising campaign' in Hong Kong – for £587. Mr Nichols paid up and, like hundreds of other people, all he ever received for his money was one advertisement in a Hong Kong newspaper alongside 60 others. None of the promised contacts materialized and the quoted success rate of 50 per cent turned out to be complete fiction. The impressive office in central Hong Kong turned out to be simply a mailing address.

Mr Nichols took London Investment Property Services to the small claims court, but the company went into liquidation before his case could be heard.

Despite 15 years of laws, codes of practice and, more recently, the introduction of an ombudsman, it is still quite easy for a company like London Investment Property Services to set up as an estate agent, make all kinds of outrageous promises and get away with it, at least for a time. When the market is poor and some people are desperate to sell their houses, these kind of estate agents flourish.

The Estate Agents Act 1979 states that estate agents must tell you their fees, how and when they are to be paid and if they have any interest in the property. The Act also states that estate agents must give you an estimate of any extras (the usual extras are advertising costs). The Act is administered by the Office of Fair Trading, which has the power to ban people from the trade. The Property Misdescriptions Act 1991 makes all estate agents responsible in law for the accuracy of their descriptions.

The trade association, the National Association of Estate Agents has a code of practice, but, like all such codes, it is voluntary. There is no requirement for estate agents to be members or to follow the code. The estate agents' ombudsman will look at complaints about its members, but its members are only corporate estate agents not independents.

How to get the best deal from an estate agent

▷ If you want to sell your house, sign on as a buyer first to test the service provided by different agents.

▷ Never give 'sole selling rights' because this entitles the agent to a commission even if you sell the house without their help.

▷ Cross out any 'ready, willing and able' clause in the contract that commits you to paying the agent's fee if a buyer is found and you decide not to proceed with the sale.

▷ The best option to take is to give one firm 'sole agency' for a limited amount of time. If your property does not sell, take it off the market for a while and give sole agency to another agent.

▷ Make sure you give 14 days notice in writing before you change from one sole agency agreement to another. If a previous agent gets in touch, tell them to go through your new agent – otherwise you will have to pay two sets of commission.

▷ Under 'sole agency' agreements, you will not have to pay commission if you sell your house privately. But you should tell the agent if someone is interested before you sign the contract with them.

▷ Try not to pay for any advertising but to pay only commission if your property is sold.

▷ Always try and negotiate on the commission. You may be able to persuade them to accept less.

DOCTORS

In June 1993, the Government announced an independent review of complaints procedures in the National Health Service. It was not before time. The present system is a shambles. Complaining about a doctor's behaviour, for example, could mean involving the Family Health Services Authority or the General Medical Council or the Health Service Commissioner and none of these people have any power to award you compensation – you must go to court to get this.

If you see a doctor under the National Health Service, you do not pay for their service, at least not yet, so the problems that crop up with other professionals about bills and overcharging do not apply. As you have no contract with an NHS doctor, the Supply of Goods and Services Act 1982 is of no use (although the Act does apply if you see any doctor privately).

Apart from this, doctors are like any other professional. They provide expertise and a service for which they are well paid. They have the same 'duty of care' that any other professional has and you can sue them if they are negligent in how they treat you.

General practitioners

GPs are self-employed independent contractors. Most GPs contract their services to the NHS through the local Family Health Services Authority, but some GPs only see private patients and some see a mixture of NHS and private patients.

The Family Health Services Authority in your area will provide you with a list of GPs (it will be listed in the phone book). It will also find you a GP if you cannot find one yourself. Under the Patients' Charter, Family Health Services Authorities can lay down standards for their GPs, but these standards are not compulsory.

Almost all specialist and hospital services in the National Health Service require a referral from a GP. In theory, a GP should only refer a patient if the GP is convinced that the patient's illness or condition needs a specialist's opinion or treatment. In practice, most GPs will refer a patient to a specialist if the patient asks or keeps asking, if only to keep them quiet. If a GP refuses to refer you to a specialist, you can try and get a referral from another doctor in the same practice. If this does not work, you could change your doctor. You do not need to tell your old doctor this or give any reason, but simply tell the Family Health Services Authority and they will let your old doctor know.

Apart from emergencies, you would normally be referred to a specialist if the GP does not know what is wrong with you, if the treatment they provide does not work or if the GP decides you need specialist treatment.

Fundholders

One in four patients now have GPs who are fundholders and the number is increasing all the time. Fundholding

GPs are still employed by the Family Health Services Authorities, but they control their own budgets. This means that they can choose which hospital and specialist services to send their patients to. Some GPs do deals to try and get the best and cheapest services for their patients.

The evidence suggests that patients from fundholding GPs get faster and better treatment from consultants and hospitals. This is hardly surprising as fundholding GPs have more bargaining power than other GPs. If they are dealing with hospitals which are trusts (see page 134), there is little stopping the GP and hospital coming to an arrangement that puts the GP's patients at the top of the waiting list.

Another advantage of a fundholding GP is that they are free to refer you to any medical specialist they want, anywhere in the country. A non-fundholding GP is much more dependent on the local Family Health Services Authority's arrangements with local hospitals. Fundholding GPs are also more likely to develop services 'in house', for example, simple surgery or regular sessions with visiting professionals like psychotherapists.

On the other hand, there is always the temptation for a fundholding GP to behave more like a businessman than a doctor, to be more concerned with balance sheets and projections than the health of their patients. You can never be quite sure what their motivation is when they recommend a treatment. Are they referring you to a particular hospital or developing a specialism in the practice because they believe it is the best for you or because it is the cheapest deal for them? It is difficult to know and sometimes the GP does not know either, so immersed have they become in the finances of running the business.

Finding a good GP

The best GPs are the doctors who have energy, commit-ment and clear ideas about what their practice is about. You should look for someone you do not feel embarrassed about visiting or calling out to visit, who seems to be in touch with new medical developments and treatments, who organizes their practice in such a way that you do not have to spend hours waiting to see them. Above all, the best GPs are good at diagnosing illnesses and this can be crucial.

Potentially fatal illnesses like meningitis or some of the cancers are treatable if they are spotted in time, but, often, the early symptoms are unclear or confusing. You need to find a GP who has that rare balance between experience and up-to-date knowledge, a GP who can sense when a condition is serious and when it is not. GPs like this are uncommon, but here are a few pointers that can help you identify them.

▷ Always go and see a new practice first and arrange an initial interview with one of the doctors there.
▷ Look at the waiting room and the information provided by the practice. What kinds of regular services do they offer?
▷ Check the specialist knowledge of the doctors. A good practice will have doctors with a range of experience and specialisms between them.
▷ Check, too, the practice's reasons for being a fundholder or for not being one.
▷ Ask what kind of flexibility they have about referrals. Could they refer you to a specialist in any hospital or are they tied to particular hospitals?
▷ Check how they handle emergencies and what kind of

deputizing service they use.
▷ Check, too, that they will talk to you over the telephone if something is worrying you.

When things go wrong

As this book went to press, the Government had not announced how it intended to change the NHS complaints procedures. The present system gives patients three options when things go wrong with a GP. All these options have their problems, and all require considerable work from the patient or the patient's family or friends.

If the GP has been *negligent*, you can go to court for compensation. If a GP has been guilty of serious professional misconduct, you can complain to the General Medical Council. All other complaints should be made to the Family Health Services Authorities, which will look into any complaint about the service provided by GPs in their area.

The main problem is that it is difficult when things go wrong to be clear whether the doctor has been negligent or guilty of professional misconduct or has failed to provide a proper service – it could be one, two or even all three.

Unless you are reasonably sure that you want to take a doctor to court for compensation, the best place to start is with the Family Health Services Authority. Most authorities will be able to give you information and advice about the appropriate action for the kind of complaint that you have. You can always register a complaint with the Family Health Services Authority and then change your mind and take court action instead or go direct to the General Medical Council.

You can get help from your local Community Health Council (under 'C' in the phone book). Community

Health Councils were set up by the Government to represent patients' views and they monitor local NHS services. The Councils vary, however, in the priority they give to helping patients with complaints, although all will provide at least some assistance. Some Councils will offer to represent patients all the way through the system.

The Family Health Services Authorities

The kinds of complaints about GPs that Family Health Services Authorities (FHSAs) have the power to investigate by law are breaches of a doctor's contract with the authority. In the contract, a GP agrees to provide appropriate services for their patients. If these services have not been provided, the Authority will investigate.

In practice, it can be difficult to distinguish between not providing an appropriate service and behaving negligently. What often happens is that cases of negligence have been brought before the Family Health Services Authority under the guise of breaches of contract, partly because the risk and cost of going to court is too great.

If you decide to make a complaint about a GP to your Family Health Services Authority, you must make sure that the complaint gets to them quickly. At present, the time limit is 13 weeks, although you can appeal if you are outside this limit.

How to complain

The patient or patient's relative sends the complaint in writing to the FHSA. They will then write to the GP and will attempt to resolve the complaint if this is possible.

If the complaint cannot be resolved by the staff, it will be dealt with either *informally* (for complaints about waiting times, untidy surgeries, rudeness of manner) or at a *formal* hearing (for more serious complaints where people's health was put at risk).

Informal hearings can prove to be a useful way of clearing the air. They ensure that a GP listens to you and that you get an explanation of what went wrong. However, an informal hearing has no power to get the GP to do or change anything if they do not want to. If you are dissatisfied, you can ask for a formal hearing.

Formal hearings are conducted by the medical services committee of the FHSA, a committee that consists of GPs and lay people. If a complaint is upheld, they can warn or fine a GP and report the GP to the General Medical Council. The system can work well, but it can also leave many patients dissatisfied.

William Powell complained to his local Family Health Services Authority after the death of his 12-year-old son Robert. Robert died of Addison's Disease, a rare hormonal disorder that can be treated if diagnosed in time. In the last two weeks of Robert's life, he was seen by five doctors from his local health centre, yet still he died. Mr Powell wanted to know why.

At the formal hearing, Mr Powell and his witnesses felt it was an entirely unequal contest. They felt that they were up against medically qualified people arguing about medical diagnoses and they had no help at all. It seemed to them that Mr Powell was the one on trial, and not the doctors. At the end of the hearing, four of the doctors were found to have behaved perfectly properly, but a complaint was upheld against the fifth. She was let off with a warning. Mr Powell felt badly let down by the experience, which he felt had not given him any explanation of why his son had died. He is certainly not alone in feeling this way.

The General Medical Council

The General Medical Council (GMC) is the regulatory body for the profession and all doctors have to be registered with it to practise.

The GMC will investigate complaints about *serious professional misconduct*, although what this means is not entirely clear. In practice it is whatever the GMC decides has brought the profession into disrepute. The classic complaints concern drunkenness, dishonesty, sexual relationships with patients, violence, and extremely poor medical treatment. Doctors who are fined over £500 by a FHSA usually have their case referred to the GMC, but patients can complain directly to the Council as well.

On average, about 1 in 10 complaints made to the GMC are thought serious enough to be considered by the Council's professional conduct committee. Unlike a FHSA hearing, legal representation is allowed. Any doctor brought before the Council will almost always be accompanied by a lawyer and the complainant can ask the GMC to pay for legal representation as well.

The GMC can suspend or strike a doctor off the register and so deprive the doctor of their livelihood. A handful of doctors are struck off the register every year, and a few doctors who are struck off do apply successfully to get back on to the register later.

Taking a doctor to court

One of the biggest difficulties with complaining to the FHSA or the GMC is that the process is laborious and time-consuming. It can sometimes take years. Taking a doctor to court for *negligence*, however, is worse still.

The problem is that you have to *prove* medical negligence and this is extremely difficult to do. For example, it

132

is not enough to show that the doctor's treatment did not do you any good, you have to show that your condition has worsened and that this was a direct result of the doctor's actions or lack of them.

Then, too, it is quite possible for a doctor to have made your condition worse without having actually been negligent. A doctor can claim that they did their best and you will have to prove that their best was not good enough for someone in the doctor's position. Finally, even if you can show that a relative of yours died as a result of a doctor's actions, you may not be able to claim compensation if the patient would have died anyway, irrespective of what the doctor did or did not do.

Getting the evidence to back your case will take considerable time and legal expertise. It could also prove extremely costly. It is possible to receive legal aid if you have a good case, but present rules mean that your income will have to be at income support level to qualify.

If you have a good case, however, for example, if you have suffered permanent injury due to a doctor's carelessness or if a relative has died after what seemed a routine operation, and you can get the medical backing to prove your case, do not be put off. The most important thing to do is to find a lawyer who specializes in medical negligence. Such a lawyer can be found by contacting Action for Victims of Medical Accidents. Be prepared for the case to take several years, although often these cases are eventually settled out of court.

Hospital doctors
GPs are generalists: hospital doctors are specialists. GPs spend more time with people who are basically well; hospital doctors spend their time with people who are sick.

Hospital doctors' titles are given according to their experience and qualifications. The two senior grades are consultant and senior registrar; the junior grades are registrar, house officer and medical student. There are one or two unusual grades, like clinical assistant, that lie somewhere in between. When you go into hospital, you will be under the care of a senior doctor but you will be seen most of the time by a junior doctor. One of the things people pay for in a private hospital is the chance to see more of the consultants, although sometimes this is not an advantage.

All NHS hospital doctors are employed directly by a health authority or by a self-governing hospital trust. Unlike GPs, they are not independent contractors. One implication of this is that if you think a hospital doctor has been negligent, you have to take the health authority or trust to court, not the individual doctor. You will, however, have to prove your case in exactly the same way as you would for a GP (see above).

You can complain to the GMC about any hospital doctor if you think the doctor has been guilty of serious professional misconduct. Your complaint is treated in exactly the same way as would a complaint made against a GP (other problems with hospitals, such as complaints about clinical care, are dealt with on page 215).

Private doctors

The GMC will look at complaints of serious professional misconduct about private doctors, but, apart from this, there is no other statutory complaints procedure. However, some private hospitals have their own methods of dealing with complaints. There are just as many difficulties taking a private doctor to court for negligence as there are with any NHS doctor.

You can, however, dispute a private doctor's bill if you think it is unreasonable by using the Supply of Goods and Services Act 1982 (see page 76).

Are private doctors worth it?

It is difficult to see any great advantage in having a private GP rather than a good NHS GP, beyond, perhaps, finding it easier to get a quick appointment. What may well be worth doing, however, is to see a specialist or a consultant privately for a second opinion, especially if you have been refused a second opinion by an NHS doctor or feel too embarrassed to ask for one or just want to try a top specialist who is outside your local area.

A consultation with a specialist can work out cheaper than you might think, especially if no testing is involved. Try to find out how much the cost will be before the appointment. Ask your GP to make sure that your medical notes and any NHS tests are made available to the new doctor (there should be no problem with this if the doctor is suitably qualified).

Stop Press

The Government has now published its proposals to change the complaints procedures about doctors outlined above. The proposals are that every hospital and GP practice should have a designated complaints officer. If the complaint cannot be resolved by conciliation, it will be looked at by the complaints executive of a family health services authority (for GPs) or by the chief executive of a hospital (for hospital doctors). Serious complaints will then be dealt with by an especially appointed panel with a lay majority.

These proposals are sensible – and long overdue. But

they are unlikely to become law until the middle of 1995 at the earliest.

DENTISTS

Like GPs, NHS dentists are independent contractors, but most do private work as well. Indeed, some dentists will accept only private patients. To have your teeth treated on the NHS, you must register for two years with a dentist who does accept NHS patients. You will then be entitled to all the dental care you need to maintain your teeth and gums, but this care is by no means free.

You must pay 80 per cent of the cost of any course of treatment unless you are receiving income support or family credit, are pregnant or have had a baby in the last year or are under 18. There is, however, a maximum payable for any course of treatment (at present £250). A course of private treatment is likely to be much more expensive. Always make it clear to a dentist that you want any work done on the NHS.

Complaints about NHS work by dentists are dealt with by the local Family Health Services Authority in the same way as complaints about GPs (see page 130). For example, if a dentist has been rude to you the complaint will be dealt with informally. If a dentist has caused you harm because of incompetence or poor service, the complaint will usually be examined at a formal hearing. The General Dental Council – the regulatory organization for dentists – works in a similar way to the General Medical Council. If you want compensation for bad or unnecessary work, you must take a dentist to court in exactly the same way as you would take a GP.

OPTICIANS

Anybody can sell glasses, but only a qualified optometrist or an ophthalmic medical practitioner can test eyesight and write prescriptions. Contact lenses must be sold under the supervision of one of these professionals. Prescriptions for glasses can be on the NHS and this part of an optician's work is monitored by the Family Health Services Authorities which will deal with complaints.

If the test is done on the NHS, you still have to pay part of the fee unless you are entitled to a free eye test, for example, if you are under 18 or on income support. The current contribution is £10. You do not have to use your prescription in the shop that carried out the test, you are free to take the prescription wherever you choose. This is a good idea as the prices for glasses vary considerably and it is worth shopping around for the best quote.

You have the same rights when you buy glasses as you have with any consumer product. If they are faulty, you are entitled to your money back. However, you are not entitled to a refund if you simply find them uncomfortable, so it is a good idea before you buy glasses or lenses to agree with the shop that they will give you a refund if you change your mind. Make sure, too, if you buy contact lenses that after-care treatment is included in the price.

The Optical Consumer Complaints Service was set up in 1993 by the optical trade to deal with disputes between customers and qualified opticians.

OTHER MEDICAL PROFESSIONALS

Many other medical professionals, such as nurses, occupational therapists, physiotherapists, chiropodists and pharmacists, have to be registered with a regulatory body to practice. Check their registration if you consult them privately. Pharmacists are regulated by the Family Health Services Authorities, which will deal with complaints, but the others are usually employed by health authorities or trusts or by local authority social services departments, so complaints need to be taken up with their employers.

ALTERNATIVE MEDICINE

Alternative or complementary medicine ranges from the old and relatively established (homeopathy, osteopathy, herbalism, chiropractic) to the more recent and mostly respectable (acupuncture and psychotherapy); from the avant-garde (aromatherapy, hypnotherapy and reflexology) to the bizarre (numerology and colonic irrigation). In all of these categories there are trustworthy professionals. In all of them, too, are deluded or fraudulent individuals who can do great harm. The problem is separating one from the other.

There are virtually no protections offered to the customer, no statutory regulations or State-approved registers of practitioners. There are some schools and councils that do check up on their members, but often they compete with each other. The umbrella term 'alternative medicine', like less conventional religious groups and small political parties, can include some unsavoury characters.

Some of the councils have codes of ethics and training that you can inspect and, if you are thinking of consulting an alternative practitioner, you should always check their qualifications carefully. Ask what the qualifications mean, check where they were trained and with whom they are registered.

If they say they are medical doctors, check their registration with the General Medical Council (it is a criminal offence to claim or advertise that you are medically qualified when you are not). Finally, always ask a practitioner how much the treatment costs per hour and how many treatments you are likely to need.

One safeguard is to ask your doctor for a referral to an alternative practitioner. Doctors can refer a patient to a non-medically qualified practitioner as long as they are satisfied with the treatment on offer.

FUNERAL DIRECTORS

Many people have difficulties when dealing with funeral directors. When people arrange a funeral, it is at a time when they are at their most vulnerable. It often seems almost disrespectful to shop around or enquire about money and people sometimes see the cost of a funeral as a measure of how much the person who has died meant to them.

The result can be high expectations, but little precise agreement about what is actually being bought. When the Office of Fair Trading investigated the funeral business a few years ago, 1 in 10 customers reported some dissatisfaction with the services they had received.

Here are some tips about how to get the best deal:

▷ Prices vary quite considerably. Ask other people which company they used and whether they were satisfied with the experience. Try to get quotes that itemize every part of the funeral from at least two firms.

▷ Check if the firm is a member of the National Association of Funeral Directors. The Association has a code of conduct that you can quote if things go wrong, although the Consumers Association considers that the code is inadequate and poorly policed. Several funeral directors have left the Association to form another organization, the Funeral Standards Council. This Council says it will be tougher on its members than is the Association and has recently appointed its own ombudsman, who will look at complaints (071 430 1112).

▷ If the service provided is not what you asked for or is unacceptably poor, deduct what you think is reasonable from the final bill and pay the difference. Make sure you have evidence from other people who were present at the funeral, especially from any priest or minister involved. The company will have to take you to court for the rest of the bill and if you have a good case, few companies will bother.

▷ If you have already paid the full bill and cannot face taking the funeral company to court yourself, you can use the conciliation and arbitration service of the National Association of Funeral Directors as long as the company is a member.

VETS

All treatment provided by a vet is private: there is no national health service for animals, nor are there any national rates – vets can charge whatever their customers agree to pay or make a reasonable charge if nothing has been agreed. The bills can be quite considerable, so it is always worth checking with vets how much they charge before any consultation. If you are on a low income, ask the vet if there is any kind of discount. The People's Dispensary for Sick Animals will see animals for free, but only if their owners are on income support or a similar means-tested benefit.

All vets must be registered with the Royal College of Veterinary Surgeons and the College will investigate any complaint concerning a vet's professional misconduct. However, if you have been overcharged or if you have received poor service, you will have to take the vet to court and you will need evidence from another vet to do this, which could be difficult to obtain. If you do have problems, the British Veterinary Association may be able to help as most vets are members and the Association has a code of practice.

Local councils have a duty to collect dead dogs, but not dead cats. The bodies will be disposed of either in a tip or in an incinerator together with other waste. All vets, too, will dispose of a dead animal, but they will charge for this and the animal will be handled in a similar way. Many pet owners opt for a private burial or cremation, which can often be arranged through vets. Unless you pay from £50 upwards, however, your pet will be cremated communally and any ashes given back are unlikely to be all theirs.

JOURNALISTS

It is perfectly possible to hire someone to write or research for you. The National Union of Journalists has a guide to freelances, most of whom are quite willing to sell their skills to the general public.

However, most people come into contact with journalists when a journalist is putting a story together. This can turn out to be a distressing experience. Here are some tips.

▷ If a journalist calls you, take their number and say you will call back in five minutes. No journalist can refuse this, even if they are working to a tight deadline. They would not have called you if the deadline was that tight. This five minutes gives you time to decide whether or not you really want to speak to them, and what you want to say.

▷ Before you call back, try and work out why they are calling you. Always ask the journalist how they got your name, who else they are talking to and what angle they are taking.

▷ Anything you say to a journalist is regarded as 'on the record'. This means that it can be used in any report the journalist is putting together, with your name as the attribution. The classic way to prevent this is to say right at the start of the conversation that, although you are quite prepared to be quoted about some things, you want to talk initially 'off the record'. At the end of the conversation, you can then decide if you are happy to be quoted or not. It is not unknown for journalists to break an off the record promise – it has no basis in law – but most journalists will respect the convention, and most editors will take a dim view of the breaking of such a promise.

▷ On or off the record, many journalists tape record their phone calls, even with members of the public.

▷ Always ask how your contribution will be used, but do not expect any kind of detailed answer. Ask them to send you a copy of the final product.

▷ Journalists will often exchange information with you, as long as they trust you will not ruin their story by passing on the information to someone else. Use them as a resource.

▷ If your name is going to be in print or if you have done a radio or television interview, be prepared to be disappointed the first time you see it. Try and read it or listen to it or watch it a few days later. You may be pleasantly surprised.

▷ Finally, always try and put across your views with passion. Like most people, journalists prefer talking to someone who really cares about their subject.

If something goes wrong

You may not like something a journalist writes or produces, but there is little that you can do if this is the only thing wrong with the report. You can write a letter for publication or contact one of the right-to-reply shows on radio or television and you will stand a reasonable chance of having your letter printed or read out, especially if you were a contributor to the programme. However, this is all, unless you have been libelled or represented unfairly.

If your views have been misrepresented or your privacy has been invaded without a good reason, you should complain. The first person to contact is the editor of the paper or the programme. Try for a correction, although you will be unlikely to be granted one as editors hate printing or broadcasting corrections because it is saying to their audience that they have got something wrong.

If you cannot gain any satisfactory response from an editor of a newspaper or a magazine, contact the Press Complaints Commission, which may decide to investigate. If they find in a complainant's favour, they can instruct a newspaper or magazine to publish a correction. The Commission has recently appointed a Privacy Commissioner who will investigate intrusions by newspaper journalists into people's privacy. As this book goes to press, the Government has also indicated that it will soon introduce a new civil law of privacy which will allow people to claim compensation from journalists for invading their privacy.

The Broadcasting Complaints Commission fulfils a similar role to the Press Complaints Commission for radio and television programmes. It entertains complaints from people who have been interviewed, contacted or mentioned on a programme and been treated unfairly, unjustly or had their privacy infringed. The Broadcasting Standards Council can investigate complaints about taste or decency. The BBC has now set up its own Programme Complaints Unit which will look into serious complaints about, for example, inaccuracies and breaches of broadcasting standards.

None of these organizations, however, can award compensation, even if you have been libelled. For this, you will need to sue. Do not consider suing for libel unless:

▷ you have an absolutely clear case, with supporting evidence

▷ the libel written or broadcast (anything spoken on radio or television is libel not slander) is a serious one
▷ you have a reputation to lose
▷ be very wary of suing anyone for slander since this is even more difficult to prove than libel.

If all these are true and you want to risk what could turn out to be a very costly process (there is no legal aid for libel), it is better not to contact the paper or programme direct, but to see a solicitor who specializes in libel. Be prepared for a long battle that will be settled, hopefully, before you get to court. With any libel action you risk losing a considerable amount of money as there is nothing certain about taking legal action, least of all for libel.

LAWYERS

Much of this book is aimed at saving you the expense of consulting a lawyer, but there are some occasions when you will need one. Beware of the cost, though – lawyers are always expensive, most charging from £50 per hour and upwards. (Lawyers are either solicitors or barristers. Barristers advocate cases in court: they are never employed directly by a member of the public, but are engaged through solicitors. To confuse matters, some solicitors now advocate cases in court, a right that used to be restricted to barristers. All major court cases, however, are handled by barristers.)

Finding a good solicitor

▷ Most high street solicitors are generalists: which means that they will take on virtually any case. Ask them about their experience of dealing with cases like yours.

▷ It may be better to find a practice that specializes in certain kinds of law. The *Regional Directory of Solicitors* can provide you with such information (a copy is available in most reference libraries or Citizens Advice Bureaux). If your case involves personal injury or medical negligence, contact the Association of Personal Injury Lawyers for a list of members in your area.

▷ Go for an initial interview to discover if you feel happy with the solicitor. It is not *necessary* to like someone who is going to represent you, but it certainly helps.

▷ Ask them how much they charge per hour, how much work is likely to be involved, what other costs you will have to pay and when you will be expected to pay. It is difficult to predict in advance how much your costs will be, but keep clear of any solicitor who is not open and frank about money.

▷ Check exactly who will be doing the work and whether or not you will pay the *same* hourly rate for *all* the work. Solicitors have a number of people working for them who are not legally qualified, but who do much of the routine work. They should charge less for this.

▷ With the solicitor go through the projected timetable for the case, what the various steps are, and what you have to do next.

How to cut down costs

▷ Ask the solicitor to let you know when your bill is nearing a certain amount, say £300. You can then take action to avoid it going over what you can afford.

▷ After every meeting, confirm in writing what you want done.

146

▷ Ask the solicitor if there is any routine work you can do yourself.

▷ Try to be as businesslike as you can. A solicitor is there to represent you and advise about your legal rights. Do not use them as a shoulder to cry on because the shoulder could turn out to be a very expensive one.

▷ Find out about all the schemes that could enable you to receive legal services cheaper or, in some cases, free (see pages 282 to 288).

▷ If you are unhappy about a bill, you can ask the solicitor to send it to the Law Society for a remuneration certificate. There is no charge for this certificate, but be warned that the Law Society can increase as well as reduce bills. (The Law Society is currently reviewing remuneration certificates.) If court work has been involved, you can apply to the court for the bill to be 'taxed'. Again, the court can increase the bill as well as reduce it. You will have to pay the solicitor's costs if the court's reduction is less than a fifth of the bill, so think carefully before asking for this.

Complaining about a solicitor

▷ Each solicitor's practice should have its own complaints procedure so ask the solicitor to use this first.

▷ If this proves to be of no use, ring the helpline of the Solicitors Complaints Bureau (0926 822007/822008). This helpline can give you advice on whether or not there may be cause for complaint.

▷ Then, put your complaint in writing and send it to the Bureau. It will be passed initially to the Conciliation Unit, which will try to mediate.

▷ If the conciliation process fails or there has been
   serious professional misconduct, the complaint will be
   dealt with formally. The Solicitors Complaints Bureau
   will consider complaints about poor service (for which
   it can award compensation of up to £1000, and order
   a refund of fees), and unprofessional conduct (for
   which it can rebuke or warn a solicitor or pass the case
   on to the Solicitors Disciplinary Tribunal. The
   Tribunal can stop a solicitor practising).

▷ If you are unhappy with the Bureau's way of handling
   your complaint, you can complain to the Legal
   Services Ombudsman. You must do this within three
   months of the Bureau's decision. The ombudsman can
   award unlimited compensation.

▷ The Solicitors Complaints Bureau cannot deal with
   claims of negligence over £1000, but it can put you in
   touch with either a solicitor who specializes in
   negligence claims or with the Solicitors Indemnity
   Fund which provides insurance for solicitors.

▷ You can also apply to the Solicitors Indemnity Fund if
   you have lost money because of a solicitor's dishonesty.

▷ In Scotland, all complaints about solicitors are dealt
   with by the Scottish Law Society. It has no power to
   award any compensation.

6

TRAVEL
AND TRANSPORT

THE HOLIDAY OF A LIFETIME
THAT NEARLY WAS NOT

There are few experiences more memorable than an enjoyable holiday, and a holiday that combined visiting Seville in Spain with the chance of seeing a performance by the great opera singer Luciano Pavarotti was not to be missed – or at least it seemed that way to Hazel and Richard McPherson. The McPhersons paid £569 to a firm called Concert Tours for a four-day holiday in Seville with tickets to see not just Pavarotti but also Placido Domingo.

The tickets, however, never turned up. Eventually, the McPhersons received an explanation. Concert Tours said they had to cancel the tour because the theatre Pavarotti and Domingo were to appear in would not be ready in time. It was a complete lie: the concert did, in fact, go ahead as planned. The McPhersons never made it to Seville and Concert Tours never refunded them their money.

For anybody, it would have been a disappointment to say the very least, but for Hazel McPherson it was worse because she was going deaf and the holiday in Seville would be one of the last chances she would have to hear Pavarotti sing, a pleasure she wanted to experience.

The business that had denied Mrs McPherson this

pleasure, Concert Tours, turned out to be the trading name of a company called Strategic Air Charter Limited. They have since gone bust.

Fortunately, after *Watchdog* had told the McPhersons' story, a newspaper stepped in and offered to pay for the McPhersons to see Pavarotti after all, although in Dublin not in Seville. It is one holiday disaster that turned out well in the end, but one of the few.

The only consolation that most people receive for an unhappy holiday is the ability to tell tales of woe to friends who naturally find these much more interesting than tales of a wonderful time. This chapter will give you advice on how to irritate your friends by making sure you have a good time when you travel.

AIR

There used to be a clear difference between scheduled flights, which were offered by airlines, and chartered flights, which were offered by holiday companies. They used different planes and often flew at different times from different airports. This difference has now become extremely blurred. Many holiday companies offer holiday accommodation combined with air tickets that are not on a specially chartered aircraft but on an ordinary scheduled flight. Strictly speaking, these are charter tickets as they are sold not by the airline or by the airline's agents, but by a tour operator as part of a holiday package. However, the tickets are the same as schedule tickets and the passengers are treated in exactly the same way.

It is still useful, however, to keep the distinction in

mind, because it matters if things go wrong. When you buy a charter ticket, your contract is with the holiday company, not with the airline. You should, therefore, always make sure that the agent selling you the air ticket has an ATOL licence (see page 178) because you will then have protection if they go bust. When you buy a scheduled ticket, your contract is with the airline. If the airline goes bust, you have no protection at all.

What makes all this even more confusing is that some travel agents sell scheduled tickets (where they act as an agent for the airline) *and* charter tickets (where they act as an agent for a holiday company). These tickets could be to the same city and on the same flight, so, before you part with your money, try to find out what kind of ticket you are buying.

HOW TO GET A CHEAP FLIGHT

On any plane going anywhere in the world, few of the passengers will have paid the same fare. The differences in the fares can be startling, particularly on the most popular routes to America and Europe. The person sitting next to you could have paid hundreds of pounds less. Here are some ways in which you can buy a cheap flight.

Airline's own discount fares
Every airline offers a range of discounted fares – including APEX, Youth, PEX, Budget and Standby fares – but they all have restrictions. For example, APEX fares have to be booked 14 days in advance and you have to stay a Saturday night.

Each of these fares may well have their own variations. APEX fares are often cheaper if you go earlier in the week, for example, and there are often special discounts if you fly out of season. You can try to book these fares through travel agents, but counter staff cannot always be relied on to come up with the cheapest fare. The best bet is to book through the airline itself.

Unknown airlines

Many smaller national airlines survive for political, not economic reasons. They are heavily subsidized and are not expected to make a profit, but they are there to provide flights from the capital of their country to the major cities in the world. Most of their flights have spare seats and the airlines try to sell these seats cheap.

Many of the seats end up in bucket shops (see below), but it is possible to cut out the bucket shop and negotiate your own discount. Bear in mind, however, two things. First, you may have to travel via an unusual route, with stopovers in obscure places in the early hours of the morning. Second, the safety record of the more obscure airlines may not be as good as the major international companies (you can find out more about the safety records of different airlines by consulting the twice-yearly survey by the trade magazine *Flight International*, which describes the major aircraft crashes that have occurred during the previous six months and notes how many people died).

Courier tickets

Courier tickets are not quite the bargain they once were. Few of them are free and the days of the £50 return to Australia have long gone. On the other hand, the companies that offer courier tickets are now better organized. You can book a courier ticket in advance and, on some tickets, you can even bring your own luggage. Sometimes you do not even have to take any responsibility for the package you are meant to be accompanying as this is all done for you. You can obtain a list of courier companies from the Yellow Pages. The real courier bargains are available to people who can travel to obscure places at a moment's notice.

Bucket shops

Few flights ever sell out. Often there are a large number of seats unsold, but the flight still has to go ahead. It makes sense, then, for airlines to sell any unsold seats for whatever money they can get. The problem for the airlines is that if cut-price tickets go through the established routes, this will bring down the price of the official fare as passengers will wait until the cut-price tickets are available.

So, what has happened is that a shadow market has developed, a murky world where contacts are everything and few names are mentioned. Airlines sell the surplus tickets to wholesalers known in the trade as 'consolidators'. Consolidators sell the tickets on to a wide range of discount agents that range from established shops to lone operators. These agents are known collectively as 'bucket shops' because they mop up leftover seats. They advertise in the local and national press.

Bucket shops come and go. They are often difficult to track down and few of them offer any protection to their customers if they go bust. However, they do provide the cheapest air fares on the market, and often these fares become available only a few days before departure. Here is how to minimize the risks when buying from a bucket shop:

▷ find out the airline and the flight number and check this with the airline concerned

▷ ask the shop if they are acting as an agent for the airline (selling scheduled tickets) or acting on their own behalf (selling charter tickets). If they are an agent for the airline, check that they are registered with the International Air Transport Association (IATA) and make sure the credit card voucher is made payable only to the airline. If they are acting on their own behalf, they must have an ATOL licence or be an ATOL agent (see below)

▷ ring the airline to see if your name is on their passenger list. Ask them if your name is 'confirmed' or not: that is, your ticket has been paid for

▷ never pay more than £50 deposit

▷ avoid any shop that advertises flights at one price and then tries to sell the flight at another price

▷ always pay by credit card

▷ only pay the full amount when you receive the ticket, even if you have to go in person to collect the ticket

▷ when you get your ticket, check the top right hand corner to see where it was issued. Beware of a foreign address

▷ when you have paid the full amount, ring up the airline and check that you are booked on to the flight and that your ticket has been paid for.

Bucket shops also sell unsold charter tickets as holiday operators have similar problems to those of airlines in selling all their holidays. These come on to the market a few days or weeks before departure, as the holiday company realizes that it will have to pay for more seats than it has managed to sell. Sometimes just the ticket part of the holiday will be available.

All bucket shops that offer these kind of tickets

must have an ATOL licence or be acting as the agent for someone with an ATOL licence. Before booking the flight, find out the name of the ATOL agent and their ATOL number and check them with the Civil Aviation Authority. The ATOL protection ensures that you will get your money back or be flown home if the agent goes bust. If the shop is acting as an agent for an ATOL licence-holder, make sure the credit card voucher is made out to the name of the ATOL agent.

WHEN THINGS GO WRONG

If your ticket is a charter ticket, you should be protected by the ATOL bonding scheme, but the scheme does not apply to scheduled tickets bought through an airline. If an airline company goes bust, you lose your money. If you are stranded abroad when this happens, you may be flown back free of charge by another airline, but they are under no compulsion to do this. So, it is a good idea, as mentioned above, to pay by credit card as you should then be able to get your money back from the credit card company. You should also make sure that your holiday insurance includes cover for the financial failure of an airline. If a travel agent who sold you a scheduled airline ticket goes bust before you receive the ticket, the airline should honour the ticket although there have been problems with this in the past.

Overbooking and bumping
As there are usually a number of passengers who book tickets but do not turn up, airlines try to sell more tickets on a flight than there are seats. One consequence is that if everyone *does* turn up, latecomers are 'bumped', which

means that they will be put on the next available flight.

The best way to avoid being bumped is to check in early. However, there are advantages to turning up late. If there are no seats left, standard class passengers will be offered an upgrade to business or first class if there is any room left there. If there is no room at all on the plane, you *will* be bumped, but this is not as bad as it may seem. You will be offered a full refund or a seat on the next available plane. And you will also be offered compensation, which is generous if you have to wait more than two hours. At European Community airports, for example, EC regulations state that, currently, this compensation must be £106 or £212, depending on the journey time involved. You will also be entitled to free meals and, if appropriate, accommodation, along with a free phone call to your destination. For any journey involving an American airport, compensation is also mandatory and is usually around half the applicable one-way fare, plus expenses.

All this can make a sizable difference to the cost of an airline ticket, for the price of being a few hours late. It is worth negotiating similar deals if you are bumped outside Europe or America.

Delays, damage and the Warsaw Convention
Most things that go wrong on a flight that are the airline's fault are covered by the Warsaw Convention. This Convention was worked out at a conference in Warsaw in 1929 when national governments decided to set limits on the liability of their airlines for things that did not go according to plan. The Warsaw Convention has been incorporated into English and Scottish law, so it has full legal status in the UK.

It obliges airlines to compensate passengers on international flights as long as the airline was in some way to blame. But it also sets out the *maximum* amounts airlines will have to pay for certain kinds of mistakes or catastrophes. For example, if your luggage is damaged or lost, the maximum amount payable by an airline under the Convention is, at present, £13.63 per kilo – less than you would get from holiday insurance (but even if you do have insurance for lost luggage, always ask the airline for spot compensation to cover any essential goods like clothes and toiletries that you may have to buy straight away).

The Warsaw Convention also obliges airlines to pay compensation for delays, unless the delay was due to something entirely out of the airline's control, such as a strike or a crash. The amount payable depends on how long the delay is and how responsible the airline was for it.

Under the Convention, the maximum limit for compensation from an airline is US $75 000. This has been updated by a new international agreement, the Montreal Protocol, to roughly £75 000, but the Protocol is not yet law as it still needs a few more countries to ratify it.

How to complain

If it proves impossible to sort out a complaint on board or at the airport, contact the customer relations department of the airline when you get home. You can also get advice and help from the Air Transport Council User Committee, a passengers' watchdog that, unfortunately, has very few teeth, apart from being able to refer problems to its parent body, the Civil Aviation Authority. The Civil Aviation Authority does have teeth: it is the regulatory body for air travel in the United Kingdom and it can take away an airline's licence.

RAIL

As this book is being prepared for publication, the privatization of railway services is taking place. The Railways Acts 1993 allows 25 of the most popular lines to be sold off as franchises, under the control of a new franchise director. Other lines will follow. The Act also allows anybody else to offer a railway service along these 25 lines under the 'open access' principle. British Rail continues to operate all the lines that have not been franchised and they will be allowed to bid for a franchise line as long as the franchise director agrees. The track is run by a new private company called Railtrack. Railtrack owns the stations, although several of the very largest stations will be franchised. Monitoring all this is the Rail Regulator.

By 1995, the first private franchises should be up and running. It will be interesting to see whether or not all the predictions made by the critics of railway privatization – and there are many – turn out to be misplaced. What is certain is that, in the next few years, railway travel is going to look very different indeed.

PASSENGERS' CHARTER
AND CONDITIONS OF CARRIAGE

Curiously enough – or perhaps not that curiously – British Rail has made some genuine efforts in the last few years to become more consumer-friendly. One example is that they have changed, at last, the notorious Condition 25 of their conditions of carriage.

The old Condition 25 stated simply that British Rail would not be liable for anything that went wrong with a train journey, even if it was their fault. This was probably unenforceable in the courts, but it was difficult to challenge and passengers did not bother.

The new Condition 25 commits British Rail to paying out for 'delays, cancellations or poor service' as long as the reason for the problem is within BR's control. A payment could cover, for example, the cost of putting you up in a hotel overnight if you cannot get to your destination.

However, there are problems with the new conditions of carriage. For example, they only allow two children under five to accompany one adult instead of four. Also, the payments are not exactly compensation, although they are a recognition that British Rail is beginning to take responsibility when it gets things wrong.

Another improvement is British Rail's Passengers' Charter. The Charter promises, for example, that you will be given vouchers if your train is delayed for more than an hour and discounts on season tickets if punctuality targets are not met.

The Government's intention is that the standards set out by this Passengers' Charter will be taken up by the new franchise companies, although it will be up to them to work out their own conditions of carriage. However, the Passengers' Charter will not apply to the open access companies, which will be free to set their own standards subject to law.

How to complain
▷ Take things up first with the company concerned or with the appropriate BR manager.
▷ For BR complaints, you should then contact the divisional Customer Relations Manager.

159

▷ If you are still unhappy with the reply, contact your
regional Rail Users' Consultative Committee
(RUCC), the rail passengers' watchdog. These are the
new organizations that have replaced the old Transport
Users' Consultative Committees (TUCCs). RUCCs
can investigate complaints and they have the power to
look at fares and charges, which the TUCCs did not.
You can get their address from the Central Rail Users
Committee. However, they cannot force British Rail or
any other franchised company to do anything,
although they have a good deal of informal influence,
and they have no power to investigate complaints
about an open access company. Any complaints about
these companies that cannot be dealt with by the
company concerned are to be resolved by the courts.

BOATS AND FERRIES

On a warm summer night in August 1989, Iain Philpott
was one of 130 young people partying on the pleasure boat
Marchioness on the River Thames. The boat had just gone
under Southwark Bridge when it was struck from behind
by a sand dredger, the *Bowbelle*, three times its size. Within
seconds, the *Marchioness* had capsized and sunk. Drowned
that night were 51 people, including Mr Philpott's girl-
friend Tamsin Cole, who was just 24 years old.

Since that dreadful night, Mr Philpott has spent much
of his spare time trying to shed light on why so many of his
friends died. What he has discovered through the back
door has horrified him.

It turns out that accidents on the River Thames involving sand dredgers are not that unusual. Before the *Marchioness* disaster, there had been 26 previous incidents involving the *Bowbelle* and her two sister ships, nine involving the *Bowbelle* herself. One was virtually identical to the tragic accident with the *Marchioness*, although no one died, but nobody knew this because the records were not publicly available.

Despite the promises that have been made about open government, the public still does not know whether or not another tragedy like the *Marchioness* may happen because the full accident records of boats ploughing up and down British rivers each day are still a secret. This is not all.

There is no official regulator, nor any government-appointed consumer body that regularly monitors the safety of boats and ferries on rivers or on the seas around the British Isles. Indeed, the entire area of sea travel is remarkably uncontrolled. Anybody can run a ferry service, but each boat must have a certificate of sea worthiness.

In March 1987, there was another disaster when the ferry the *Herald of Free Enterprise* capsized off Zeebrugge. There were 192 deaths. As a result, new safety standards were introduced for RoRo (roll on, roll off) ferries, but these standards only apply to ferries built after April 1990, although some older ships have been rebuilt according to them.

If you are concerned about safety standards on a ship, you should get in touch with the Marine Safety Section at the Department of Transport, which will put you in touch with the relevant district office that will investigate your complaint.

One positive development is that the standards of cross-Channel ferries have improved dramatically over the last few years, at the same time as prices have fallen. The Channel Tunnel seems to be having far more impact than critical consumer reports.

COACHES AND BUSES

All coach services and most bus services are run by private companies. (The exception is in London, where all bus services will not be under private control until the end of 1994.) There is open competition between these private operators and there is no regulation nor any passengers' watchdog, although there have been many calls for one.

To obtain an operator's licence, a bus or coach company has to ensure that its vehicles meet safety standards. The company is then free to operate any route it may choose, although it must give 42 days' notice to the local traffic commissioners. The commissioners, who are part of the Department of Transport, can only turn down a proposed route on safety grounds.

When deregulation was introduced, there were many warnings that it would lead to chaos. In some towns like Sheffield this has happened, but, in other towns, the new private companies have delivered a service at least as good as the local authority's services that they have replaced. The main problem has been that their services have concentrated, hardly surprisingly, on the most profitable routes and have left the remoter parts of town unserved. Local councils are allowed to subsidize routes if there is a 'social need', but, even if a social need can be shown to exist, the local council can always plead lack of cash.

If you do not think a company deserves an operator's

licence, it may be worth complaining to the traffic commissioners, but only if you can get the support of other passengers as well, as the commissioners can only deal with group complaints, not with ones from individuals. One of the complaints traffic commissioners will be interested in is any concern about safety, although the main impediment to coach safety – mandatory seat belts – has still not been introduced. Another 16 people were killed in a coach crash in Kent as this book was being written. Their lives might have been saved if seat belts were compulsory on coaches and minibuses.

TAXIS AND MINICABS

There is total confusion about the licensing of taxis and minicabs across the United Kingdom. London taxis – purpose-built black cabs – are licensed by the police. Every other car touting for business in the metropolis is a minicab and does not need to be licensed. The only restrictions on minicab drivers are that they must have a full driving licence and that their car must be roadworthy and have adequate insurance. The Government has given some commitment to changing this anomaly, but does not see it as a top priority, to say the least.

In the rest of England and Wales, local authorities must regulate taxis, but are free to choose whether or not to regulate minicabs. Most councils, in fact, do choose to regulate minicabs. In Scotland, local authorities can choose between licensing both taxis and minicabs or not licensing them. In Northern Ireland, all taxis and minicabs are licensed.

What distinguishes a taxi from a minicab is that taxis have a set fare shown by a meter, while minicabs are free to negotiate their charges with passengers. Taxis are only allowed to set their own fares if the journey goes outside the area in which they are licensed.

Minicabs are almost always cheaper than taxis, but they are not allowed to tout for business in the street. Taxis are allowed to do this, although they do not have to stop for you. If they do stop, they have to take your fare as long as your journey is inside their licensing authority's limits. In London, this is six miles from Trafalgar Square and journeys to and from Heathrow airport.

Another distinction between taxis and minicabs is that taxis have more to lose if they upset their passengers, because you can complain to the licensing authority about a driver's behaviour and it could mean their licence being taken away from them. But making a complaint is a difficult business as you need the taxi number and registration plate and these are easy to forget in the middle of a dispute.

CARS

With an average one and a half cars per household, car ownership in the United Kingdom is the highest in Europe and it shows no sign of changing. After a depressed few years, new car sales are booming once again, but how can you ensure that you get a good deal?

BUYING A NEW CAR

We pay too much for our new cars in Britain. Virtually all makes of car are cheaper in the rest of Europe and

America, sometimes considerably so, and although some of this difference can be explained by tax, not all of it can. One reason car prices are high is the influence of the company car market, which is more important in Britain than elsewhere. Often companies negotiate discounts of up to 50 per cent on new cars and private customers end up paying for these. Another reason is the franchised dealer system. This system ensures that all new cars are sold by dealers that have a franchise to sell the cars of one manufacturer in their area. It is difficult for customers to compare cars without visiting half a dozen different garages. Despite all this it is still possible to find a new car bargain, although there are some questions you should ask first.

▷ *Do you really want to buy new?* Cars depreciate heavily in value in their first two or three years. This depreciation is far greater than any decrease in a car's reliability. Most new cars should last 150 000 miles if they are looked after. So, it makes sense to buy a car that is two or three years old as it will be much better value than a new car.

Unfortunately, the pleasure of buying a second-hand car comes nowhere near the sheer excitement of taking possession of a new car straight from the showroom. So, a useful thing to remember before deciding to buy a brand-new car is to ask yourself what *exactly* is new about the new car you are buying apart from the shine. Successful models last for about 10 years. To persuade the public to keep buying an old model, car manufacturers give their new cars a new look and a new marketing strategy every three years or so, but, inside, it is the same old car.

▷ *Do you really want to buy this car?* Most people who set out to buy a new car have a pretty good idea about which make and model they would like. These prejudices should be challenged by consulting the car press. Car magazines test new models regularly and compare them with the competition. *Which?* magazine does similar tests, concentrating particularly on car safety, which matters because, although every new car must meet the Government's standards on safety, these standards are not stringent enough. Only half of all new cars were acceptable to *Which?* researchers, and, as 12 people die every day on the road, the argument for buying a safe car is a very strong one. The Government has produced a booklet, *Choosing Safety* (from HMSO bookshops) which reports on how cars fare in a crash.

In all the tests done by *Which?* and the car magazines, some cars do much better than others. If you read enough surveys, a pattern begins to emerge of the cars that motoring experts like and trust, the cars that keep their value and their reliability over the years. It is never worth buying a car that you hate the look of just because other people recommend it, but it is well worth avoiding a car that you have fallen in love with that has performed consistently badly in objective tests.

▷ *Bargaining and discounts:* Discounts are endemic throughout the British car trade. They are available on every car, even on brand-new models, but only to customers who are prepared to bargain. Half of all new car customers do not get a discount simply because they do not ask for one or are too embarrassed to ask.

So they end up paying hundreds and sometimes thousands of pounds more than they need to. If you are not the kind of person who likes bargaining, bring a friend along with you who does.

It is only worth bargaining once you have made up your mind which car you want to buy as a car salesperson will only offer a discount to a serious buyer. Your aim is to try to get the car at the lowest price that the salesperson can afford to let it go.

New cars have a list price and this is the maximum price for which a car can be sold. Curiously enough, the on-the-road price may be *more* than this maximum as it may include road tax plus the cost of delivering the car from the manufacturer to the garage.

New cars usually have a dealer margin of some 17 per cent although some manufacturers have cut this margin to 10 per cent for some popular new models. On top of these percentages, garages often receive bonuses for meeting sales targets. These are the margins with which you can bargain.

The classic bargaining technique is to convince the salesperson that they *will* get a sale from you today, but only for the right price. You must allow the salesperson to make all the running. Never say what price you will pay – that is their job, not yours. In stages, the price will come down. You can get the largest discounts at slow times in the car-buying year, like Christmas. It is more difficult, although not impossible, to obtain a discount on brand-new models, basic models, Japanese cars and other cars in short supply.

▷ *Buying a car abroad:* Another way to buy a new car cheap is to buy it abroad and then import it into

Britain. The best countries to try are Holland, Belgium, France, Portugal and Spain and the savings can amount to some 30 per cent less than the British price, depending on the model.

In theory, what you do is order the car you want from a dealer in one of these countries (you can order a right-hand drive car). You then go to the country concerned and bring it back into Britain as a personal import (customs will provide you with the right forms to fill in). You will have to pay British VAT on the car at the British border, but you do not have to pay the VAT of the country where you bought the car, as long as the dealer knows you will be taking it back to Britain.

That is the theory. In practice, things have been more difficult, mainly because European car dealers have been under pressure not to supply right-hand drive cars to British customers. The European Commission has been trying to stop this.

Faulty new cars

If the new car you buy turns out to be faulty, you have the same rights under the Sale of Goods Act 1979 as you have with any other item you buy. However, garages have long refused to refund a customer's money if things go wrong after the first few drives. Instead, they have offered to repair a faulty new car and sometimes this has meant repair after repair after repair for cars that are particularly problematic.

If a customer disputes this approach, the garage or, more likely, its legal adviser will quote the Bernstein case (see page 49). The effect of this case is that, unless a major problem emerges with a new purchase in the first few weeks, a customer loses their right under the Sale of Goods Act 1979 to claim a refund. All they are entitled to is compensation and, in practice, this adds up to a free repair.

In countries like the United States and Germany, there are 'lemon' laws and manufacturers' guarantees that enable a customer to reject any new car that consistently goes wrong. Under these laws and guarantees, people can get their money back for a car that turns out to be a 'lemon'.

This approach is slowly spreading to Britain. Vauxhall have introduced a scheme where customers can return a new car in the first month after they bought it for any reason whatsoever and they will exchange it. Rover go one better and offer an exchange or a refund. Ford have a similar scheme to Vauxhall's, but they also offer to replace a car or provide a refund if a new vehicle has a persistent defect within the first 12 months of ownership. There have, however, been one or two problems with this last promise.

Ron Sinkinson, a teacher from Liverpool, bought a new Ford Orion. The car turned out to be a lemon. The gearbox went within the first week and this was not the only problem. However, when Mr Sinkinson tried to return the car under the Ford commitment, Ford said that there were no similar Orions available in the country. Eventually, after repairing his Orion 10 times, Ford did find Mr Sinkinson another car, an Escort, but Mr Sinkinson's experience illustrates that there are limitations on these new promises: ask about them before you buy. Still, they are much better than what has gone before.

Apart from these new deals, there is little alternative, if

your new car goes wrong after the first few weeks, to accepting a garage's offer of a repair. Make sure, though, that the garage provides you with a spare car while your car is being repaired. If they refuse, tell them that you will claim the cost of hiring a car from them.

BUYING A SECOND-HAND CAR

Three out of four car owners choose to buy a second-hand car rather than a new one. Even though the average price for a second-hand car is only £3000, the second-hand car market is worth almost as much as the market for new cars.

There are three main ways to buy a second-hand car: privately, from a dealer or at a car auction. Each way has its attractions.

Private sales are usually cheaper than garages but should always be conditional on an inspection by an engineer, which costs from £75. Unfortunately, if a car is a particularly good bargain, the seller may not wait around while an inspection is completed. Beware, too, of any garage who says they have sent the registration documents off to be amended. They should have kept a photocopy.

If you are buying a second-hand car from a garage, you should ensure that it has some kind of insurance-backed warranty. Ask to see the policy and make sure that it is signed over to you before you buy so that you are protected if the garage goes bust. You should also consider getting an engineer's report. If a garage advertises that its cars have been inspected, ask them for a copy of the report. The reports done by garages are usually less extensive than those commissioned by individual buyers directly from the AA or the RAC, however. Be wary, too, of any dealer that will not guarantee the mileage of any of its cars.

Whether you buy a second-hand car privately or through a garage, there are three things you should always look out for.

▷ *Clocking:* Clocking is when a car that has done, say, 135 000 miles becomes one with only 45 000 miles on the clock. Tampering with a clock is a criminal offence and if you discover that a car you have bought has been clocked, report the seller to your local trading standards department. However there are a number of ways in which you can discover whether or not a car has been clocked before you buy.

The most obvious is to look at the wear and tear of the car and see if it is consistent with the mileage. Check things like the seat covers and steering wheel, as both can indicate high mileage. Also, take a look at the clock itself. If the digits do not sit in a straight line, this is a sign that they may well have been tampered with. Be wary of any car that does not have a registration document or a documented service history or any car that comes from a garage with notices saying that the mileage cannot be guaranteed.

▷ *Stolen cars:* As many as 1 in 40 cars are stolen at some time or another and many of them end up in the second-hand market. They are then sold on to unsuspecting buyers. If a car you have bought turns out to have been stolen, you generally have no right to keep it. The rightful owner can reclaim the car and you will have to try to get your money back from the person who sold it to you.

How, though, do you know if a second-hand car is stolen? The registration document – or its absence –

may help. Check that the seller's name and address is on the document and ask them for proof of their identity, preferably by seeing their driving licence.

If you have any doubts at all, contact HPI Autodata, a privately run used car information line in Salisbury (see below).

▷ *Hire purchase:* If you buy a car that has an outstanding hire purchase agreement, you can keep it as long as you did not know about the agreement. However, it is probably better to find out in advance and avoid any possible trouble. HPI Autodata, based in Salisbury (0722 422422), has records of all cars with outstanding HP agreements on them. They can also tell you if a car is an insurance write-off, if it has been reported to them by the police as stolen and if the registration licence plate has been changed. A search costs £15.

Buying a car at an auction

People do make wonderful savings at car auctions, but these people are usually professionals in the car trade rather than ordinary members of the public. About five million cars are sold through auctions every year, most at least £2000 to £3000 cheaper than anywhere else. The trouble is that auctions are not run for the public, but for the trade and it is easy to become completely confused by the jargon used and the hectic pace of the sale. Here are some tips on how to get the best buy at a car auction.

▷ Go to a few auctions first before you make any bid.
▷ Always bring someone with you who knows about cars.
▷ Get to the auction early so you can inspect any car that seems suitable.

▷ Never go over your limit – there will be other cars. Generally, it is not worth buying anything under £2000, unless you have good mechanical knowledge.

▷ Avoid cars that are labelled 'total loss' as this means that they have been involved in an accident and are an insurance write-off.

▷ Go for cars that have a guaranteed mileage – any other car has probably been clocked.

▷ The best bargains are ex-company cars. These are known as 'direct' cars. If a car is not 'direct', look for the phrase 'all good' as this gives you an hour to check whether a car has any faults after your bid is accepted.

▷ The best buys are not the £100 or £200 bargains – they will *not* be a bargain – but cars that are two or three years old and priced between £3000 and £4000.

▷ If you do buy a car, pay an indemnity fee, which will allow you to claim a refund if the car turns out to have been clocked or stolen.

CAR REPAIRS

After a long holiday drive, Stephanie Cartwright and David Morgentern stopped off at a motorway service station. They were filling their car with petrol when a garage attendant pointed out that there was something wrong with one of their tyres. To the holidaymakers, the tyre did not seem to be the least bit dangerous, but they decided it was better to be absolutely safe and they swapped the tyre for the spare. However a mechanic at the garage then said that the car was dangerous to drive as the treads on the spare were different to those of the other tyres. So, once more, they took the garage's advice and bought a new tyre from the garage. When they arrived

173

home, they found that the garage had misled them: there was nothing wrong with any of their tyres. However, there was little they could do as the garage was in France, several hundred miles away.

It could not, of course, happen here – or could it? The Consumers Association did a survey recently of car servicing. They asked 36 garages to service a car and only two did a good job. The remainder provided a sorry catalogue of missed faults and sloppy workmanship. There was little difference between large franchised dealers and small independents.

If you put a car in for repair or servicing, you have all the usual rights under the Supply of Goods and Services Act 1982 (see page 76). The trouble is that it can often be difficult to show that a garage's bill is unreasonable or that the work done was unnecessary. Make sure you tell the garage that all work has to be authorized first and never pay for work that has not been authorized.

For straightforward repairs, the fast-fit centres are usually much cheaper than conventional garages, but the single best way to find a reliable garage is by personal recommendation.

If your car is damaged when it is being repaired or if it fails to function properly after a repair, you can claim compensation, which is likely to be the cost of having the damage repaired, plus any out-of-pocket expenses.

If you dispute a garage's bill, the garage has the right to keep your car while the dispute is sorted out, although, of course, they will have to keep it safe. So, if you need your car back, you may have to pay the disputed bill and sue the garage in court for any overcharging. Make sure when you pay that you write on the receipt 'paid under protest'. This will be evidence that you did not agree with the bill but were only paying it to get your car back.

HOLIDAYS

In March 1990, Amanda Cochrane was staying at a five-star hotel in Cairo. A fire broke out and the air conditioning, which should have been shut off, instead pumped smoke throughout the building. When Miss Cochrane realized what was happening, she found that the floor was full of thick, acrid smoke and everything was black. She managed to find a bannister and went down the stairs two at a time, but, when she came to the ground floor, there was no door to be found.

Her head was spinning, the smoke was starting to overpower her and she thought she was going to die. Fortunately, someone outside the hotel smashed a door open and she tumbled out. Miss Cochrane was lucky. Two of the hotel's fire exits were locked that night and the hotel had no proper sprinkler system to put out a fire. Seventeen people died.

The last thing people think about when they book a holiday is whether or not their hotel is safe, but it is not just hotels in the more exotic countries that may have slack fire standards. When *Watchdog* asked fire safety expert Stuart Kidd to check hotels on the Algarve, he concluded that seven out of the eight hotels he looked at would not have been given fire certificates in the UK. These hotels were all used by British tour operators. All tour operators have to do is to ensure that the hotels they use meet *local* standards and these standards are usually lower than those in Britain. There is no compulsory European standard.

Apart from fire, there are other concerns to bear in mind. Faulty gas heaters have killed several British tourists over the years as a result of carbon monoxide poisoning. Lack of warning signs in swimming pools have caused dreadful injuries to tourists who have just dived in without checking the water depth. Several foreign tourists have been murdered in Florida when they ventured away from the tourist areas.

Travel agents now provide advice for people going on holiday to Florida, but it will still be up to you to check for fire, gas and swimming pool risks. You can ask a tour operator or travel agent about them, but all you will be told is that the operators would not use facilities that were unsafe. As the *Watchdog* research shows, you cannot rely on these assurances.

When you arrive at a hotel or apartment abroad, try to spend just a few minutes making sure you know where the fire exits are. Check any gas heaters that there may be in your apartment and take a good look at the swimming pool. Then you can relax and enjoy your holiday.

HOLIDAY FIRMS

Although most people still take their holidays in Britain, foreign holidays are catching up. Nearly 22 million people took holidays abroad last year and most of them choose a 'package', a combination of travel, accommodation and other extras provided by a holiday company at an all-inclusive price.

Package holidays have changed considerably since they became common in the 1960s. The two-week full-board family hotel in Majorca is still available, but the trend is towards self-catering rather than hotels, low-rise rather than high-rise buildings, a dozen other Mediterranean countries rather than just Spain. However, the foreign package holidays that are sold in Britain are still cheaper and offer a far greater range than those sold in most other countries.

In fact, packages are probably too cheap. The average profit margins for the top operators are less than 3 per cent, and this has meant that the standards of many holidays remains poor, particularly at the bottom end of the market. *Holiday Which?* magazine does regular 'best-buy' surveys of holiday companies among its readers, and the small operators, many of whom sell direct to the public, usually come out ahead of the larger companies like Thomson, Airtours, Horizon and the Owners Abroad group.

Many of these small firms are – like the large operators – members of the Association of British Travel Agents (ABTA), but some are members of the Association of Independent Tour Operators (AITO) and some have no membership of any trade association at all.

How to get a good holiday deal

▷ Before you book a holiday package abroad, look up any hotel the operator intends to use in the *Agents Hotel Gazetteer* or one of its rival directories – most travel agents will have a copy. The *Gazetteer* is written for the trade and describes hotels as they are, not as the tour operator's brochures may imagine them to be.

▷ Consider using a mail-order holiday company rather than a travel agent. These specialist companies are more expensive, but they can give much better advice than high-street travel agents on whether or not the holiday you like the look of is really suitable for you.

▷ If you use a travel agent, be wary if they recommend their own company's holidays rather than a company you prefer. Going Places and Hogg Robinson Business Travel are owned by Airtours; Lunn Poly is owned by Thomson; Thomas Cook have strong connections with Owners Abroad.

▷ Once you have found the holiday you want, it is perfectly possible to negotiate a discount, especially if you book late. You can obtain discounts from ferry companies (especially if the ferry ticket is part of a package), travel agents (air fares and car hire) and, above all, hotels. Virtually every hotel in Britain and many hotels abroad will bargain for the cost of a room, especially if they are not full and you phone or turn up on the day you would like to stay.

▷ Finally, never book a holiday from an operator that is not bonded (see below).

If things go wrong

As a result of a European Community Directive, all companies that offer package holidays must have some form of protection for their customers if they go bust.

Although various options are allowed by the Directive, most companies have chosen a *bonding scheme* and these kinds of schemes are the only ones at the moment that have a proven record of success.

There are seven bonding schemes operating as this book went to press. The ATOL scheme guarantees all holidays that involve air transport. The other six schemes cover surface transport. They are run by ABTA, AITO, the Bus and Coach Council, the Passengers Shipping

Association, the Tour Operators Study Group and the Association of Bonded Travel Organisers Trust. They work by guaranteeing you a refund if the tour operator goes bust before you travel. If you are already abroad, the schemes allow you to continue your holiday and come back as planned.

So, the most important thing to do when you book a holiday is to check with the tour operator which bonding scheme applies. Also check that your contract is with the operator, not with the travel agent, because even if the travel agent is a member of ABTA, this kind of membership offers you no protection if the tour operator goes bust.

If the operator is not part of a bonded scheme, do not travel with them. The holiday business is a precarious world where even the most secure companies risk insolvency. One consequence of the severe competition between rival operators is that several companies go into liquidation each year, owing customers hundreds of thousands of pounds. If your money is not protected, it will be lost.

Some rogue operators have been known to quote membership of the ABTA, AITO or ATOL bonding schemes when they have nothing of the kind. It is sensible always to check with the organization concerned. Another useful tip is to pay at least some of the cost of the holiday by credit card. This will allow you to make a claim against the credit card company if things go wrong (see page 53).

The new compulsory protection requirement is not perfect, but it does sort out the small reputable companies from the incompetents and crooks, even if an inevitable result is to push prices up (somebody has to pay for the cost of regulations and insurance schemes and this somebody is usually the customer). It only covers uncompleted holidays, however. If a tour operator provides you with a lousy holiday, but makes sure that you get there and back safely, you have no claim under any bonding scheme. You will have to claim compensation from the operator instead.

What holiday companies have to provide

Trevor and Carol Kilby booked into the Hotel Atlantis in Madeira with one of the major operators. The brochure described the island as peaceful and secluded, which it was. It also had a picture of the hotel, implying that the hotel, too, was peaceful and secluded, which it was not. It was right next to the airport and extremely noisy. The Kilbys' holiday was ruined.

Another major operator sold a Greek holiday to the Morgan family. When they arrived, they found that the beds that were going to be used by the children were wringing damp. The kitchen had no workspace and there was no door preventing the children walking up on to the roof.

The Johnson family's holiday in Minorca was also ruined. They were unable to enjoy the impressive views of the island because there was drilling going on 12 hours a day. The tour operator had called the place a 'peaceful spot'. When they complained, they were originally offered a token amount by the operator, but they persisted with their complaint and eventually they received £450 in compensation.

These are just three of the thousands of complaints about holidays that *Watchdog* receives every year, and it is not just us. ABTA deals with some 13 000 complaints a year and this number does not include complaints that have been sorted out by their members before ABTA become involved.

Of course, some of these complaints are ridiculous. There are people who complain that their Spanish holiday was ruined by Spanish food or that they could not pick up British television in the Greek Islands. There are also some people who seem determined to find something wrong with their holiday, almost as if they had some bizarre wish not to enjoy themselves. Then there are the professional complainers, the people who will try to save themselves a few pounds by finding something they can claim compensation for when they return.

Most complaints are, however, perfectly reasonable ones, at least to the complainant. What people expect from a holiday is that the brochure's promises are met, any special requirements that they have been promised are honoured and for the accommodation to be clean and adequate, even if it is the cheapest on offer. What happens, though, if these promises are not kept?

▷ *Brochures*: All holiday brochures should tell you the price, destination, type of transport, itinerary, meal plans and deadlines for cancellation. Any description that the brochure makes, whether in writing or in the pictures, must be accurate. If it is not and you are misled as a result, you can claim compensation for breach of contract. You should also report the company to trading standards for any possible offence under the Trade Descriptions Act 1968 (see page 56).

▷ *Changes before the holiday:* If the operator makes a major change in your holiday plans – for example, by changing the resort – you can cancel and claim a full refund. If these changes end up costing you more, reserve your right to claim compensation. All brochures must tell you the deadlines for cancellation

181

and how much money you will receive back if you cancel for your own reasons.

▷ *Increased costs and flight surcharges:* Companies are only allowed to increase their prices if this is stated in their terms and conditions. Prices cannot be increased within 30 days of departure.

▷ *Problems with the hotel or other accommodation:* If the accommodation turns out to be poor, you must make this clear straight away to the company representative. If they cannot remedy the situation, tell them you are accepting it 'under protest' and that you will be claiming compensation. If the accommodation is just too poor to enjoy your holiday, ask the rep to find you other accommodation and, if they cannot, find other accommodation yourself. Tell the rep that you will be claiming compensation for the extra cost involved. (You will, of course, have to be reasonable about this. If you were booked into a one star hotel that was completely unacceptable, you must try to find another one star hotel that is suitable.)

How to complain

Three out of four complaints about a holiday end up being successful, but almost all of them take time to sort out. This is because most holiday companies indulge in delay-ing tactics. They will first try to ignore your complaint. Then they will offer a very small sum without admitting any liability. If they are pushed, they will increase this offer, often in stages, until they are threatened with court action. This is how to make them respond quicker.

▷ If something goes wrong on holiday, tell the company immediately. First, inform the rep and ask them to sign

182

your complaint. Ask them, too, for the fax number of the company's customer relations department and fax your complaint to them.

▷ If nothing is done, collect evidence while you are still on holiday. This could include photographs, a video recording (although this may not be accepted as evidence if your complaint goes to arbitration), signed statements from other people at the resort (hotel manager, local police, the company rep) and the names and addresses of other holidaymakers who feel the same as you.

▷ Write to the company immediately you return home. Explain your complaint and indicate your evidence. Then ask them for compensation, which should include money for:

loss of value the difference in value between what you paid for and what you received.

loss of enjoyment how much something present like noise or something absent like a promised swimming pool detracted from your holiday.

out-of-pocket expenses anything you had to pay out because the tour operator did not deliver what it had promised (your costs, however, must be reasonable).

▷ Most companies will ignore your complaint or offer you a token sum. Some companies will claim that they were not responsible for what went wrong. Ignore this: they will have to prove that there were circumstances that they could not have foreseen.

▷ Send back a recorded delivery letter saying that you will take them to the small claims court within 14 days if they do not pay up.

▷ If they still do not respond, take out a summons (see

page 273). If they send you a cheque that you do not want to accept, send it straight back to them.

▷ Instead of going to court, you can contact ABTA or AITO with your complaint. They will try to conciliate. If this does not work, ABTA has an independent arbitration scheme that is an alternative to court action. It is certainly worth considering if your claim is over the small claims limit or if you would prefer to have the matter sorted out without attending court (see page 293). AITO have a similar scheme, although it works by mediation rather than arbitration. It is called an Independent Disputes Settlement Service and the mediator will talk to you on the phone as well as look at the documents (arbitration is a documents-only system). At £30, it has the advantage of being cheaper than ABTA's arbitration or most holiday claims in the small claims court.

TIMESHARE

Timeshare has its place in consumer mythology alongside such products as used cars and double-glazing. They are all linked inescapably to dodgy salesmen and misleading sales techniques. Of course, there are good timeshare deals and reputable companies, but there are rogues as well and the rogues have now come up with a new scam: selling more timeshare to existing timeshare customers.

Their timeshare in Tenerife was adored by Anthony and Betty Houghton, but when Mrs Houghton was diagnosed as suffering from cancer, they both decided, reluctantly, that they would have to sell it. So they approached the sales rep at the resort who handled resales and he promised them he could get £20 000 for their three weeks, but there was one condition: they would have to put a deposit of £1000 on an extra week at the resort. This was a 'purely paperwork transaction' and would be cancelled after three months if the Houghtons' timeshare was unsold.

At the end of the three months, the Houghtons' three weeks was unsold, the salesman had vanished and the company denied all knowledge of any promise. The Houghtons had to cancel this 'purely paperwork transaction' to buy an extra week's timeshare and lost their £1000.

When you buy a timeshare, what you are buying is the right to stay somewhere for a limited amount of time every year. Most timeshares are sold at special presentations and the companies use prizes and special gifts to lure people into buying. The sales techniques are very clever and the prizes are often very poor. If you do want to buy a timeshare, do not go to these presentations, but write instead to the Timeshare Council and ask them for a list of their members who have property in the resort you are interested in. Visit the resort and look at the different developments. Talk to any residents there already. Find out how much they paid, what the facilities are like, what the extra costs are and how easy it is to exchange with other resorts.

When you have made up your mind, find out from the company what deals are on offer and ask about any resale companies. Always make sure that you check the contract with a British solicitor before you sign. If you sign in this country, you have a 14-day cooling-off period in which you can change your mind, but this does not generally apply outside the UK, so it is best not to buy a timeshare when abroad, no matter how persuasive the promises are.

7

PUBLIC SERVICES

Public services are different to virtually everything else described in this book. Unlike the goods and services that we pay for, most public services are provided free of charge and paid for out of taxation. One effect of this is that people lose an important lever if things go wrong – the lever of money. You cannot stop paying PAYE if a promised new road is cancelled, you cannot cancel your Council Tax if the rubbish is not collected. This does not mean that you have no rights at all, but it does mean that if you want to get a good deal from public services, you have to go about things slightly differently.

WHO RUNS WHAT

There has been so much reorganization in public services over the last few years that it is difficult to remember who is responsible for what. Some services have contracted out; others have opted out. Some services are now responsible directly to the Government; others are now no longer provided by the Government but by a semi-autonomous agency.

There is very little logic (but a great deal of politics) in all this continual reorganization of responsibilities. As this book goes to press, the Government is committed to removing much of the present split of responsibilities between county and district councils. The Local Government

Commission is currently examining how best to do this and the changes should happen by the end of 1996. They would make a great deal of sense if they did not come on top of all the other changes that have been made during the last 20 years. Here is the present situation.

▷ *County councils* are responsible for social services, some roads and highways, libraries and museums, trading standards, fire, waste disposal, strategic planning and conservation matters. They are also still the main organizations responsible for education, although many schools have now opted out and are managed by independent boards answerable directly to the Department of Education.

▷ *District councils* look after rubbish collection, planning, housing, local parks and leisure, environmental health and most pavements.

▷ *Metropolitan councils* combine the district and county council roles in most major cities. (In London, they are called *borough* councils.)

▷ *In Scotland* all council services are provided by *regional* councils.

▷ *In Northern Ireland* most council services are run by government Boards, although district councils have some responsibilities there, too.

▷ *City councils* Some are the same as metropolitan councils. Other city councils are just another name for a district council.

▷ *Town and parish councils* are really historical anomalies. They have few direct powers, but act as a forum for local views.

Most other public services are provided by the Government, either directly or through a semi-autonomous agency. These include the major roads (Department of Transport), social security (the Benefits Agency, responsible to the Department of Social Security), pollution and safety control (various inspection agencies, responsible to the Department of Environment), Jobcentres (local TECs, responsible to the Department of Employment), prisons and probation services (the Home Office) and the courts (the Lord Chancellor's Department).

The UK's police services report to their regional police authorities, which consist of local council representatives and magistrates (apart from London, which reports directly to the Home Secretary). Most of the NHS's services are provided by health authorities. The majority of hospitals, however, have opted out of health authority control and are run by trusts, which report directly to the Government.

WHEN THINGS GO WRONG

In December 1988, a retired couple bought a bungalow in Redditch that had been built originally by Redditch District Council. Six weeks later, after a neighbour had put a similar bungalow up for sale, they discovered that the bungalow needed to be rebuilt completely because it was a 'Dorran-type' house, and the concrete blocks used for its construction had deteriorated over time. The Housing Act 1985 said that houses built in this way were defective and grants had been made available to have the houses repaired, but Redditch Council did not register the bungalows of the couple and their neighbours with the Government as they thought, mistakenly, that the houses were not Dorran ones. By the time the mistake was realized, the Council had long since relinquished ownership of the bungalow.

The couple faced a massive bill as a result of the Council's mistake and the Council refused to help them. As they had not bought the bungalow directly from the Council, any legal claim they had against the Council was likely to be complicated and expensive. But they also had another option: to make a complaint to the local government ombudsman. This they did, and the ombudsman ruled in their favour. The result was that Redditch Council had to pay the couple 90 per cent of the repair costs, the same as the grant would have been, plus a further £250 in compensation.

Local government ombudsmen are just one of three ombudsmen who provide a final appeal for complaints about public service incompetence and maladministration: the other two are the parliamentary commissioner and the health service ombudsman. However, they are all a last resort and they have their limitations as well as their advantages. Here is what you should do first.

WHEN COMPLAINING
ABOUT A LOCAL COUNCIL

▷ Ring the council and find out what council department is responsible for the service. You will need to find out if the service has been contracted out or not and it is useful to establish whether or not the department has published any kind of customers' charter, with targets for particular services.

▷ Contact the Director of the department. Council departments are still responsible for services that they have contracted out, but, for these types of services, complain first to the private firm as they will usually want to resolve matters without involving the council. If you are not satisfied with the department's response, complain to the council's Chief Executive.

▷ If your complaint is not dealt with satisfactorily, contact your local councillor. Consider, too, involving your local paper or radio station if you think other people would be interested in your complaint and you do not mind the publicity.

▷ If all else fails, you can then take your complaint to the local government ombudsman. There are three ombudsmen in England and one each for Wales and Scotland. In Northern Ireland, the Commissioner for Complaints performs the same role.

Local ombudsmen are interested mainly in cases where individuals have been unfairly or unjustly treated because of council maladministration or incompetence. You usually have to complain within 12 months of a council's decision.

The majority of ombudsmen's published investigations have been in favour of the complainant and there is no limit to the amount of money they can award. While any ombudsman's decision is not binding on a council, only 1 in 20 decisions have *not* been accepted by the council concerned.

TAKING LEGAL ACTION AGAINST A COUNCIL

Anybody who provides a service that people use has a duty of care to them and their possessions. This duty of care applies as much to local authority services as to private ones. So, a council would have a duty of care, for example, to people who visit its leisure centres and to pedestrians who use council pavements. If you are injured while using a council service or if your property has been damaged and you can show that the council has broken a duty of care to you, you can sue for compensation.

As with any negligence claim, you will have to show that your suffering was the fault of the council or one of its employees. This can sometimes be difficult to prove. After all, it is possible to be injured quite badly using a council service without it being the council's or, indeed, anybody's fault. So, it is important to obtain legal advice from a solicitor who specializes in personal injury. Most personal injury cases are settled out of court.

If you are unhappy with a council's decision or policy, it is possible to challenge its decision by means of a process called *judicial review*. This kind of review cannot decide on the fairness of a council's decision, only on whether or not the process by which a council reached a decision was fair. An example of a case that would qualify for review would be if an interested party was not consulted properly before a decision was made. The process of judicial review is expensive, complicated and requires skilful advocacy. You should only consider it if you have some kind of backing or can get legal aid.

However, there is another method local council taxpayers can use to challenge one of their council's decisions and, unlike judicial review, it does not cost anything at all. You can ask the District Auditor to see if councillors have gone beyond their powers in making a decision. The Auditor will see if there has been any impropriety or if the decision that has been made is within the council's powers and offers value for money. Often the best time to approach the Auditor is after you have read the council's annual accounts which are thrown open to public inspection for a few days each year.

COMPLAINING ABOUT SERVICES RUN BY CENTRAL GOVERNMENT

▷ Find out who runs the service. Is it a local branch of a government department or one of the newer agencies?

▷ Write to the Director with your complaint.

▷ If the complaint is not dealt with satisfactorily, ask your MP to raise the matter with the department's or agency's Chief Executive or the government minister responsible. This will take time, but a letter from an MP will always receive a reply.

▷ Your MP (but not you) can then take up the complaint with the Parliamentary Commissioner for Administration, the ombudsman responsible for investigating complaints about government departments.

Like the local government ombudsmen, the Commissioner can only look at complaints about injustice or unfair treatment that has occurred as a result not of government policy, but of civil service maladministration. However the Commissioner can investigate complaints about all government departments and about many public bodies and quangos, for example, the Arts Council.

The Parliamentary Commissioner has the power to award unlimited compensation, and more than nine out of ten of the 1000-odd complaints the

Commissioner hears every year are resolved in the complainant's favour, although it can take up to a year to sort a complaint out. In Northern Ireland, this ombudsman's role is performed by the Commissioner for Complaints.

THE VALUE OF CAMPAIGNING AND PUBLICITY

Most of the time, ensuring that we get a good deal from the goods and services that we buy is a private matter. The laws and regulations that help us negotiate with traders give us rights as individuals and we usually pursue these rights on our own. After all, there is little need to be aware of other customers' problems, especially as this may well hamper any deal you might be able to sort out as an 'exceptional case'.

However, the opposite is true when it comes to negotiating with public services, particularly with local and national government departments. What matters here is not so much the law and *ex gratia* settlements, but politics and political consent. If enough people are against a policy or come up against the same problem, there will be considerable pressure for things to change. Because of this, it always makes sense when you have a problem with public services to combine with others, especially if the problem seems insuperable. Officials start paying attention when complaints come from more than one or two isolated individuals, when they appear to have a constituency that needs to be taken into account, especially if that constituency includes respected members of society, like local doctors, businessmen, vicars or community leaders.

The other important weapon is publicity, particularly the local press and local radio. Good tales involving some kind of injustice are always in short supply and, with luck, you might be able to persuade a local paper not only to feature your story, but to mount a campaign on your behalf, particularly if other people come forward with similar experiences. At the very least, a story in the papers will usually force a council or department to defend their decisions in public.

COUNCIL TAX

Unlike the old Community Charge, or poll tax, Council Tax is based on the value of your house rather than on the number of adults living there. Every house has been put into one of five valuation bands and local councils set the amount payable by each band. All the adults resident in a house are equally and jointly liable for the Council Tax bill and any of them could be prosecuted for non-payment.

If you think your Council Tax bill is unreasonable, there are two ways in which you may be able to appeal.

▷ If you have bought a brand-new house, you can appeal against any decision by the council to put your house in a particular valuation band. You should contact the Listing Officer at the council's Valuation Office. This right only applies to newly-built homes: the right of appeal against Council Tax valuations for all other houses and flats ended in November 1993.

▷ Any appeal against the bill that does not involve the valuation of your house should be made directly to the local council. Most councils have special Council Tax

194

departments to deal with queries. They will look at appeals from people who contest responsibility for a bill or who think they are entitled to a discount.

Like the poll tax, the Council Tax is a civil debt. It is not a criminal offence not to pay the Tax, and you cannot go to gaol for not paying the bill, at least not at first. Like poll tax, too, if you do not pay Council Tax, the council can (and usually will) take out a court summons against you.

If you do not answer the summons, the council has three main options: it can apply to have the money deducted from your pay (but it will have to find out who your employer is to do this), or it can send bailiffs in to seize property or, if you are on benefit, it can deduct money from your income support (although there are restrictions on this power).

If none of these methods of recovery work, the council can then go back to court and ask for a charging order to be put on your house (if you are the owner) or sue you for bankruptcy. It can also claim that your failure to pay is a criminal act and should be treated as a criminal offence.

In practice, as was the case with the much more unpopular poll tax, few, if any, people will ever be imprisoned as a result of not paying their Council Tax. However, the power to put an order on someone's house is quite new and it will be interesting to see if councils use this power in the next few years. Despite all the publicity, nine out of ten people paid their poll tax and the Council Tax is predicted to do even better.

If you have *paid* your Council Tax and you are still summonsed to appear in court, write to the City Treasurer by name and say you will be counterclaiming for compensation and damages. That should soon clear the matter up.

195

THE ELECTORAL REGISTER

Councils obtain people's names from the electoral register. Electoral registers are available in public libraries and most, but not all, councils sell their electoral registers to mailing list companies. It is possible for you to be registered to vote but not have your name listed on the electoral register, but you will need a convincing reason, for example, if you have been a victim of domestic violence. In such cases, your name can be entered on a separate list that is not published or you can use another name with the electoral officer's permission.

PAVEMENT AND ROAD REPAIRS

Most major roads are the responsibility of the Department of Transport, but minor roads are owned, run and maintained by local traffic authorities. These authorities are usually county councils, although some are district councils. Virtually the only way to make sure a road is repaired or made safe is to join with others and lobby council staff and councillors. Copy all letters to the local press.

The major difficulty in making sure a pavement is repaired is finding out who owns it and who is responsible for repairing it. They are not always the same people. Sometimes district councils are involved, sometimes county councils. Sometimes it is up to a water company or a gas or electricity supplier. The local council should be able to help you with the question of ownership.

It is perfectly possible to sue a council for damages if you have been hurt because of a hole in a road or pavement. Some people do claim damages and win, but many with just as strong claims, do not. What you have to do is show that the council was negligent in not repairing the hole. If you have been injured, take legal advice from a solicitor who specializes in personal injury. Any damages awarded may be reduced if you were partly to blame, for example, by ignoring any warning notice.

PLANNING

Planning decisions are made by the local council's planning committee after taking advice from the council's planning officer. These committees must have a good reason to refuse any request for planning permission. One reason often given is that a proposed building contravenes the council's local plan or is in a conservation area, but four out of five requests for planning permission are granted.

If your request for planning permission is turned down, you have six months to apply to the Department of Environment or the Scottish, Welsh or Northern Ireland Offices. The Department will appoint an inspector who will look into the case and decide whether or not to hold a public inquiry. The inspector will grant planning permission unless there is a very good reason to refuse it.

In Scotland and Northern Ireland, local authorities are obliged to notify anybody who may be affected by a planning application. In England and Wales, this is not a legal requirement, although most councils do try to inform neighbours.

If you want to oppose someone else's planning permission, you will need to get as much help as quickly as you can. You must register your objections with the local planning department and try to get the support of other people and the local press. Your case will be strengthened if you can show that the proposed plans contravene the style of a local neighbourhood or are against the council's own local plan. If planning permission is granted, you can ask the appropriate secretary of state to reconsider, although the secretary does not have to grant your request.

The only people who have the power of compulsory purchase of a house or land are public authorities; no private developer has this power – if the latter want your land, they have to negotiate with you. (If someone does need your land for building, a good figure to agree to is the full market price, plus 10 per cent, plus the costs of moving.) Similarly, if a private developer is developing land near you, you cannot force them to buy your house, even if you are seriously affected by the development, although you can try and claim compensation under the Land Compensation Act 1973.

If a local authority is doing major work near you that affects the value of your property, you can serve a *blight notice* on the authority. This notice compels the authority to buy your property. You will have to show that your property cannot be sold at its original market price because of the work.

If you discover that a building is being put up without planning permission, contact the local council straight away. Once a building is up, it is quite rare for a council to insist that it is demolished, even if no planning permission has been granted.

Building regulations are quite different to planning permission, although both are often supervised by the same council department. They lay down the rules for constructing a building and building inspectors must approve the building at various stages prior to its completion. Contact the council's Building Officer if you think building regulations may be being broken. Unfortunately the building regulations do not cover everything.

A few years ago, a five-year-old boy, Ashley Ewins, was playing with a ball outside his home with several of his friends. The ball went into a neighbour's garden and Ashley went after it. He then noticed a small ornamental wall and he could not resist trying to climb it. The wall gave away and one of the blocks fell on Ashley and killed him. The wall was just 1.2 metres (4 feet) high. Like many such walls, it was put up haphazardly with little thought to what might happen if it gave way.

It was no consolation for Ashley's parents to discover that while houses have to be built to building regulations, the regulations do not apply to free-standing walls. Builders and other individuals can build a garden wall with as much or as little care as they please. The result is that Ashley was just one of some 30 children who have died over the last few years as a result of a badly built wall falling down on them.

Local authorities do have the power to inspect and demand the demolition of any unsafe structure, including walls, but too often they hear about an unsafe wall *after* a tragedy has occurred.

THE ENVIRONMENT

The divisions of responsibility between central government, executive agencies and local councils are at their haziest when it comes to environmental matters. Everybody seems to be involved in preventing pollution or prosecuting polluters. The Environmental Protection Act 1990 accepts the argument that the polluter should pay for any pollution caused, but, in practice, this has not happened.

One difficulty is that of finding out who the actual polluter is because, in many situations, it is not clear. Another problem is that it is still quite easy to get away with breaking the rules. Cash restraints on the inspection agencies mean that the notion of a green police force is more an idea than a reality. It may become a reality if the Government's promise of an environment agency is ever kept. The proposed agency would combine the roles and expertise of the Inspectors of Pollution, the Waste Regulatory Authorities and the National Rivers Authority, but the agency requires legislation in order to be able to operate effectively and, although this has been promised, it has been continually postponed. Much of the watching over of the environment is done not by the regulatory authorities, but by voluntary organizations and pressure groups, like Greenpeace, Friends of the Earth or the National Society for Clean Air and Environmental Protection.

LAND: SOLID WASTE, RUBBISH, LITTER

The responsibility for collecting rubbish usually lies with the *district* councils: it is one of the few duties they have to fulfil by law. They are obliged to collect household rubbish at regular intervals, although they can impose their own conditions on this, for example, by asking householders to use particular bags or bins. Councils are also obliged to provide a service to pick up any larger items and they must also take away the bodies of dead dogs, as long as they are hygienically wrapped.

District councils are also responsible for street cleaning. If you are dissatisfied with the way your streets are kept clean, you can apply to the magistrates' court for an order compelling your council to clean your street properly under the Environmental Protection Act 1990.

This law can also be used to make sure the council clears up dog mess. If there is a particular problem with dog mess in your street, you can ask the council to declare it a '£100 fine area', which should deter dog owners, at least in theory. Under this law, too, councils have the power to fine people whom they catch dropping litter. The problem is that both regulations are rarely enforced.

Most household waste ends up buried in the ground in a landfill tip. These tips and other council dumps are the responsibility of the local waste disposal authority, which, in most parts of the UK, is the *county* council. The authority licenses the various landfill tips, and there are strict regulations concerning the disposal of waste there. In practice, however, many tips are never checked and all kinds of chemicals are dumped in them. If you have any suspicions about a local tip, particularly if there has been any sign of methane gas, contact your county council at once.

It is an offence to dump rubbish or dispose of waste anywhere else apart from a designated rubbish tip and individuals or companies can be fined for doing this. Local councils are responsible for clearing up waste dumped in their area. They also have a duty to collect abandoned cars and supermarket trolleys.

INLAND WATER: RIVERS AND LAKES

All inland water in the UK is the responsibility of the water companies. They are obliged to keep lakes and rivers clean and this obligation is monitored and regulated by the National Rivers Authority, which will investigate complaints brought by the public.

Many factories are still allowed to dump solid and liquid waste through the sewerage system or directly into rivers. Water companies themselves are allowed to get rid of treated and sometimes untreated sewerage in this way.

This disposal of waste is regulated by licences that specify what can be disposed of where and in what quantity. These licences should be open for public inspection at the water company's offices, but in reality it is often difficult to work out whether or not any pollution in a river is legal or illegal.

AIR POLLUTION
AND LOCAL FACTORIES

Local factories are allowed to dispose of noxious gases into the air, but only according to the regulations laid down by the various clean air acts. There is yet another regulatory body responsible for monitoring this kind of pollution: Her Majesty's Inspectors of Pollution (HMIP). These pollution inspectors have the responsibility for the combined pollution control of all large factories and plants.

Eventually, the factories will all need discharge consents from the HMIP, and these consents will be available for inspection by the public. Air pollution by smaller factories is monitored by local authorities.

NOISE

Noise from neighbours

Most noise problems come from neighbours, but these are some of the most difficult problems to resolve. If all your attempts to reduce the noise fail and you want to take further action, you will have to prove two things. First, you will have to show that the noise is a nuisance, that is, it is an unlawful interference with the use and enjoyment of your property. Second, you will have to prove that the noise is continuous. To prove both these things, you will need evidence like a noise diary, photographs, comments from other neighbours and, if possible, a professional recording of the noise involved.

If you think you will be able to establish all this, you can threaten a noisy neighbour with either or both of the following.

▷ *Your local council's environmental health department:*
They can write informally to the neighbour asking them to stop. If the neighbour does not stop, environmental health officers should then take 'all reasonable steps' to investigate the complaint. This may mean monitoring the noise out of office hours with professional equipment. Some councils finance this work, while others give it low priority.

If a council investigation concludes that the neighbour's noise is a statutory nuisance, the council can serve an abatement notice, which usually gives the neighbour a month to comply. If nothing is done after this, the council can get a court order from the magistrates' court, and the neighbour can be fined.

It is a long process and it cannot deal with one-off problems like parties. In Scotland, the police can shut down noisy parties and confiscate equipment, but in England and Wales there are no such powers.

▷ *Taking them to court:* If the council cannot or will not do anything about the noise, you can take court action yourself and often this is the quickest option. You can use the civil courts to get an injunction, but the best approach is to use Section 82 of the Environmental Protection Act 1990 and go to the magistrates' court to obtain a nuisance order.

As court orders go, this is a relatively simple and inexpensive procedure. You can do it without a solicitor and your local magistrates' court should be able to give you advice. You must give your neighbour three days' notice in writing that you will be going to court under the Act. You then go before the magistrates who will ask you to prove your case and give the neighbour the chance to reply. If the magistrates are convinced by your arguments, the court can serve an order on the neighbour to stop the noise. If the noise does not stop, the neighbour can be fined.

Other sources of noise problems

Apart from noisy neighbours, the usual noise complaints are about transport (road, aircraft and rail) and building construction.

Noise pollution from fixed premises is covered by the

Environmental Protection Act 1990 and the Control of Pollution Act 1974. These Acts allow a local authority to deal with noise from shops, factories, building sites and other construction activities if they consider the noise to be a nuisance. The council will take out a noise abatement notice and this will lay down various conditions. If these conditions are broken, the companies can be taken to court. They can argue, in turn, that the noise is a by-product of a necessary part of their work and that they are using the best practical means to limit the noise.

One problem with these laws is that they apply only to noise from fixed outlets. The Noise and Statutory Nuisance Act 1993, extends noise control to car alarms, machinery, vehicles and equipment in the street. The Act also gives police officers the power to break into cars and turn off car alarms. However, there are still no noise restrictions on those traditional country pursuits of motorcycle scrambling and clay pigeon shooting. Road improvements are also exempt, although you are entitled to the cost of double glazing if a new road is built near you or an existing one is improved and the result is excessive traffic noise. You may also be entitled to compensation for the loss in value of your house. Your local council should have details about these schemes.

There are restrictions on night flights at some, but not all, airports, restrictions that have come about after pressure from local residents. You can complain individually about aircraft noise (the Department of Transport runs an Aircraft Noise Complaints Line: 071-276 5323), but the only action that will make any real difference is to join a campaigning group.

British Rail has always tried to resist any attempts to

restrict the noise levels of its trains or its construction works as well as most demands for compensation. However, recently, they agreed to help pay for noise barriers on the new Channel Tunnel line and this could well set a precedent for complaints about railway noise in future.

THE EMERGENCY SERVICES

The three emergency services – ambulance, fire and police – are all organized quite differently.

THE AMBULANCE SERVICE

The 57 ambulance services of the United Kingdom are part of the National Health Service. The Government's Patients' Charter (part of the Citizens' Charter initiative) lays down targets for ambulance response. In urban areas, nine out of ten ambulances should arrive within 14 minutes. In rural areas, this time is increased to 19 minutes. As with other Patients' Charter targets, these are guidelines: there is no penalty for the service if they do not meet them.

If you want to complain about an ambulance service, write to the service's Chief Ambulance Officer or, if the service is a trust, to its Chief Executive.

THE FIRE SERVICE

The 65 fire brigades are organized and paid for by local authority fire committees. They, too, have attendance targets, although these targets predate the Citizens' Charter and they are *mandatory* for each brigade. The targets vary according to which part of the country you live in and according to the level of risk the fire brigade decides a fire in your local area poses. Thus, in Central London, two fire appliances have to be at a fire within five minutes of a call, but, in rural areas, the target is likely to be one fire engine within 20 minutes. Every fire brigade has to do regular time-runs to make sure that they can meet these targets and, if they are not met, an internal inquiry usually takes place.

It is possible to sue a fire brigade if they arrive late at a fire, but very few people ever do. If you want to complain about a fire brigade, write to its Chief Fire Officer.

THE POLICE SERVICE

There is no national police force in Britain, although there have been many arguments made for one and some specialist police work is organized on a regional or national basis. Police services are provided by 52 different forces, which correspond mainly to county boundaries. Each force is responsible to a police authority that is made up of local council representatives and magistrates, although as this book went to press the Government is proposing that some police authority members will come from the 'wider community'. In London, the Metropolitan Police answers directly to the Home Secretary.

Police authorities can only deal with problems about the level of police services provided. They have no power to investigate complaints about individual police officers or to decide on operations.

Getting the best deal from the police

▷ Each police force has a Customers' Charter. If you get poor police service, ask to see their Charter.

▷ The police are organized hierarchically. The main ranks are constable, sergeant, inspector, chief inspector, superintendent, chief superintendent, assistant chief constable, chief constable. Police officers tend to be very sensitive about rank so, if you have a problem with any particular officer, ask to speak to the next rank up. Most police stations are under the control of a superintendent.

▷ If you suspect a crime, ask to speak to the Duty Officer or CID Desk. It is far quicker to ring your local police station than to ring 999, even in an emergency.

▷ If you are charged with a motoring offence, it is often worth challenging the offence in court if you have a reasonable case. Most motoring offences are heard in magistrates' courts and the police evidence can be poorly prepared. If you have a reasonable response to the charge, especially with any kind of supporting evidence, it is easy to represent yourself, so you will not incur the cost of a solicitor if you lose.

▷ Most police officers who deal with the public will respond favourably to a reasonable manner; one thing they are not impressed by is threats of any kind or attempts at bribery.

How to complain about a police officer

Peter Smart knew all about the police. His father used to be a policeman, his brother still is a policeman and Mr Smart himself has many dealings with the police because he is the owner of a security alarm business. Indeed, Mr Smart's respect for the police was extremely high until, that is, a few years ago.

At 4.30am one morning, 12 police officers, some carrying guns, broke into Mr Smart's home and ordered him, naked, to march out of his house at gun-point. His terri-fied wife and children were ordered to follow him and Mr Smart was arrested. Within hours the police realized that they had made a dreadful mistake: they had arrested the wrong man.

Mr Smart expected to be offered an immediate apology and compensation for his terrifying ordeal, but he had to wait several weeks before the police eventually paid for the £1800-worth of damage they had done to his home. They offered no apology and no compensation.

Mr Smart complained to the Police Complaints Authority, which investigated his case, but he did not find their investigation at all useful or helpful. Instead, he felt it was traumatic, drawn out and secretive. His complaint was rejected by the Authority, although the police did apolo-gize for the distress they had caused.

As the Police Complaints Authority itself has acknowl-edged on *Watchdog,* its complaints procedure does not inspire public confidence. If a complaint leads to a disciplinary hearing, the hearing is in secret and can be extremely intimidating. Complainants are not even allowed to stay throughout the complete proceedings. If their complaint is upheld, all complainants will receive is an apology.

With all these limitations, it may be better to consider taking civil court action against the police for damages if you have a serious complaint like being assaulted or harassed by police officers. Civil liberties organizations like Liberty or Justice can help put you in touch with solicitors who specialize in actions against the police.

There is, however, nothing stopping you taking civil action after your complaint has been investigated by the

Authority. If your complaint was upheld and the police apologized, this can be used to support your case in court.

To make a formal complaint about a police officer, you should write to the Chief Constable of the officer's force and ask for your complaint to be investigated. What will happen then is one of three things:

▷ a senior officer will meet with you and see if your complaint can be resolved informally.
▷ an investigating officer will make a formal investigation.
▷ the Police Complaints Authority, an independent body, will supervise the investigation or look at the investigating officer's report.

As a general rule, the Police Complaints Authority will be involved in all complaints that involve death or serious injury.

HEALTH SERVICES AND HOSPITALS

The National Health Service consists of services run by Family Health Services Authorities, like GPs, dentists, opticians, pharmacists and so on, and hospital and community services, which are provided by the 140-odd district health authorities or by self-governing hospital trusts.

Private patients are treated in private hospitals, which are separate from the NHS, or in pay-beds in NHS hospitals. Most private patient costs are met by private medical insurance.

There is nothing stopping a GP referring a patient to any hospital they choose, near or far, NHS or private. The problem is that the hospital may not accept the patient, especially if there is no guarantee that they will be paid. GPs who are fundholders (see page 126) can make their own arrangements with any hospital in the country, but most of them have arranged special deals with hospitals near them and they may well be reluctant to refer a patient elsewhere. One exception may be if a waiting list for an operation is much shorter elsewhere.

It is possible for GPs who are not fundholders to refer patients outside their local area, but they will have to make a case to their district health authority for what is termed an 'extra-contractual referral'. District health authorities now have contracts with hospitals in their own area for services and they may be reluctant to grant a GP's request without a good reason.

CHOOSING THE RIGHT HOSPITAL AND CONSULTANT

In certain parts of the United States, hospitals compete with each other for patients. This has lead to hospitals providing detailed information listing the survival rates for operations performed by their surgeons. There is no valid reason why this kind of information could not be provided here, but at the moment these figures are collected anonymously.

It is common knowledge among hospital staff who the best doctors are. So, if you have a relative or friend who works in a hospital, try to find out which doctors it may well be prudent to avoid, especially for a serious operation. You should also try to avoid having an operation on a bank holiday or weekend. A report by the National Confidential Enquiry into Perioperative deaths in 1992 concluded that patients are more at risk of dying if they have an operation at these times than during weekdays.

In 1993, the Government published figures that suggested that the risk of dying after an operation is six times higher in some parts of the country than in others.

This kind of information is useful, but it is piecemeal. What is missing is a comprehensive 'good hospital' guide, although the Government has recently published the first 'league tables' which compare hospital performance (although not clinical care). For a free copy telephone 0800 555777. Here are some suggestions for choosing the right hospital, if you are allowed a choice.

▷ Try to discover the reputation of a hospital for the treatment you need. Ask friends as well as your GP and check with your local community health council.

▷ If your problem is routine, a local cottage or district hospital is best, but for anything more complicated – and particularly for a diagnosis of anything with unusual symptoms – ask to be referred to a *teaching hospital*. You may have to put up with medical students traipsing around (although you do have the right to refuse to have them present), but you will also be seen by doctors who will be aware of current research and who will have immediate access to specialists. For example, the diagnosis, treatment and survival rate of an illness like cancer could be entirely different in a hospital with access to current research and the presence of oncologists (surgeons who specialize in cancer), than in one that did not have these.

▷ Find out how long the hospital's waiting list is. Hospitals have to treat patients if their life is at risk, but if the patient's condition is chronic rather than acute, they are put on a waiting list. The Government has put considerable emphasis on bringing the waiting lists of some common operations down, with some success. Unfortunately, the waiting lists for other operations have lenghtened and there is still considerable disparity between hospitals.

An NHS helpline (0800 665544) will connect you to your local health authority's information service. They should be able to tell you the waiting times for key operations in different hospitals in their region. You can also call the College of Health's freephone number (0800 591220) for lengths of waiting lists across the country.

One thing to bear in mind is that you may be able to jump up the list if you can be available at short notice for when there has been a cancellation, a kind of hospital stand-by.

IS IT WORTH GOING PRIVATE?

There are no published comparisons between the treatment provided by private hospitals and that available on the NHS. The general view among doctors is mixed: some private hospitals attract the best consultants and so do better, while some others do worse.

The disadvantages of private hospitals are that many neither have the range nor the ability to deal with emergencies, complications or with unusual developments in an illness or condition. If this happens, patients are often rushed to a specialist NHS hospital, although, to be fair, this can happen in an NHS hospital, too. The quality of junior doctors (and other medical staff) is often poorer in private hospitals as these hospitals are not part of the NHS career structure and training rotations that have to be completed to qualify for a consultant post.

The advantages of a private hospital are quicker non-emergency treatment, considerably better food and service and the guarantee of a private room (although this can sometimes be a mixed blessing).

THE PATIENTS' CHARTER

The Patients' Charter has made some difference to patient care in the NHS, although less than the Government claims. It does not give patients any new rights, but it does clarify rights that have never been written down before and ones of which many patients were only dimly aware, for example, the right to be given a clear explanation of any treatment. The Charter also sets out some national standards, for example, out-patient waiting times should not be more than 30 minutes. You can get hold of a copy by ringing 0800 665544.

MEDICAL RECORDS

Under the Access to Health Records Act 1991, patients have a right to examine any medical record kept on them after 1 November 1991. Most records are held by GPs, but the right also extends to any hospital or clinic records. The only exception is that doctors may hold back part of a patient's record if they think their health may be at risk (this exception is used mainly in cases of psychiatric illness).

You do not have to give any reason for asking to see your medical records, but a doctor can charge £10. Some doctors will also allow you to see your records before this date, although it is entirely up to them. Children are allowed to see their own records, but the doctor can exercise discretion regarding whether or not to allow a parent to see their child's record. If anything on your record is incorrect, you can ask for it to be changed and if the doctor disagrees, you have the right to put a note in the file.

The right to see medical records also applies to other professionals working in the NHS, such as clinical psychologists. Patients also have the right to veto any medical reference sent on their behalf, for example, a medical report for insurance purposes.

WHEN THINGS GO WRONG IN AN NHS HOSPITAL

The Government's review of the NHS' complaints procedures has not been published yet but is long overdue. The present system seems to offer little to patients who are dissatisfied with their treatment, but, for the moment, this is what you should do.

▷ If your complaint is about *non-medical services,* complain to the General Manager of the hospital or to the Chief Executive if the hospital is a trust.
▷ If your complaint is about *clinical care,* write to the General Manager of the unit in charge of your care or to the Chief Executive if the hospital is a trust. If your complaint is serious and you are not satisfied with the response you receive, you can ask to have the complaint referred to the Regional Director of Public Health, who can arrange an independent professional review. This review, however, will not investigate a complaint if there is any legal action pending. As it is

difficult to imagine any serious complaint about clinical services in which legal action *could* be ruled out, the whole procedure is rather unsatisfactory.

▷ Complaints about *serious professional misconduct* of a hospital doctor can be made to the General Medical Council (see page 130).

Taking legal action

When things go wrong in hospital – someone dies unexpectedly after an operation, for example, or complications turn a minor illness into a major event – it is natural to want some kind of explanation, apology or compensation. The only remedy in law, however, is to sue for negligence, and this can be extremely difficult to prove. The procedure is much the same as proving medical negligence against a GP (see page 132), but there are some additional hurdles.

You will only win your case for compensation if you have actually been harmed and this is not the same as not being cured. The doctor or hospital may well have done all they could. Even worse, just because your condition has been made worse by a doctor does not mean that you will automatically win your case because, for example, the doctor may have taken an acceptable risk and the dice may just have fallen against you. Finally, if a doctor is accused of being negligent because they did not see a patient who subsequently died, the relatives of the patient will still have to show that the patient would not have died anyway. All this makes legal action extremely complicated, which is why the services of a solicitor who specializes in medical negligence is essential. You can find one through the Action for Victims of Medical Accidents.

You can take a private doctor to court for negligence in the same way as a health authority or NHS trust, but if something goes wrong, it is better to sue for breach of contract. This is much easier to prove than negligence as you will not have to show any fault, but prove only that the service offered was not of the kind you could reasonably expect to have received for the money. (You cannot sue an NHS hospital for breach of contract because you have no contract that can be breached.)

Who can help

It is often extremely difficult for patients to obtain even an apology, let alone an explanation when something has gone wrong with their treatment. However, there are a number of organizations and campaigning groups that can give advice and information and, sometimes, will be able to help with a complaint.

▷ Community Health Councils are the government-appointed NHS watchdogs of local NHS services. They can give advice about complaints and many will take up a complaint on your behalf.

▷ National organizations, such as the Action for Victims of Medical Negligence, the College of Health, the Patients Association and the Consumers Association magazine *Which? Way to Health* all keep a watchful eye on patient concerns.

▷ The Health Service Commissioner is the ombudsman for the NHS, but the Commissioner's powers are less impressive than the title suggests. The Commissioner can only look into complaints about personal injustice or hardship that have occurred due to poor service or maladministration. The Commissioner is not allowed to look into matters involving clinical judgments (although this may well change after the Government's review) or into cases where there is any legal action pending, although they can investigate if they think it unreasonable that a patient has to go to court. You must normally contact the Commissioner within 12 months, although this time limit can be waived in exceptional circumstances.

The Commissioner can make an *ex-gratia* award to a complainant and, while this is not binding on health authorities or trusts, it is usually adhered to. The Commissioner also has all the powers of a High Court Judge to demand documents. In Northern Ireland, the Health Commissioner's role is performed by the Commissioner of Complaints.

Stop Press

As this book goes to press the Government has published its review of the NHS Complaints system (see page 135). One of its proposals – which should become law – is to extend the Commissioner's powers to cover GPs and complaints about clinical judgement.

8

MONEY

WHAT CAN HAPPEN TO IT

When Samantha Harris was 19, she decided to start saving up for a car. She visited her local bank and the counter staff directed her to their Insurance Adviser who sold her a 'savings plan'. After two years, she had paid in some £360, which she thought would be enough to put down as a deposit on a second-hand car. She went to withdraw her money, but found it was only worth £134. She had been sold a life insurance policy and the first £200 of her payments had gone towards the salesman's commission and setting-up charges.

Clive Johnson knew what he was buying: a mortgage, backed by an endowment insurance policy. The endowment policy cost him £60 per month. After six years, he decided to cash in the policy, but he only got back £2000, less than half the payments he had made during this time. The £2120 difference had gone, like Miss Harris' money, on the salesman's commission and setting-up charges.

Holly and Adele Ashton trusted the Nationwide Building Society to look after their money. Neither of them knew a great deal about investment and returns, which is hardly surprising as they were aged just six and eight years old at the time. A Nationwide Cashbooster account, aimed especially at young people, seemed fine to their mother Beverley, particularly because the interest rate was 6 per cent. Two years later, Mrs Ashton discovered that Nationwide had introduced a new young people's account, Smart to Save, with a similar interest rate, but the old Cashbooster account, which still had all of Holly and Adele's money in it, had cut its interest rate to just 2 per cent. They now keep their pocket-money in a Post Office account.

Three consumer tales. Three stories of financial institutions behaving perfectly legally, but in which customers are left feeling that they have lost out.

It is curious how even the most careful shopper seems to place a kind of blind trust in their bank, building society, insurance company or financial adviser to provide them with the best deal. It is as if we do not want to see these companies as they are: perfectly reputable (for the most part) businesses whose main aim is to not to help us, but to make a profit from our money. Because we do not want to see this, we sometimes lose out.

This is not just because of fraudsters and con men, although they exist in financial services as much as in any other trade, perhaps more so. It is not just because of clever selling techniques, although some insurance salespeople make double-glazing and timeshare salespeople seem like ingénues. It is more than this. Something happens with money that makes most people almost incapable of getting a good deal. We all trust too much.

This trust may be based on sound financial judgment, but it is more likely to be based on a friendly chat years ago with a bank manager or financial adviser or insurance salesperson who has since become a friend. Too often, this relationship can cloud the fact that things have changed and that there might be a much better deal elsewhere.

BANKS

The last 10 years have been very odd for banks and their personal customers. Previously, the competition between the banks had been for new customers, but, in the 1980s, this market became saturated and a new kind of banking emerged. The major high street banks kept their identities and images, but underneath they became very different creatures indeed.

Individual bank managers were given targets for profitability, and profitability could be increased by commissions from the new kinds of financial products: pensions, mortgages, life insurance and investments. So, the banks started showering their personal customers with all kinds of financial information, selling them on the basis of the trust their customers placed in them.

However, this trust began to ebb away. Many customers started noticing that if they went overdrawn, the interest and charges made by the banks were extremely high. As the recession started to bite and the profits of the major high street banks collapsed, some overdrafts were called in at a moment's notice, not because of decisions made by individual bank managers who knew the circumstances, but because of rulings from regional headquarters. The result was that many small businesses that were struggling to survive in the late 1980s were driven out of business by their banks. This produced an outcry and even the then Prime Minister voiced her concern.

The banks are now under considerable pressure to offer their customers a better deal. In March 1992, they introduced a voluntary code of banking practice, partly to offset the pressure for new banking laws. Among other promises, this code pledges fair conduct, an end to 'charges on charges' and an internal complaints procedure. A revised edition of the code, published in 1994, promised to end one of the most annoying aspects of banks' behaviour: imposing charges on customers without notice. Banks have, however, up to 1997 to stop doing this.

Almost all of the British banks have agreed to uphold the code of practice, but as competition for customers has increased, so clear differences between banks have developed. Some offer much better service and are much better value than others.

HOW TO PAY LESS

▷ Some current accounts pay better interest than others. Some do considerably worse.

▷ If you have had your money in a deposit account for some time, check that it has not been replaced by a better-paying account that the bank has introduced to lure in new customers.

▷ Banks can make considerable mistakes in how they calculate interest and charges. It is worth always checking your statements and querying anything that seems high. Some estimates say that 1 in 10 bank statements are wrong, the errors being, somewhat unsurprisingly, in the bank's favour.

If you have been charged unreasonably, here is what to do.

▷ *Complain*: You can often have charges refunded if you have a good case. Ask the bank to explain how they have worked out your charges and what interest rates they have used. They will probably find it easier simply to reduce the bill. The main charges you must watch out for are fees rather than interest.

▷ *Have more frequent statements:* Ask your bank for weekly statements so that you can spot immediately when you are going over your limit and thus triggering very high charges. If your bank refuses, threaten to move your account.

▷ *If your charges are very high, consider having your bank accounts checked.* Several private companies now offer this service, using sophisticated computer software. They estimate that they can save people hundreds, if not thousands, of pounds. You can claim back wrongly worked out charges for up to six years.

▷ *Try to work out an informal agreement with your bank manager:* They may well have considerable discretion. You could get them to agree to always phone or fax you when your account goes overdrawn so that they will not charge you for letters that often take several days to arrive. See if you can get your bank manager to agree to tell you in advance before any charges are made to your account.

▷ *Always try to get an overdraft authorized:* It is quite possible to obtain authorization for a temporary overdraft over the phone, thus avoiding the high interest rates and charges imposed on unauthorized overdrafts.

▷ *Remember, your account is important to your bank:* For most customers, it is relatively easy to change accounts and find a good deal elsewhere, but when bank managers lose an account, they have to explain to their manager why this has happened and this can put them on the spot. If you have been a customer of the bank for some time and have a regular job, you will be in a good bargaining position, even if your account is always overdrawn – your bank manager will not want to lose you. Also, other banks will be happy to take on an overdraft if you have a steady income.

CASHCARDS AND MACHINES

Another area of concern for bank customers has been 'phantom withdrawals', money disappearing from a bank account as a result of an unauthorized cashcard withdrawal.

The banks have claimed that these withdrawals are the result of poor security on the part of their customers. Customers who lose money in this way, the banks claim, do so because other people have found out their PIN number and gained access to their cashpoint card. A number of cases have proved that this explanation is not always correct.

A few years ago, a Midland bank customer had £50 deducted from his account. He claimed he was nowhere near the cashpoint that had been used at the time. The bank disputed this and the customer returned his card to them. Then, another £50 was withdrawn from his account. An investigation by the Midland revealed that a card which belonged to another customer had been given the wrong account number. In other words it was the bank's mistake.

It is not the only mistake that can happen with these cards. Cards can be sent to the wrong address, thieves can look over shoulders, computers can go wrong, staff can make errors putting in information and, finally, of course, there can be staff fraud.

Some of these reasons have been accepted by the banks. In the code of banking practice, the burden of proof for a phantom withdrawal has shifted from the customer to the bank. As this book goes to press, several cases are wending their way through the legal process. Many smaller cases have been settled out of court, when banks have made *ex-gratia* payments.

HOW TO COMPLAIN ABOUT BANKS

▷ Ask to see the Manager who deals with your account. They will often have the power to waive charges. A good tactic to use is to threaten to move banks, even if you have an overdraft (see above). If the Manager agrees with your complaint, ask them how much the bank charges you to send you a letter. You can then claim a similar amount for all the letters you have had to send them to sort out the problem. They can hardly refuse your claim.

▷ If the Manager cannot resolve your complaint, ask to use the bank's complaints procedure. Under the Code of Banking Practice, all banks must have one. Most complaints procedures involve some kind of investigation of your case at regional level.

▷ If the complaints procedure does not sort out the problem, take your complaint to the banking ombudsman. You will need a letter from the bank acknowledging that your complaint has reached a stalemate. All the major banks subscribe to the banking ombudsman scheme, and the ombudsman can look at most kinds of complaints, apart from ones about commercial policy – for example, the reasons for refusing a loan. The ombudsman can award compensation up to £100 000, including compensation for distress as well as for financial loss, as long as the distress is substantial and can be proved. Banking ombudsman awards are binding on the bank, but you can still go to court if you are not satisfied with the decision. In one third of cases the ombudsman investigates, they have ruled in the complainant's favour.

BUILDING SOCIETIES

There are differences between banks and building societies but, for many customers today, the differences mean less than the similarities. Since banks started offering mortgages and financial advice, and building societies started offering current accounts, unsecured loans and overdrafts, choosing a building society over a bank and vice versa is often a matter of personal style than of anything else. Here are a few arguments to bear in mind.

REASONS FOR CHOOSING A BUILDING SOCIETY OR A BANK

▷ Who has the nearest branch to you? This can make quite a difference to being able to sort out problems quickly.
▷ Banks are more likely to offer a wider range of overdrafts, loans and other financial services. They also clear cheques much quicker than do most building societies.
▷ Building societies usually offer wider ranges of accounts and better interest rates on deposit accounts.

▷ There have been fewer reports about building societies getting interest rates and charges wrong. In surveys, customers prefer building societies.

▷ You can probably get a better interest rate for an unauthorized loan from a building society than you can from a bank.

Building societies are becoming more like banks, but it is a gradual process. They still have three quarters of the mortgage market, but only 1 in 10 current accounts. Much of the specific advice given above about banks applies equally to building societies, but there are a couple of specific building society problems that are worth mentioning here.

Interest rates and old accounts

In 1989, a *Watchdog* viewer opened a Guaranteed Premium Share Account at her local branch of the Woolwich Building Society. She thought that its competitively high interest rate would suit her well, but a year later, in 1990, the Woolwich introduced several more attractive accounts and they did not tell her. By the time she found out, a year on, she calculated that she had lost £700-worth of interest. This was not only because the new accounts offered a higher rate of interest, but also because the interest rate on her account had been cut.

She was just one of a thousand building society customers who contacted *Watchdog* about this topic. There were customers from all the major building societies and they all claimed they had lost money by leaving their savings in accounts that had been good value when they had opened them but that had since been downgraded.

When *Watchdog* investigated, we discovered a plethora of different accounts with different names, all introduced at different times. For example, the Nationwide alone had Capitalbuilder, Cashbuilder, Bonus Builder, Capital Bonus 90, Capital 90, and Bonus 90. It was not exceptional in this – all the other major building societies had their own long lists.

The only way to make sure that your money is earning the best interest rate is to contact the building society every few months and ask them if any new accounts have been introduced that have a better rate than yours. Keep a note of what they say, because if they give you the wrong information, you could claim compensation.

COMPLAINTS ABOUT BUILDING SOCIETIES

All building societies must have their own complaints procedures, but the way different societies deal with complaints varies considerably, as does the time they take to do so. If your complaint cannot be resolved by the Manager, ask to use the society's complaints system and if you are not satisfied after this, take your complaint to the building societies' ombudsman.

In a National Consumer Council survey published in 1993, half of the people who had complained about their building society to the building societies' ombudsman thought that the ombudsman was not at all or not very fair. Most thought that the whole process of complaining about a building society took too long – the average time from the initial complaint to the decision by the ombudsman was not far short of two years.

However, short of legal action – which is not recommended – the building societies' ombudsman is the only recourse people have if their building society refuses to budge. If the ombudsman does decide in the customer's favour, their decision is not binding on the society, although only one award has not been honoured in five years. They can award up to £100 000.

CREDIT

Credit is money you have borrowed that you can pay back. If you cannot pay it back, it becomes debt. The following are the main forms of credit available.

▷ *Credit cards:* Over 27 million credit cards are now in circulation. Their interest rates vary and it is well worth shopping around to find the cheapest card or cards available. You can even use a new card to pay off the old card's balance. Two thirds of credit cards now charge an annual fee.

▷ *Debit cards:* like Switch, Delta and Connect are *not* credit cards at all as nobody ever lends you money. They are more a kind of electronic cheque.

▷ *Charge cards:* These are like credit cards, but customers have to pay off the full debt every month. The most popular charge cards are Diners Club and American Express.

▷ *Gold cards:* These are either credit or charge cards and are offered to high-income customers. Apart from the cachet, a gold card usually has perks, like the availability of cheap overdrafts. You should be able to get one if you earn over £30 000 a year.

▷ *Store cards:* Most store cards are credit cards that restrict your spending to one store or group of shops. Some store cards are based on a monthly account like charge cards. With one or two notable exceptions, these cards are a very expensive way of borrowing and are not recommended.

▷ *Hire purchase:* When you buy something on hire purchase (HP), you never own the item until after the final payment is made. A very similar form of credit agreement is a *conditional sale* agreement.

▷ *Credit sale:* This is a loan that has been arranged to pay off a particular item in a shop.

▷ *Bank and building society loans:* These are usually the cheapest ways of borrowing, although you have no equal liability protection (see page 233).

▷ *Finance company loans:* Many credit sale agreements are made with finance companies and there are many such companies around, some less than respectable. One useful check is to see if a company is a member of the Finance and Leasing Association. The Association offers a conciliation process if things go wrong and an independent arbitration service for disputes. Finance company loans are usually comparatively expensive, although they do offer you equal liability protection (see page 233).

With all these different forms of credit around, it can be extremely easy to mistake one form for another.

To have a permanent record of her wedding, Rebecca Read decided she wanted a video camera. She found one she liked for just over £700 and what attracted her most was that it came with what seemed to be a very good credit arrangement. Apart from a small deposit, all Miss Read would have to pay was a monthly instalment of £30. In two years' time, the video would be hers, or so she thought. However, after 17 months, she contacted the finance company to discover that although she had paid £510, she still owed another £517.

What Miss Read thought she had bought was a very low interest loan with regular monthly instalments, but what she had actually bought was a very high interest credit sales agreement with minimum instalments. Under this credit sales agreement, all the customer was required to do was to meet a minimum monthly payment. However, if this was the only payment made, the bill simply mounted up so that the final amount could be much more than the cost of the original item.

In Miss Read's case – and in many others *Watchdog* investigated – the salesperson had not made it clear to her what kind of credit she was buying. If you are buying something on credit, ask the shop for a written quotation – they have to provide this by law. The quotation will tell you how much the total cost of the credit will be if you pay the suggested monthly instalment, and you can then compare this with the price on offer. The written quotation will also tell you another, most important figure that will allow you to judge if the credit is a good deal or not – the APR.

APR

APR stands for Annual Percentage Rate of charge. It is important not simply because it tells you how much the credit is going to cost you, but also because it allows you to compare the costs of the different forms of credit that are available. All lenders must work out the APR in the same way, by including all the charges they make for the credit as well as the interest they are charging. The APR is, therefore, an easy way of comparing credit deals, and you should be very wary of any salesperson who says that the

APR does not matter very much. Be wary, too, of any credit on offer that is more than 10 to 15 per cent over the bank rate. This includes many store cards as well as more dubious finance houses.

APR has proved to be a very useful comparison of credit, but the signs are now that it needs to be overhauled. It cannot deal with some of the new financial services like complicated mortgages deals. Often the APR quoted in the mortgage advertisements is completely misleading.

SECURED CREDIT

Most forms of credit are unsecured. However, this does not mean that credit companies cannot pursue you if you fail to pay back their money – they can, and they will – but they are unlikely to be able to seize your home even if they take you to court. Secured creditors, though, are allowed to do this as their loans are usually guaranteed on your home. If you do not meet the repayment conditions, the lender can apply for your home to be sold. By law, advertisements for secured credit must include a warning about this.

The classic secured loan is a mortgage, but all other forms of secured loans should be avoided, even though the interest rates on offer seem attractive. It is very easy to lose your home as a result of not being able to meet the repayment terms.

Pawnbrokers offer a kind of secured loan as you borrow money by leaving behind something valuable as security. If you do not repay the loan plus the usually quite high interest, the item is sold.

CREDIT AND THE LAW

Everybody who offers credit over £30 has to have a credit licence from the Office of Fair Trading. The Director-General of Fair Trading can investigate complaints about lenders and revoke their licence. Unfortunately, this is not as strong a threat as it sounds. Since 1976, there have been 330 000 licences issued and, on average, only a few hundred are revoked every year.

Most forms of credit are controlled by the Consumer Credit Act 1974. The Act gives customers a number of rights when they take on credit that are well worth knowing about:

Equal liability

Section 75 of the Consumer Credit Act 1974 states that if someone buys an item on credit and the item turns out to be faulty, the credit company is equally liable with the retailer to repay the customer. This is a very useful Act indeed because credit companies, or at least the respectable ones, do not go out of business at nearly the same rate as shopkeepers and traders do, and it gives customers a guarantee that they will get their money back if the trader turns out to be insolvent or fraudulent.

There are, however, some limitations. The goods must cost more than £100, and less than £30 000, although the most you can pay by credit is £15 000. Also only some kinds of credit are covered. These include credit cards, store cards, finance house loans, credit sales and HP, but charge cards and bank and building society loans are not covered. (However, some charge card companies will refund any money their customers may have lost because of a trader going bust. And occasionally a credit card company will refund amounts less than £100 due to complicated 'charge-back' agreements. All this is up to the company concerned: they are under no legal obligation to make a refund.)

One thing to bear in mind is that you can claim all your money back from the credit card company, even if you have paid only a small amount of the total price by credit. So, if you buy an £800 holiday and pay a deposit of £20 by credit card and the rest in cash, you can claim the whole £800 back, plus any compensation due from the credit card company if the holiday turns out to be a fiasco. Some other credit card situations that are not covered by equal liability are explained on pages 53 to 55.

Cancellation rights

Some forms of credit give you the right to cancel for up to five days if you change your mind. If you have this right, there will be a box in the corner of the credit agreement form outlining it. Generally, you will be allowed to cancel if you sign for credit in your home, but not if you sign for it in a shop or office. Do not believe any company that says you have a right to cancel if there is no indication of this on the form.

Debt

If you start to be unable to afford credit repayments, the credit has turned into debt. The moment you start defaulting regularly on any form of credit, you should try to see a trained debt adviser (your local Citizens Advice Bureau should be able to put you in touch with one).

Trained debt counsellors can contact creditors for you and help work out agreements with them that should stop you ending up in court. They can do this not because the creditors take pity on you, but because the creditors know that a County court judge is unlikely to offer them a better deal than any a debt adviser has been able to work out.

If you do not contact your creditors, sooner or later they, or a debt collection agency acting on their behalf, will start trying to get their money back. However, no debt collector is allowed to harass a debtor for money, irrespective of how much money they owe. Harassment could include contacting an employer or repeatedly coming around to the house. If you are being harassed, report the company to the police.

It is possible to challenge an interest rate that seems extortionate in court, but few people have ever tried this because it is not at all clear what kinds of rates are considered extortionate.

Credit companies usually sell debts on to debt collectors because it is not worth them spending very much money pursuing people who are unlikely to be able to pay. Eventually, debt collection agencies will give up, too, but not before a County court judgment has been obtained. These judgments matter because other credit companies, including banks and building societies, consult them before making a decision about giving credit. Anybody who has an unsatisfied County court judgment against them is seen, quite reasonably, as a bad credit risk.

SETTLING CREDIT EARLY

You can settle all forms of credit early, but credit companies can charge you an early payment penalty. These penalties are, however, regulated by the Consumer Credit Act 1974. If you want to settle early, ask the company how much it will cost.

HIRE PURCHASE

Hire purchase agreements under £15 000 are regulated by the Consumer Credit Act and this regulation includes provision for paying a HP debt off early. Ask the company how much it will cost. If you want to sell an item you have bought on HP, a car perhaps, you must settle the HP debt first. Another useful thing to remember when you buy something on HP is that your contract is not with the trader, but with the HP company. Thus, if the item turns out to be faulty, you are entitled to a refund from the HP company, and this right extends throughout the time you are paying for it, much longer than any right would last if you purchased it directly from a shop.

INSURANCE

Credit insurance is often a good idea, especially if it covers redundancy or sickness, but the insurance offered by a credit company may not be the best deal or give you the best cover. Check the exclusions and the competition before you sign up. Sometimes this insurance is added on automatically by the credit company unless you tell them not to, so check the application form carefully.

CREDIT COMPANY CHECKING

Before granting a new customer credit, a finance company will check them out. They will first work out what kind of risk a new customer may pose by means of a process called *credit scoring*. This gives marks for things like income, age, home ownership, job security and so on. They will then check a customer's credit history by consulting a credit reference agency.

Credit reference agencies collect information about people from two kinds of sources: public information (like the electoral register and County court judgments) and information from other companies that have lent you money in the past (they should not have any information about your bank account, which is confidential – if they have, complain to your bank). All this information will be put on a computerized file.

The main credit reference agencies have information about virtually every adult in the UK. You have the right to see any credit file anyone has on you by paying £1 for each credit file you want to look at (under the Consumer Credit Act 1974) or by paying £10 for any other file (under the Data Protection Act 1984).

If any of the information is incorrect, you can ask for it to be corrected. If the company refuses to do this, you can ask for a 200-word statement to be inserted in your file. The company must put this in, unless they believe it to be incorrect, frivolous, defamatory or scandalous. You then have the right of appeal to the Director-General of Fair Trading (for credit files) or the Data Protection Registrar (for other files). You have the right, too, to ask any finance company that refuses you credit if they have used a credit reference agency. They must tell you, if you apply within 30 days of their refusal.

You may disagree strongly with a credit company's decision not to give you credit, but you cannot force them to lend their money to you. Just like any other trader, they have the right to refuse any potential customer as long as their decision is not based on race or gender. However, if you are refused credit, many credit companies will tell you why if you ask them.

MORTGAGES

In 1991, Colin and Marianne Dobbies needed a larger house for their new family, but, as mortgage rates were then over 11 per cent, they did not think they would be able to afford one. They then spotted an advertisement from a company called Daca Finance in Northampton offering 8 per cent fixed-rate mortgages. After checking the company out through their bank, they signed up. The £800 advance fees seemed cheap at the price, until it became clear that Mr and Mrs Dobbies and 2000 other Daca customers were not going to get their money. The company simply could not deliver what it promised. It closed down and offered no refunds. The Dobbies lost their cheap mortgage and their £800.

However, this was not the end of the matter for the Dobbies. There was a further shock. The Dobbies lived in Scotland, and with the offer of a Daca mortgage, they had put an offer on another house near where they lived. When the mortgage fell through and they had to withdraw the offer, the Dobbies were forced to pay compensation, because under Scottish law, once an offer has been accepted on a house, it is binding on everyone concerned.

The Dobbies suffered considerably as a result of Daca finance and advice, but they were not entitled to any compensation. Unlike other forms of financial advice, mortgage selling is not covered by any watchdog or compensation scheme.

Daca Finance are not the only mortgage company to have collapsed over the last few years. There are a bewildering array of small and large mortgage sellers on the market, including building societies you may never have heard of and foreign banks that are obscure even in their own countries. However, the mortgages on offer all fall into a few categories, though the packaging and the names may be different.

THE DIFFERENT TYPES OF MORTGAGES

Repayment mortgages

Most of the monthly payment on a repayment mortgage goes, initially, to pay off the interest on the loan. After about 17 or 18 years, the capital owed is much less and the monthly payment then goes, mainly, to pay off the capital. The last monthly payment is the last money owed on a house.

Endowment mortgages

Two payments are made each month: one to the mortgage company (which pays off the interest on the loan) and one to a life assurance company (which builds up an endowment fund to pay off the capital at the end of the mortgage term). Most endowment policies used are *low cost* (where premiums are used to buy an investment-type insurance policy), but you can also find *interest-only mortgages* (recommended for people with low incomes, but large amounts of capital), *pension mortgages* (useful if you have no pension, but restrictive), *unit linked mortgages* (where the premiums are used to buy shares) and *PEP mortgages* (a more sophisticated form of unit-linked endowment). Most people opt for a repayment or a low-cost endowment mortgage, but which is the best?

If you believe what the banks, building societies, insurance companies and financial advisers say, endowment mortgages offer the best deal. But since the commission all these companies earn from selling endowment policies is much more remunerative than that earned on selling repayment mortgages, this advice is hardly surprising.

There are two basic advantages of repayment mortgages. They guarantee to pay the mortgage off at the end of the term, and they give people the flexibility to re-arrange payments if they get into difficulty.

Endowment policies are more of a risk: they depend on how well the stock market does. If the market does well over the next 25 years, customers will end up with a bonus. If it does not, the endowment policy may not build up enough cash to pay off the mortgage. The risk is small – endowment policies have done well in the past – but it is a risk, none the less.

Endowment policies offer life insurance as well, but it is an expensive form of life insurance. You would be better to buy it separately if this were your only reason for preferring an endowment policy.

Endowment policies are better if you move house regularly as you can switch them easily from one mortgage to another, but they work out as a bad deal if you are older (the premiums are higher) and if interest rates are high.

If you choose an endowment policy, the one thing you must not do is cash it in early. Endowment policies are designed to be long-term investments. The benefits to be gained from them do not really start to add up until towards the end of the policy and there are usually terminal bonuses paid at the end as well. If you cash in an endowment policy in the first few years, you will be unlikely to get back even the money you have paid in premiums. This is because the commission earned by the person who sold you the policy (from £800 upwards) is deducted from the first few years' premiums. From 1 January 1995 anybody who sells you an endowment policy must tell you in writing how much their commission is.

If you really have no option but to cash in an endowment policy early, do not surrender it to the insurance company, but try to sell it on to someone else. There are several firms that will buy endowments or auction them for you and you will get a better rate than from your insurance company.

DIFFERENT RATES AND DISCOUNTS

The traditional mortgage is based on a *variable interest rate*, which is set by the mortgage company. This rate goes up and down as the base rate is put up and down by the Government. In the early 1990s, mortgage rates spiralled up to 14 per cent, and over, doubling the mortgage premiums of a few years before and making it impossible for many homeowners to budget.

The response from mortgage lenders was to introduce the *fixed-rate mortgage*. With fixed-rate mortgages, in exchange for an arrangement fee, the lender promises to keep the mortgage rate at the same level, irrespective of what is happening to the base rate. Thus, 10 and 11 per cent fixed rates seemed good deals in 1992 – until the variable rates tumbled down to 7 and 6 per cent a year later as the base rate fell. The tumbling interest rates also revealed another disadvantage of the fixed-rate mortgage: they often come with penalties for any customer who withdraws from the agreement early.

Another kind of mortgage on offer is the low-start mortgage. With these mortgages, the interest rate is reduced for the first few years. These mortgages are good bargains if the interest rate is *discounted,* but not if it is *deferred.* Discounted mortgages are genuine reductions, but deferred mortgages are agreements to pay less at the start of the mortgage then more in the future. They are only worth considering if your income is likely to go up considerably over the next few years.

IS IT WORTH CHANGING YOUR MORTGAGE?

With the wide range of fixed and variable rates on offer recently, many people have been switching their mortgages to cheaper companies. It can be extremely worth while. In 1993, *Which?* magazine calculated that you could save over £3000 if you chose the cheapest lender of the 100 or so they surveyed. However, there is a catch – it does cost money to change a mortgage. Typical costs include the cost of redeeming the old mortgage, the valuation cost for the new lender, the arrangement fee for any new fixed mortgage, solicitor's costs to arrange the mortgage and, perhaps, an indemnity charge if the new mortgage is worth more than 80 per cent of the valuation of the property (indemnity charges are an insurance paid by customers to guarantee that the lender will get their money back if the customer defaults, they do not give the customer anything at all, least of all any protection from being repossessed). Some of these costs can be added on to the new mortgage, but some will have to be paid up front.

The only way to know if it is worth switching your mortgage is to add up all the savings you will make on a lower mortgage rate and take away the costs involved in changing the mortgage. You can then decide if the savings are worth the trouble. If you do change your mortgage, do not change any endowment policy. Most mortgage lenders will accept old endowment policies, but if they will not, find another lender.

FINDING A MORTGAGE

There are two ways to obtain a mortgage. You can go direct to the bank or building society and negotiate one yourself or you can use a financial adviser or mortgage broker to arrange one for you. Before you go to either, it is well worth checking with specialist magazines and the weekly financial press to find out who is offering the cheapest deal.

If you go to a financial adviser or broker, make sure they are registered under the Financial Services Act 1986. They do not have to be registered if they are just selling mortgages, but the most responsible ones will be. Find out, too, if they are a tied agent or an independent adviser. If an adviser is tied to one company, you may as well go direct to a bank or building society and obtain advice from one of their financial advisers, most of whom are tied agents as well. Independent financial advisers and mortgage brokers should be able to offer you a range of different companies.

It is worth getting quotes from independent brokers and then comparing these with quotes from high street banks and building societies. Brokers often have access to small and obscure English or foreign companies, some of which offer the cheapest deals on the market. If the best deal turns out to be a foreign bank, make sure the mortgage is in sterling and that problems are dealt with here, not abroad.

REPOSSESSIONS

If you have any problems with monthly payments, you must get in touch with the mortgage company as soon as you can as it may well be possible to rearrange payments.

If the problem seems likely to persist for more than one or two payments, it is a good idea to get some debt counselling advice from a Citizens Advice Bureau or a specialist debt counsellor. They will help you negotiate with your lender to try and avoid repossession. If it does look as if you will have to sell your house, the most important thing is to try to sell it yourself and not hand it over to the mortgage company; you will get more money for the house than they will. If the company receives less money from the sale than the outstanding balance on your mortgage, it may pursue you for the difference.

INSURANCE

When fire broke out in an attic room of Reg Osbourne's house one winter Thursday, he lost not just the roof, but also three knitting machines and £1000-worth of precious knitting yarn that he had collected over the years. Mr Osbourne's hobby and passion was machine knitting and so this was a disaster to him.

The insurance claim was likely to be complicated, but someone soon turned up to help – a loss assessor. In return for his professional services helping Mr Osbourne put in his claim, the assessor would take 10 per cent of the payout. The next day was a Friday and another person turned up – a loss adjuster who had been asked by the insurance company to work out Mr Osbourne's claim.

The loss adjuster and the loss assessor discussed the damage and agreed, among other things, that a tarpaulin should be put over the roof to prevent further damage.

However, when the assessor discussed this with a local builder, the builder said it would be impossible because there was no strength left in the roof. Something had to be done before the weekend. The assessor gave the builder the go-ahead to put a temporary roof on the house and then place a tarpaulin over it, at a total cost of some £5000. Mr Osbourne was told not to worry because he was insured, or so the assessor said.

When the loss adjuster and the insurance company found out what the builder had done, they refused to pay. They did not think that the work was necessary and they had not agreed to it. The loss assessor claimed that it was an emergency and that it had not been possible to get through to them over the weekend, a claim that the insurance company denied. Mr Osbourne was left in the middle and had to pay the £5000 builder's bill himself.

Mr Osbourne may well have a claim against the loss assessor, but he would have to show that he did not receive the best advice and this could be difficult. His experience does reveal an important point regarding insurance claims: never do anything major to repair damage until you have the loss adjuster or insurance company's approval.

Insurance claims are complicated and one reason is because insurance companies seem to talk a different language to everybody else. It is a language well worth knowing because if you do not, your claim may well fail. Here are some key words and phrases used by the insurance industry which will clarify the type of insurance you have and therefore the sorts of claims you can make.

▷ *'Material or relevant fact'*: You must tell an insurance company anything that may affect their decision to insure you. Most of the time, this is obvious and it is stated on the proposal form. Examples are any accidents you may have had if you want to take out motor insurance, or any illnesses you suffer from if you want to take out medical insurance. Sometimes, however, material facts are not at all obvious, even though they may still affect the insurer's attitude to your application. If you are uncertain whether or not something is relevant, check with your agent before you complete the form and include it to be on the safe side.

▷ *'Indemnity'*: If your insurance policy is an indemnity one, you will only get back the present value of your possessions, how much they were worth at the time of the claim. You will not get the replacement cost of them, which could well be a lot more. If you want to make sure that you receive the replacement value, make sure your policy is *'new for old'*.

▷ *'All risks'*: There are no insurance policies that cover *all* disasters. What usually happens is that you are insured against certain specific risks and if something else goes wrong, you will not be insured. A policy offering 'all risks' works the other away round: everything is included apart from anything specifically mentioned on the policy as an exclusion.

▷ *'Insurable interest'*: To claim for property that is not your own, you have to show that you have an insurable interest in the property. This interest must mean that you will be at a financial loss if your claim is denied. An example is if you have a television stolen from your house. If it was rented, you could claim for it, but if it was borrowed free from a friend, you could not claim, although your friend should be able to on their household insurance.

▷ *'Reasonable care':* Some insurance contracts, particularly for travel insurance, impose a duty of care on you to look after your property. If you behave recklessly, your claim could be invalid. An example of this is if your valuables are stolen when you are on holiday. If they were stolen from the back seat of an unlocked car, the insurance company could refuse your claim on the basis that you did not take reasonable care of the items.

Most insurance contracts also stipulate that you must take reasonable steps to minimize further damage, although if this involves major expenditure, you must make sure you have the approval of the insurance company first.

▷ *'Wear and tear':* Insurance contracts only cover accidents or one-off events. You cannot claim for things that have simply worn out.

▷ *'Exclusion clauses and the small print':* The reason it is always worth reading the small print on a policy is because this is where insurers put their exclusion clauses and conditions. Insurance companies are exempt from the Unfair Contract Terms Act 1977, so none of their exclusion clauses can be challenged as unreasonable.

A typical exclusion clause to watch out for in some insurance contracts is fire damage. You may need extra insurance for this. A typical condition is that all claims must be made within seven days of the incident.

▷ *'Betterment':* The idea of insurance is to put you back in the same position as you were before an accident or event. You are not meant to be in a better position than you were, even though sometimes this is impossible to avoid. Insurance companies can deduct any 'betterment' from a final claim.

BUYING AN INSURANCE POLICY

Most insurance policies are bought through insurance agents or brokers rather than direct from the insurance company.

The insurance *broker* is the traditional independent salesperson in the industry. Brokers have to be registered with their regulatory body, the Insurance Brokers Registration Council (IBRC), which can investigate complaints. Brokers are obliged to give you the best possible advice and they must have professional indemnity insurance to safeguard their customer's money if they go bust.

Everyone else selling insurance is an *intermediary*. If an intermediary sells policies from six or more different insurance company policies (two or more for life insurance), they are *independent*. Make sure such independent intermediaries have indemnity insurance. If an intermediary sells policies from fewer than six companies, they are an *agent*. The insurance companies they represent are responsible if anything goes wrong.

Some *direct only* insurance companies have chosen not to deal through brokers, but sell their policies direct to the public. Direct only companies save on the commission that would have to be paid to a broker or agent, but they have to pay for marketing and advertising costs and many also pay their salespeople similar levels of commission to those earned by independent brokers or agents. Nevertheless, they can be a good deal. When *Which?* magazine tested out the best buys in motor insurance, direct only companies came top.

All insurance companies have to be authorized to sell insurance by the Department of Trade. Contact the Department if you discover any insurance company that offers suspiciously low premiums. If an insurance company goes bust, policyholders can claim their money back through the Policyholders Protection Board.

HOW TO MAKE A CLAIM

When an insurance claim is made, most companies appoint a loss adjuster who deals with the claim and is paid a fee by the insurance company. Many customers who have a large or complicated claim find it useful to appoint a loss assessor to represent their interests. You can find one through your broker or through their professional association, the Institute of Public Loss Assessors.

The advantage of using a loss assessor is that they will make sure a claim includes everything a person is entitled to. This could include intangible things such as pain and suffering and additional expenses that are often forgotten about. The assessor should also make sure that the claim meets all the terms and conditions of the contract. On the other hand, a loss assessor usually takes 10 per cent of a claim as their fee.

HOW TO COMPLAIN

If you are dissatisfied with how your claim has been dealt with or, indeed, with any other aspect of an insurance company's behaviour, here is what to do.

▷ Write and ask for your complaint to be investigated.

▷ If you have no success, you can complain either to the Association of British Insurers or Lloyds, if the company is a member of one of these organizations. They will make sure that your complaint has been seen by senior management at the company.

▷ If senior management still reject your claim, you have six months to complain to the insurance ombudsman or the Personal Insurance Arbitration Scheme (PIAS). Most major insurance firms are members of one scheme or the other.

The insurance ombudsman can make an award of up to £100 000, except for permanent health insurance where the limit is £10 000. The award is binding on the company, but not on the complainant, who can reject it and go to court instead. The ombudsman cannot look at complaints that involve someone else's policy or relate to a commercial business or any complaints where legal proceedings have started. Life Insurance complaints are now dealt with by the Personal Investment Authority, not the ombudsman.

The PIAS scheme works in a similar way, except that its findings are binding on the complainant as well as the company and that you will need the agreement of the insurance company to use the scheme.

In a survey done by the National Consumer Council, only half the people who had used the insurance ombudsman service thought the process was fair, although most of them would use it again.

LIFE INSURANCE

There are three main types of life insurance: *term* insurance (which only pays out if you die within the term of the insurance), *whole life* (which pays out when you die, although you may stop paying the premium at a certain age) and *endowment* (which pays out after a fixed period).

Term and whole life insurance are usually cheap. Endowment policies are expensive, partly because they combine basic life assurance with long-term investments. They are only worth buying as part of a mortgage.

BUILDINGS AND CONTENTS INSURANCE

These are two quite different insurances, although they are often sold together. It is usually cheaper to find *buildings* insurance yourself rather than through a mortgage company. Most mortgage companies will allow you to do this if you insist, but they will also want to approve the policy as well to make sure events like subsidence are covered.

You can arrange house *contents* insurance separately. By shopping around and comparing prices, you can save yourself hundreds of pounds, but be clear about what you need. Go for a new for old policy and for one that will allow you to claim for your property if it is stolen or damaged elsewhere. Always look for a policy that covers injury to any people who come on to your property, from visitors to the milkman. This is the kind of insurance often forgotten about until an accident happens and then it is crucial.

MOTOR INSURANCE

Motor insurance premiums also vary considerably and it is well worth obtaining several quotes. You can bring the premiums down by restricting drivers, garaging your car overnight and by increasing the excess. A no claims bonus earned with one company can usually be transferred to another. You will not lose your no claims bonus if, when making a claim, the insurance company can get back their money from the other insurance company. However, if you were partly to blame or the other party was uninsured or has disappeared, you will have to balance the claim against the bonus you will lose. It is, after all, a no claims bonus, not a no blame bonus. If you have a claim against an uninsured or an untraceable driver, the Motor Insurers Bureau may be able to help.

HEALTH AND MEDICAL INSURANCE

Permanent health insurance provides you with an income if you stop work as a result of an accident or illness. A *hospital cash plan* pays you a lump sum if you go into hospital and *critical illness (or 'dreaded disease') insurance* provides you with an income or lump sum if you come down with a serious illness, like cancer.

They are all cheaper and very different to *private medical* insurance (PMI). This covers the cost of private medical treatment for acute conditions.

There are three types of private medical insurance: standard plans; budget or low-cost plans (which only cover certain kinds of treatment, for example ones for which there is a waiting list on the NHS); and over-60s plans (on which you can get tax relief). There are considerable variations between different companies in what they include and exclude in these plans. It is worth checking if the following are covered:

▷ chronic conditions (illnesses that will need continuing treatment after their acute stages)
▷ psychiatric problems (surprisingly common)
▷ childbirth and pregnancy
▷ pre-existing conditions.

You should also find out where you will be treated, what the financial limits are, what other benefits are offered (like health insurance), what happens in an emergency and what will happen if your money runs out. If your treatment is not an emergency, try to make sure that your consultant gives you an estimate of the cost and check that the estimate is inside British Medical Association (BMA) or insurance company guidelines. Insurance companies can and do refuse to pay over-inflated bills.

HOLIDAY INSURANCE

Most tour operators insist that you have holiday insurance. The operator and the travel agent will try to ensure that you take it out with *them* as their commission for this is considerable. You can go elsewhere and pick up a better deal, although the important thing is to make sure you do buy some.

It is perfectly possible to claim compensation for many of the hazards you may come across on holiday, like lost luggage or injury. You can also receive free medical treatment in EC countries by bringing an E1/11 form with you (a good idea, particularly in Spain where public hospitals have higher standards than many private clinics).

However, in most situations, it is best to claim for these eventualities from your holiday insurance company. The most important thing is to make sure everything is covered before you buy. In particular, check that

▷ *the exclusions* in the policy are acceptable as some policies will have fewer exclusions than others
▷ *unattended luggage* is covered – it is worth paying extra for this if it is not
▷ *the cancellation circumstances* are acceptable to you
▷ *all health problems* that may occur are covered
▷ *all possibly dangerous pastimes* like windsurfing or skiing are covered.

INVESTMENTS

The standard financial advice about investing money is pretty straightforward. Once you have decided how much you want to save or invest, you then need to decide how much risk you are prepared to take and how quickly you might need your money back in an emergency.

▷ If you want *no risk*, you should stick to building society and bank deposit accounts (most of which give immediate access) or the various forms of national savings, government bonds and gilts.
▷ If you are prepared to take *some risk*, for a greater return, you should consider the various forms of group ownership of shares like unit trusts or PEPs that are managed by specialist companies. An endowment policy or life insurance savings plan is similar, except it is very long term.

254

▷ If you really want to make money, you need to take *considerable risks* by buying and selling individual shares, either through a stockbroker or through the various share shops there now are. You can make a great deal of money this way, but you have to know what you are doing and be prepared to sustain losses. You should aim to spend about £1000 each on shares from 12 to 15 companies, some blue-chip (companies like British Telecom and ICI, which are safe but will give unexciting returns) and some small and new (where the real returns or losses will happen). You can get advice from the weekly financial press or from stockbrokers, although you may do better to rely on your instincts or some knowledge of the company concerned. A recent experiment in Scandinavia compared the advice given by stockbrokers with the stocks chosen at random by monkeys. The monkeys won.

FINANCIAL ADVISERS

Most people rely on the advice of some kind of financial adviser to sort out their investments and insurances. The financial adviser could be from a bank or building society or be an accountant or a lawyer or a life insurance agent or an independent financial adviser. Whatever they call themselves, all people giving financial advice are regulated by the Financial Services Act 1986, an Act that is enforced by the Securities and Investment Board. The only exceptions are advice about mortgages and advice about general insurance, although life insurance advice is covered under the Act.

Financial advisers must give you 'best advice' and they

must tell you if they are independent or acting on behalf of one company. All advisers must be registered with the Securities and Investment Board, either directly or through one of five self-regulatory bodies (SROs) or through one of the nine recognized professional organizations (RPOs), like the Law Society or the Insurance Brokers Registration Council. You can check if an adviser is regulated by phoning the Securities and Investment Board on 071 929 3652, although this will only confirm that a business is registered, not an individual.

All this protection sounds impressive and, indeed, it is an improvement on what went before. It has not, however, stamped out bad practice, incompetence or criminality. It has not stopped poor salespeople selling inappropriate investments, insurances and pensions and earning large commissions in the process.

Like many pensioners, Joyce Cottrell had a low income, but she had paid off the mortgage on her house. She was attracted to a 'retired income plan' that was advertised by a company called Acorn Insurance and Mortgage Consultants, independent financial advisers based at Princes Risborough. The plan involved Mrs Cottrell buying a £50 000 bond by taking a mortgage out on her home. The bond would pay the mortgage and provide a regular income for Mrs Cottrell to add to her pension.

What the company did not explain to Mrs Cottrell was that this all depended on three things: low interest rates, a buoyant stock market and high property prices. The company also did not explain to her that her home could be at risk if the market changed. This is exactly what happened. The bond behaved so poorly that, instead of giving her an income, Mrs Cottrell had to pay more money into it from her pension to make sure her new mortgage payments were covered and to keep her house from being repossessed. This could have been foreseen because Mrs Cottrell was sold the bond in 1989 and these bonds were already regarded by many experts as a very poor buy indeed.

Mrs Cottrell took her complaint about the company to FIMBRA, the SRO that regulates the 6000-odd independent financial advisers. However, her complaint was rejected at first by FIMBRA because they considered that she was given sufficient warnings about the risks involved. After 50 other people had complained, FIMBRA suspended the company and Mrs Cottrell was able to claim compensation from the Investors Compensation Scheme although it is unlikely that it will cover all her losses.

There have been many other complaints about independent financial agents and about tied agents who are regulated by another of the SROs, LAUTRO. Like FIMBRA, LAUTRO has been criticized for how it has dealt with complaints and for how it investigates its members. As this book goes to press, FIMBRA and LAUTRO are being replaced by the Personal Investment Authority, which is intended to have greater scope and powers. It should be fully operational by the summer of 1995.

Choosing a financial adviser

Many people still choose a financial adviser who is a 'friend of a friend'. This is unfortunate as many of these 'friends' are tied agents rather than independent financial advisers, that is, they only sell (or should only sell) the policies of one company.

One way to find an independent financial adviser is to call IFA Promotions (0483 461461). They can send you a list of six financial advisers near you and they have on their books two thirds of the independent financial advisers in the country. You should try at least three independent advisers and compare the advice you get with the advice from your bank or building society, whose advisers are usually tied agents.

Ask them how much they charge and which regulatory organization they belong to (make sure you check with the organization concerned, too). See how many questions they ask about your circumstances and be very wary of any promises or guarantees of returns they make that are much higher than you could get elsewhere. Be wary, too, of anyone who wants a cheque made out directly to them. Ask them how much commission they will make from your investment and do not be impressed by any claims made about how funds have done in the past; this does not predict future performance.

If you have a reasonable amount of money to invest, it is worth reading the weekly financial press so that you can check the advice your adviser is providing.

If things go wrong

▷ Ask to use the complaints procedure. All people or companies registered under the Financial Services Act 1986 must have one.

▷ If they do not have one, complain to the SRO or professional body the adviser is registered with. Apart from LAUTRO and FIMBRA (and the new Personal Investment Authority), the other SROs are the TSA, IMRO and AFBD. Each of the SROs will investigate complaints and will attempt to conciliate.

▷ If this does not work, you will be directed to an

arbitration scheme. Each arbitrator has the power to make binding awards, usually up to a maximum of £100 000.

▷ If you have invested money in a company that is registered under the Financial Services Act 1986 and the company goes into liquidation, you can make a claim from the Investors Compensation Scheme up to a maximum of £48 000. You can also apply to the scheme if you have an arbitration award against a company and the company cannot afford to pay it to you, but the scheme does not cover any losses from normal investment risks.

PENSIONS

Many *personal pension* plans are arranged by financial advisers and these are covered by the Financial Services Act 1986 (see above). They are much like any other long-term investment, except that the problems investors have experienced with them are, if anything, even worse. Currently the Securities and Investments Board is reviewing the private pension plans of some 500 000 people who were advised, badly as it turned out, to switch from their company pension to a personal pension plan. They should be paying compensation to people who have lost money as a result of bad advice.

Occupational pensions are not regulated in this way. They vary according to the company that offers them, but the best schemes are independent of the company and run by independent trustees.

The problem with at least some occupational schemes

is that they have been raided by their parent companies when the company has got into trouble. You can try to ensure that this will not happen by questioning the scheme's manager before signing up and making sure that the independent trustees are able to resist company overtures. You should also check what the position of the scheme will be if the company collapses.

In general, occupational schemes are better deals than personal pensions because the employer is contributing as well (one exception is if you expect to change employers many times in your career). All pension schemes have to offer you the right to buy additional years (AVCs). You should also find out what the arrangements are for early retirement.

If you have problems in tracing a company pension scheme, contact the Pensions Register, which is run by the Occupational Pensions Board in Newcastle. If you have any other kind of problem or dispute, contact the Occupational Pensions Advisory Service which may be able to help. They can refer unresolved disputes to the pensions ombudsman who will investigate complaints about the maladministration of a company pension scheme. There is no limit on how much compensation they can award.

TAX

It is not necessary to employ an accountant to sort out tax affairs. The Inland Revenue have made the annual tax form much easier to complete, and all offices can answer queries by telephone. There is also a Taxpayers' Charter.

If you think you have paid too much tax or you receive a demand for tax that you do not think you have to pay, write to your local tax inspector and give your reasons. If you have been sent a notice of assessment, appeal and ask for a postponement. You must do this within 30 days. You should then send your own assessment to the inspector. If this does not resolve matters and you are still unhappy with the final assessment, you can appeal to the Commissioners of Tax, who will hear your case.

All this can be done without an accountant, but most accountants claim that they can save people money, even taking into account their charges of £50 per hour and upwards. They do this partly by remembering rules like people's rights to claim tax back for six years, partly by knowing well all the allowable expenses against particular businesses or professions, partly by other extremely useful pieces of knowledge.

It is certainly a good idea to employ an accountant if you are self-employed, at least for your first couple of years, if only to find out all the expenses you can claim. You should try to find an accountant who already deals with the kind of business you intend to follow and check their qualifications and their membership of a professional organization.

9

USING THE LAW

Frank Bicknell had been looking forward to his retirement, yet, when it came, it was ruined by a very bad form of photosensitivity. Light made Mr Bicknell's skin extremely itchy and when he scratches the skin it hurts, sometimes unbearably. It even hurts when he wears clothes. Most of his life is spent living in twilight, unable to enjoy sharing everyday activities with his family.

Mr Bicknell is convinced that his suffering came about as a result of taking Opren, an anti-arthritic drug introduced in Britain in 1980 and withdrawn just two years later after more than 60 people had died from side-effects after taking the drug. Mr Bicknell wants compensation for the damage he claims Opren has done to his life. The manufacturers of Opren, Eli Lilly, deny responsibility for Mr Bicknell's symptoms.

The only way to resolve the dispute is through the courts, yet Mr Bicknell has come up against a virtually insuperable legal problem. He was told initially that the side-effects from the drug would be temporary, but, by the time he realized that the photosensitivity was not going to go away, it was outside the three-year period in which claims for personal injury have to be made. Other people who have put in their claims inside the deadline have had their cases settled, but, unless Mr Bicknell's appeal is successful – and the omens are not hopeful – he will not be given the chance to prove his case in court.

The British legal system is not designed to be unfair, it

just has this effect sometimes for people like Mr Bicknell. In the other chapters in this book, we have stressed that getting a good deal is about using rights and practices that are underpinned by laws, laws that people can use or threaten to use to win their case. Much of the time, mere threats are enough, but a threat has no meaning unless it can be followed through. Unfortunately, there are times when following through a legal threat by taking action in the courts can make the original problem seem small in comparison.

The main problem is inequality of bargaining power. The resources available to people like Mr Bicknell and those available to a multinational company like Eli Lilly are not comparable. Resources mean not just money, but expertise, skills and know-how.

Fortunately, most common disputes are not as complicated as Mr Bicknell's. They can be taken to court without needing a great deal of money – you will not have to risk losing your house and savings. Any expertise you may need you should be able to hire, and this chapter will provide you with the necessary skills and know-how required.

THE LEGAL SYSTEM IN THE UK

There are three legal systems in the United Kingdom: English law (which covers Wales as well), Scottish law and Northern Ireland law.

In practice, there is very little difference between the English legal process and that in Northern Ireland: laws introduced in England usually apply to Northern Ireland as well. However, Scottish law is quite different: the courts have different names (the Scottish sheriff court is the equivalent of the English County court) and, to some extent, they have different procedures. Some English laws do not apply in Scotland and vice versa. The similarities between the systems, though, are much stronger than the differences and in practice, it makes sense to talk of one legal system and to point out, if appropriate, where Scottish law departs.

Law consists of *common law* (decisions by judges over the years that are based on precedent) and *statute law* (specific acts, orders or regulations made by Parliament). Statute law often extends or clarifies rights that have existed in common law. An example will illustrate this difference.

If a shop sells you a faulty item and refuses you a refund, you can take them to court under the common law of contract, but it will be easier to prove your case if you take the shop to court under a statute law, the Sale of Goods Act 1979, because this Act lays down the specific conditions that apply to contracts between traders and customers.

Cases brought under both common law and statute law are ruled on by the courts and, over the years, this leads to interpretations of the law that are known as *precedent*. Decisions made by higher courts are binding on lower courts, but decisions made in the small claims procedure of the County court, where many consumer disputes are resolved, are not binding on anyone and set no precedent.

Another basic difference between laws is whether a law is a *civil law* or a *criminal law*. Criminal law is used when somebody has behaved in a way society has deemed unacceptable. They face investigation and prosecution by law enforcement officers in the criminal courts: the magistrates' court or the Crown Court.

Civil law is used by individuals or organizations to resolve disputes about their respective rights and duties when no criminal law has been broken. Civil cases are heard in the County courts (which includes the small claims procedure) and the High Court. Despite their name, there are over 300 County courts in England and Wales alone: most major towns have one. The newer court buildings often combine magistrates' courts and County courts.

To confuse matters slightly, some civil law cases – like claims for compensation due to unfair dismissal or racial discrimination – are dealt with not by the courts, but in *tribunals*. Also, a few civil matters like Council Tax and remaining poll tax disputes are heard at magistrates' courts and not County courts.

Some laws that affect consumers are criminal laws. An example is the Trade Descriptions Act 1968. If you suspect that somebody has broken one of these laws, you should get in touch with trading standards officers. They can investigate and prosecute offenders, but they have to gather enough evidence to win a conviction beyond reasonable doubt. This can often be difficult.

Most of the laws that affect consumers are not criminal, but civil laws. An example is the Sale of Goods Act 1979. Nobody can be prosecuted, fined or imprisoned for breaking a civil law, and trading standards officers, the police or other law enforcement officers can do little more than give advice.

If you want to take action against someone under a civil law, you will have to act yourself or pay a solicitor to act for you and use the civil courts. It is easier, however, to win a case in a civil court than a criminal court as all that has to be shown is that a claim is right on the balance of probabilities, not beyond reasonable doubt. You will, of course, still have to provide evidence for your claim. Very few civil cases are ever heard by a jury; they are mostly decided by a judge.

Much of the rest of this chapter is about using the civil courts, but there are a couple of points worth making about how the criminal courts affect consumers.

THE CRIMINAL COURTS

▷ The criminal courts can award compensation to people who have been affected by a crime. If a toy injures your child, trading standards officers can prosecute the manufacturer under the Consumer Protection Act 1987. If the manufacturer is found guilty, the court can order the manufacturer to pay you compensation. Criminal courts are not obliged, however, to award compensation and some magistrates take the view that this is not their role, but the role of the civil courts.

If you have the option and your claim is very straightforward, it is a good idea to try and claim compensation in the magistrates' court. For one thing it will mean that there is no need for another court case, and, if the person found guilty does not pay you, the sanctions of a criminal court are tougher than those of a civil court.

A drawback, however, is that there is a limit of £2000 in the magistrates' court and this £2000 will have to be shared with anybody else who has been awarded compensation as well. You may well get more than this in the County court.

If you want to claim compensation at a criminal trial, make sure that the prosecution know this and that they are prepared to raise the matter at the end of the trial. If you are not granted compensation, you can still use the result of a criminal trial as evidence in your claim for damages in the civil courts.

▷ If you have suffered personal injury as a result of a crime of violence, you can apply for compensation to the Criminal Injuries Compensation Board. You will have to provide evidence for this, but the case does not have to be brought to court. The new time limit for claims is one year, but some exceptions are made, particularly claims concerning child abuse.

▷ Prosecutions in the criminal courts are brought by the Crown Prosecution Service (with evidence from the police) or by other law enforcement officers like trading standards officers, environmental health officers, the British Transport Police and others. You may be able to convince any of these people, including the Crown Prosecution Service, to prosecute a case on your behalf. You can also take out a private prosecution yourself, but it is unwise to do this as very few private prosecutions ever succeed and, if you lose, you will face not only high costs, but possible legal action against you for libel.

CIVIL LAW: CONTRACT AND TORT

There are two kinds of civil law that affect consumers: laws concerning *contracts* and laws concerning *torts*. Contract law covers agreements between people to do things that involve payment. A contract normally includes an offer, the acceptance of an offer, payment, intention and capacity. It does not have to be written down, although if you take someone to court for breaking a contract you will have to show that the contract existed in some way and the easiest way to do this is if there is some evidence in writing. Most consumer disputes concern the breaking of terms of some contract or another, and these terms may be stated directly or be implied.

The laws concerning torts are more complicated. A tort (an old French word meaning 'wrong') is a wrongdoing that is actionable only in the civil courts, that is, it is a civil wrong. The main torts cover things like hurt, injury, nuisance, inconvenience or financial loss as a result of someone being negligent. It is much easier to sue someone for a breach of contract than for a breach of tort.

Some laws have what is called *strict liability*. This means that, as long as you can show something has happened, you do not have to show that any individual was at fault. Two examples are the Sale of Goods Act 1979 and the Consumer Protection Act 1987. If a shop sells a faulty item or a manufacturer makes a dangerous item, all you have to prove under these laws is that the item was faulty or dangerous. You do not have to show that the shop knew the item was faulty or that the manufacturer knew the item was dangerous.

All cases heard in the civil courts, apart from the small claims court, have to follow what are called the *rules of evidence*. These forbid 'hearsay': statements based on what someone else has said has happened. An example would be stating in court that an expert supported your case. This would be dismissed as hearsay evidence; you would need the expert to appear in court in person or to provide a written statement in a form acceptable to the court. Because the rules of evidence are complicated, appearing in court without a legal adviser can put you at a strong disadvantage compared with your opponent. In the small claims court, the rules do not apply. It is up to the District Judge to decide on what evidence is admissible and what is not, although most will frown on hearsay evidence.

Generally, you have six years to bring a civil claim to court, but there are a number of exceptions. Personal injury claims have to be brought within three years of the event. Claims for defective building work can sometimes be brought up to 15 years after the work and, under marine law, you have only two years to bring a claim concerning an injury that takes place at sea.

Claiming damages

When you claim money in a civil court as a result of a breach of contract or tort, you can claim for *general damages* or for *special damages* or for both. They are not as their names imply: special damages are much easier to obtain than general damages.

The category of special damages includes compensation for things that are easy to figure out, for example, money lost or the replacement value of goods that have been damaged. There is usually little dispute about special damages as they can be easily measured.

The category of general damages includes things that are more difficult to quantify – intangible things like pain, suffering, reduced quality of life, distress and inconvenience. Often these damages will be disputed and it will be up to the Judge to decide how much to award.

In all civil cases you have the right to claim general as

well as special damages, as long as they are reasonable and you are not trying to profit from your case. However, it is likely that general damages for distress and inconvenience will only be allowed by judges when enjoyment could be considered to be an essential part of the contract, for example, a claim for compensation for a poor package holiday.

THE SMALL CLAIMS COURT

Taking someone to court can be time-consuming and risky: if you lose, you may well end up paying not only your own costs, but those of your opponents as well, and these could be considerable. There is, however, one exception: the small claims procedure of the County court, known more commonly as the small claims court.

All cases brought before the County court where the amount in dispute is £1000 or less are referred automatically to the small claims procedure. This decision can be appealed against, but appeals are uncommon. It is possible for the small claims court to hear a case regarding more than £1000, but both sides have to agree to this. If the other side will not agree, you can ask the court to hear a case over the limit as long as you restrict your claim to £1000. You should put the exact amount in dispute on the form, along with a note underneath confirming that you are only claiming £1000.

The usual claims that people bring to the small claims court are debt, bad workmanship, accidents, goods not supplied, faulty goods and loans. Although originally aimed at consumers, most of the claims are, in fact, brought by businesses. The court can deal with claims for personal injuries, but, unless a claim is very straightforward, and few of such claims are, it is best to obtain legal advice first from a lawyer who is a member of the Association of Personal Injury Lawyers.

HOW SMALL CLAIMS ARE HEARD

What happens in a small claim is that the case is heard by a District Judge in private, in their chambers at the court building. Apart from the Judge, the only people present are the plaintiff (who brings the case), the defendant (the person or representative of a company whom the case is being brought against), their representatives and any witnesses. The whole process is called arbitration, although this should not be confused with the other forms of arbitration referred to throughout this book, which are *alternatives* to court action.

The idea behind the small claims procedure is that everything should be as unintimidating and as informal as possible. It is relatively easy to represent yourself and most individuals appearing at the small claims court do so. Most district judges interpret their role as being inquisitorial as well as adversarial which means that they will try to find out what has happened as well as pronounce on whether or not a case has been proved.

The great advantage of the small claims procedure, however, is that nobody can claim legal costs, so you can bring a claim without risking having to pay the other side's legal costs if you lose. All you will be liable for, normally, is the plaint fee (10 per cent of the claim up to a maximum of £60) and any out-of-pocket expenses of the other side. Even these expenses are set down. They can include loss of earnings (but only up to a maximum of £29), travelling costs and expert fees, up to a maximum of £112.50. Of course, all this means that you cannot claim any legal expenses of your own if you win and *your* expenses and loss of earnings are restricted to these limits as well.

Most small claims usually involve taking a couple of days off work to appear at the preliminary hearing and then the main hearing. They also require a considerable amount of paperwork and correspondence, even if the case runs smoothly.

Although you cannot claim legal costs, you are quite free to use a solicitor to help with your case and present it for you in court. Alternatively, you can ask someone else to speak for you in court, although you have to be present as well. The defendant may also use a solicitor and, indeed, all representatives from large companies and many smaller businesses will turn up at court with a solicitor to present their views. When this happens, district judges usually try to ensure that anyone in court without a solicitor is not at a disadvantage.

The District Judge decides a case on the basis of evidence, which can be spoken, written or expert. The Judge works out which side's evidence is most likely to be right, on the balance of probabilities. If it is impossible to decide, or if both the plaintiff and the defendant's stories are equally likely, the case will be dismissed. It is up to the person who brings a case to prove their version of events.

You can appeal against a district judge's decision, but only on the basis of law, not fact. Appeals are quite rare.

Small claims in Northern Ireland and Scotland
The small claims procedure in Northern Ireland is very similar to that of England and Wales. The upper limit is

£1000, although the plaint fees are cheaper. The major difference is that there is a strict 'no expenses' rule. The District Judge will decide if any expert report is needed and the report will be paid for by the court.

In Scotland, small claims is a procedure of the sheriff court. The maximum limit is £750, but there is also a similar summary cause procedure for amounts between £750 and £1500 in which limited legal costs can be claimed. In small claims, there is an expenses limit of £75. Unlike England, Wales and Northern Ireland, both the small claims and the summary cause procedures are heard in public by a Sheriff. Both procedures are adversarial, so, unlike an English District Judge, the Scottish Sheriff does not try and find out what happened, but simply hears the evidence and makes a decision.

TAKING SOMEONE TO THE SMALL CLAIMS COURT

▷ You can start a claim in any County court, although if the person you are claiming from contests your claim, it will be transferred to their local County court. Courts are open from 10am to 4pm, weekdays only.

▷ The form you need is the County court default summons form. It is pretty straightforward: the main thing to get right is the 'particulars of claim' section, which outlines your case. Court officials can advise on filling in the form, but they cannot advise you on the substance of your case. When you take out a summons, you are known as the plaintiff and the person you are sending the summons to is known as the defendant.

▷ You will need three copies of the form – one for you, one for the court and one for the defendant. You must have the defendant's name and address.

▷ The court will give you a receipt for your fee and a case reference number (do not lose this). It will then post the summons to the defendant, who will be asked either to pay the amount you are claiming into court or to dispute the claim by filling in the form of defence. If the defendant does not respond within 14 days of receiving the summons, you can ask for a judgment in default.

▷ If the defendant contests the claim, the District Judge may go straight to a full hearing, but it is more likely that they will call both of you to a preliminary hearing at a date that suits you both. At a preliminary hearing, the Judge will go through the evidence you and the defendant intend to present and see if there is any possibility that the dispute can be settled without a full hearing. If not, the Judge will agree the number of witnesses to be called, decide whether or not you need to inspect each other's documents and arrange the date and likely duration of the full hearing.

▷ The full hearing should take place within six months of your claim. On the day of the hearing, you should check the special arbitration list pinned up in the court and give your name to the usher. At the hearing itself, you present your case along with your evidence. You are then cross-examined by the defendant. The defendant then presents their case and any counter-claim they may have against you. They then sum up, and you do the same. The District Judge will then make a decision, but may ask for some time to think about it.

▷ If you win, the defendant will be asked to pay the award, which could be all or part of your claim, and any expenses the Judge approves. If you do not get your money straight away, write to the defendant after the case and give them seven days in which to pay.

▷ If the defendant does not pay, it will be up to you to enforce the debt. The usual way is to go back to the court and ask for an order so that the court bailiffs can seize property of the defendant up to the value of the award. This will cost about £50, although it can be added on to your claim.

For most of the 80 000 claims made every year in the small claims court, things go as smoothly as all this implies, but for some people they do not.

PROBLEMS WITH THE SMALL CLAIMS COURT

John Davies was having considerable difficulty selling his house in Cheshire, so he paid £500 to a London company to advertise and sell his house abroad. The company did not live up to its promises and Mr Davies demanded his money back. When they refused, he took out a summons against them in Crewe County court.

The company requested that the case be transferred to a London court but then the problems began. Mr Davies' papers were lost in the transfer and he was not told. He discovered eventually that his case had been decided by default: the company had not bothered to reply. Mr Davies instructed the court to send in the bailiffs and paid his £50, but it then became impossible to find out what was happening. He rang the court up every week, but the bailiffs never seemed to be around. He was told that the bailiffs *had* visited the company, and then that they *had not*. Then Mr Davies heard some more bad news: the company went into liquidation and so he was very unlikely to get any of his money back. The entire experience left Mr Davies feeling as annoyed with the civil courts as he was with the company that had let him down.

Mr Davies' experience is not exceptional. There is considerable variation in the efficiency and customer service of different County courts. It is not unusual for papers to be mislaid or lost. Some County courts are good at replying to phone calls, some are not. Some have made great efforts to improve their relationship with the public. Some have not.

It is true that there is a Courts Charter, part of the Government's Citizens' Charter. This Charter encourages the County court system to give better information and service to people who use it, and certainly the leaflets are better and some staff are more helpful. The problem is that there has been an ever-increasing amount of business going through the County court and the small claims procedure and the County courts just cannot cope.

There are other problems as well. District judges vary considerably in how judicial they are and in how friendly. Many enjoy small claims and the flexibility it allows them to adopt an inquisitorial role. Other district judges treat small claims like any other court dispute. Some can get impatient with a poorly presented case and often seem unsympathetic to any plaintiff who has not thought their case through.

Finally, it is fairly easy for any company, firm or individual to spin the whole process out. They can do this by trying to postpone every stage, rearranging all appoint-ments and hearings and then by trying to avoid paying any award made against them. In practice, there is little you can do with someone determined to avoid paying you, except realize at the start that you will probably not get your money.

TIPS ON USING
THE SMALL CLAIMS PROCEDURE

▷ If you are claiming against more than one person, sue them all and try and get judgment 'jointly and severally', which means that each person is responsible for all the debt. If you are claiming against a firm that is a partnership, sue the partnership, not just the individual involved.

▷ Before you take out a summons, send a final letter to the person who owes you money, saying you will be going to court if you do not hear from them within seven days.

▷ If there is no response, ask yourself how likely it is that the company or individual will pay up if you win. Is it the kind of firm that has any assets? Is it likely to go bust any moment? Consider, too, how far away the defendant is. Many defendants will ask for the case to be transferred to their local court and if you live in Scotland and the defendant lives in Cornwall, the effort and the expense involved in travelling to the court will hardly be worth it.

▷ Before you fill in the 'particulars of claim' part of the form, try to predict what the response from the defendant is likely to be, what defending arguments they will put forward and how you will answer them.

▷ Keep your claim short and specific.

▷ You must have evidence to back your claim, otherwise it will be dismissed. If a witness does not want to appear in court, you can get a summons ordering them to do so, but you must give them seven days' notice of this and you will have to pay all their expenses.

▷ Pay the small extra charge to have your summons delivered and signed for, rather than relying on the ordinary post.

▷ If you think it will help your case, ask the court for a 'site visit'. For example, if your claim is against a builder for faulty work, a site visit to your house may be far more convincing than any photographs or expert reports. It is up to the Judge to grant a site visit or not.

▷ Once you have sent your summons, it is quite possible to carry on negotiating with the defendant, but you should make sure that all letters are marked 'without prejudice' so that the contents of any deal you may offer cannot be brought up in court if it falls through. If a deal is agreed, always make sure that you have the money before writing to the court to cancel the summons.

▷ It will be up to you to contact the court to find out what is happening. The court will not ring you. Always quote your case number when you ring.

▷ If judgment is passed in your favour, there are a number of options other than the bailiffs if the defendant does not pay up. To find out which one is most likely to work, you can apply to the court for an oral examination of the defendant (who is now known as the debtor). At this examination, you can ask for details of their income and employer, bank account and other assets and any property they own. If the debtor fails to attend, they can be sent to prison for contempt of court. If the debtor is a company, you can request any officer of the company to attend. Depending on the information you receive, you can then use the bailiffs or ask for an attachment of earnings or use what are called garnishee proceedings, which means that an instruction is given to the debtor's bank to pay the debt from their account.

▷ If you feel that the County court has dealt with your claim badly or inefficiently, you should complain to the Chief Clerk of the court. If you get no response, contact the Lord Chancellor's Department. It is possible to claim compensation from a court if you have lost money, for example, because of court maladministration or because of the illness or death of a judge. Write to the Chief Clerk of the court which dealt with your case and ask for an *ex-gratia* payment to cover your losses. Your claim will be investigated. If your claim is over £400, it will be referred to the Courts Administrator for your region.

DEFENDING A SMALL CLAIMS SUMMONS

▷ If you receive a summons, it is important to respond within 14 days. Otherwise the judgment may well be entered against you.

▷ It is possible to set a judgment aside if you can show that you never received the summons or you did not have enough time to do anything about it. To do this you have to appeal directly to the District Judge.

▷ When you receive a summons, consider if you want to make any counterclaim against the plaintiff. This does not have to have anything to do with the plaintiff's claim, although obviously you will have to provide evidence to back your counterclaim up.

▷ Although it is up to the plaintiff to prove their case, it is best to act as if you have to prove your case as well. Make sure you find out at the preliminary hearing all the witnesses and experts the plaintiff is going to use, and ask for copies of any documents they intend to present at the final hearing. Consider if you need to commission an expert report of your own.

THE FUTURE OF THE SMALL CLAIMS COURT

As this book goes to press, the Lord Chancellor's Department has indicated that the maximum limit for the small claims court in England and Wales should be increased, probably to £2500. The Government is also proposing that all personal injury claims that are unliquidated, that is, the amount of damages claimed is left open for the judge to decide, should start in the small claims court. At present, if a claim is unliquidated, it goes straight to the County court, unless the plaintiff states that the amount claimed is likely to be less than £1000.

USING THE COUNTY COURT

If your claim is for an amount over £1000 and less than £25 000, you will almost certainly have to use the County court (it is possible to use the small claims procedure for claims over £1000 and less then £5000, but only if the defendant agrees).

The County court is a 'proper' court, although the actual procedure is not that different to that followed for a small claim. You take out a summons, there is a preliminary and then a full hearing and so on. The main differences are that cases are heard in public and that they are usually presented by lawyers, although it is quite possible to present your case yourself.

County court cases are heard by Circuit Judges and may be reported in the local press, although few are. If you lose, you will almost certainly have to pay some or all of the other party's legal costs, as well as your own legal costs and all other expenses, although you can agree with the other side before you start to pay your own legal costs, win or lose. Even with this waiver, your costs could still be high, especially if you are represented in court.

So, it is important before you take County court action to make sure that you have:

▷ good legal advice that confirms you have a very good case
▷ some kind of evidence that any person you take to court has the money or professional indemnity insurance to pay up and that they are unlikely to disappear or go bankrupt
▷ similar evidence that any company you take to court is unlikely to go into liquidation or cease trading.

In all but the most straightforward of cases, it is best to get a solicitor to represent you, and it is essential if you have any claim for damages due to negligence.

It is probably not a good idea to take a cowboy trader to

the County court, unless you are quite sure they have the assets to pay up if you win. However, one kind of case that may well be worth bringing is if you have a personal injury claim against an institution, established firm or professional. Solicitors who specialize in personal injury cases estimate that there are thousands, perhaps tens of thousands, of people who suffer as a result of an accident caused by someone else's negligence, but only a small number of them ever take legal action for damages to cover pain, suffering and time off work. If you have a good personal injury case, backed up with evidence, it is well worth considering a claim. Most of these claims are settled by insurance companies out of court, although often not until they realize that the claim is serious. You can show you are serious by using a solicitor who is a member of the Association of Personal Injury Lawyers and taking out a summons.

All civil cases now have to start in the County court, but claims for more than £25 000 or cases where the legal issues are extremely complicated are transferred to the High Court. This is no place to be without good legal advice as the costs if you lose will be very high.

GETTING LEGAL HELP CHEAPER

For any kind of complicated case, legal help is essential. Unfortunately, it does not come cheap. The average cost of a solicitor is around £80 per hour and some are a lot more. Barristers can be more costly still. A court case involving two days in a County court could well cost £5000 in legal expenses if you lose, sometimes more. A medical negligence case that ends up in the High Court could well cost more than £20 000 in legal expenses if you lose. Most people do not have this kind of money to risk in this way, even if they can find a solicitor who will not require a substantial down payment. This is the main reason the British civil justice system is so unfair.

It is possible, however, to obtain legal help more cheaply than these costs imply, although to qualify for it has become more difficult in the last few years.

LEGAL AID

Legal aid for *civil* cases is available and free to people whose income is at income support levels. If your income is above this, you may qualify for legal aid, but you will be expected to make a contribution to your costs. These contributions can be quite high: usually around a third of your disposable income. About half the population do not qualify for legal aid at all.

You have to go through quite a complicated process to obtain legal aid. Here is what to do.

▷ Find a solicitor whose practice handles legal aid cases. You can find this out by looking through the *Solicitors Regional Directory,* a copy of which is available at your local reference library.

▷ The solicitor should be able to tell you if your case is of the kind that may be presented using legal aid (some claims, like those for libel, are barred). If it is, the solicitor will send your application to a legal aid area office.

▷ This office will first check with the Department of Social Security legal aid assessment centre in Preston to see if you qualify for legal aid. If you do, the office will then decide whether or not your case stands a *reasonable* chance of success. If so, legal aid will be awarded. All your legal costs will then be paid for, apart from any contribution assessed to come from you. If you win your case, however, you will have to pay back all your legal costs if the court does not cover them.

Legal aid is much more readily available for *criminal* cases (although it is not if you decide to prosecute somebody yourself). Legal help is free and not means tested if you are held by the police for questioning or appear in court with no representation. You will have to accept, however, the Duty Solicitor and you will not be able to claim the costs of your own solicitor.

THE GREEN FORM SCHEME

This scheme is part of legal aid. If your disposable income is less than £61 per week, you can qualify for two hours free legal advice (three hours in matrimonial cases and the time can be increased on application from a solicitor). It only applies to solicitors who are part of the scheme, but many are. In Scotland, the scheme is called a pink form scheme – presumably because the form is pink.

CHEAP LEGAL ADVICE

The Law Society's fixed fee scheme – where participating solicitors offered an initial interview for £5 – has now been abolished. In its place, there are a number of 'local referral schemes', where solicitors will offer free or cheap initial advice to people referred from a Citizens Advice Bureau.

It is possible to discover the solicitors who offer this service by looking through the *Solicitors Regional Directory* at your local reference library. In the *Directory*, there will be notes next to each solicitor listed there, indicating what kinds of services they offer, including free or low-cost initial interviews. Many solicitors, in fact, offer these, if you just ask first. Some solicitors have surgeries at particular times, usually Saturday morning, when they offer drop-in low-cost interviews. However, all of these initiatives just cover the first interview, where a solicitor diagnoses a problem and outlines various options; if you then employ the solicitor to take up your case, they will charge their usual rate.

ACCIDENT LINE

This is the new name for ALAS (Accident Legal Advice Service). It is run by the Law Society, and they will give you the name of a specialist accident solicitor in your area who is part of the scheme. The service entitles you to a free initial 30-minute interview if you have been injured in an accident. Research indicates that 85 per cent of people who have a serious injury (serious enough to take two weeks off work) do not claim compensation, so it is certainly worth using Accident Line if you have been injured. You may well be surprised at the strength of your claim, even if you were partly responsible for the accident.

OTHER CHEAP DEALS

Two other schemes are worth knowing about, if you qualify for them. The Lawyers for Your Business scheme in England and Wales and its equivalent in Scotland offers a cheap diagnostic service for small businesses. Union Law offers a number of fixed-cost legal services, including conveyancing and wills, to members of affiliated unions. The Law Society can provide details of these.

'NO WIN, NO FEE'

There is nothing stopping any solicitor taking on your case for nothing, but there used to be restrictions on solicitors taking on cases on a speculative or contingency basis, that is, they would only get paid if they won. This is a common practice in the United States and many other countries. In Scotland, the practice has been allowed for a number of years, but, as this book goes to press, it is in the process of being introduced in the rest of the United Kingdom. Here it will be called a 'conditonal fees' arrangement.

Solicitors who take on a case on a no win, no fee basis are not allowed, as they are in the United States, to charge a percentage of the final award if they win the case. All they can charge is their normal fee plus a success fee, which cannot be more than the normal fee. The normal lawyer's fee can be claimed back from the other side, but the success fee will have to be paid for out of the award.

If a solicitor accepts your case on a no win, no fee basis, you will not have to pay their costs if you lose, but you will still have to pay the other side's legal costs. In a typical personal injury claim in a County court, these could amount to several thousand pounds. Because of this the Law Society has launched a new insurance scheme, available from participating solicitors, where you can insure against paying the other side's legal costs, if you lose, for the payment of a single premium. It is only available when a solicitor takes your case on a conditional fees basis. The premium will be around £100.

FREE REPRESENTATION UNIT

This is a scheme that was set up by the Bar Society, the organization that regulates barristers. It provides help from barristers (who are often trainees, but they can be more senior) for people at *tribunals,* but not at court. If they take on your case, all the legal help and the representation are free to anybody, irrespective of income. Unfortunately, because of funding problems, it is only available for tribunals within one or two hours' train journey from London as tribunals start at 9.30 in the morning and the Unit's barristers cannot afford to stay overnight. There are one or two similar schemes run by university law departments around the country.

LAW CENTRES

There are over 55 law centres in the country, mostly in the poorer parts of large cities. They offer free legal advice, often provided not by solicitors but by trained workers and volunteers, although all law centres must have a solicitor on duty. Most law centres are geared to tribunal work and criminal law rather than civil disputes. Their expertise is in areas like housing, social security, welfare rights and immigration, rather than consumer disputes.

LEGAL EXPENSES INSURANCE

Legal expenses insurance is still uncommon in Britain although not in other countries. There are a number of policies on the market and most cover legal advice and representation up to a set limit, usually £10 000 cover for about £200 a year. There is often an annual limit for claims as well.

As so few people in Britain have it, the insurance is quite expensive. Some employers have taken it out for their employees and some household insurance, car insurance and mortgage policies have legal expenses insurance built in, or available at a small extra cost. If this option is open to you, take it up.

Another kind of legal insurance is offered by The Consumers Association. *Which? Personal Service* costs about £20 per year and offers legal advice, help and letter writing for many of the typical consumer problems featured in this book. The catch is that it is only available to people who subscribe to *Which?* (currently about £50 per year for 12 issues), and it does not cover any representation in court.

OTHER LEGAL HELP

Because legal advice and representation is so expensive, some pressure groups will offer free legal advice in their area of interest. They may even take up your case if it seems to be one of national importance. Examples are the Commission for Racial Equality (for problems with race discrimination), the Equal Opportunities Commission (for sexual discrimination) and MIND (for mental health problems).

If they are unable to take up your case, campaigning groups should be able to put you in touch with specialist solicitors and, occasionally, these solicitors will defer payment, reduce their fees or work for nothing if they have particular sympathy with your case and you have no money. The Environmental Law Group, for example, advises residents' groups for free on the environmental implications of planning disputes.

OTHER KINDS OF HELP

There are a number of organizations and individuals who can help with everyday consumer problems as well as provide some legal advice. It is worth knowing about them all.

CITIZENS ADVICE BUREAUX

There should be a Citizens Advice Bureau in every town and city, but as local Bureaux depend entirely on local councils for funding, there are some gaps. Advice is free and so, for most Bureaux, it is advisable to ring beforehand and book an appointment. The advice is provided mainly by trained volunteers, although there is professional back-up and access to specialist advice, including solicitors.

The commonest problems dealt with by advisers are straightforward consumer complaints, such as those regarding faulty goods, poor service and problems with bills. Some Bureau workers may ring a trader up on your behalf, although they have no powers of enforcement and can only persuade people to act. In practice, a Bureau worker is unlikely to be able to do more than you can do by yourself if you have read this book.

Where a Bureau can be extremely useful is for problems with debt, repossession, eviction and social security, particularly if the Bureau has built up expertise in these areas, as many have. They should know of any specialist debt or money counsellors or clinics and they should be familiar with the methods of interceding with the courts and with debt collection agencies.

TRADING STANDARDS OFFICERS

All county councils or their equivalents in Great Britain must employ trading standards officers (in Northern Ireland, they are part of the Department of Economic Development). The council department in which they work is not always called a trading standards department – it may be known as a consumer protection or a consumer services department – but whatever their name, a trading standards officer's main duty is to enforce the criminal consumer law. Thus, they will look into complaints about misleading descriptions or prices, unsafe goods, inaccurate weights and measures and certain problems with credit. Trading standards departments vary in the weight they give to prosecuting traders. Most authorities are more likely to warn or formally caution a trader for a first offence, although some will prosecute. Several thousand firms are prosecuted every year for consumer offences, although most only receive a fine and this is unlikely to deter the serious rogue.

Trading standards officers can also report a trader to the Office of Fair Trading if they suspect unfair trading, but the powers the Office of Fair Trading has under the Fair Trading Act 1984 are limited. Certainly, neither the Office nor the Companies Investigation Department of the Department of Trade and Industry seem able to stop any but the most blatant con man from continuing to trade.

If you have a complaint that does not involve someone breaking a criminal consumer law, the advice you will receive from trading standards officers may well be limited. Most trading standards departments will give advice and some will contact the trader, but, after that, it will be up to you to pursue your claim through the civil courts.

CONSUMER ORGANIZATIONS

There are a number of consumer organizations in Britain, but, with the exception of *Which? Personal Service* run by the Consumers Association and mentioned earlier, none can provide individual help. The Office of Fair Trading keeps an eye on general trading practices; the National Consumer Council and its sister organizations in Wales, Scotland and Northern Ireland looks into any area in which consumers have a legitimate interest and pays particular attention to the needs of less well-off consumers. Both the Office and the Council are funded by the State.

The Consumers Association is funded by its members through their subscriptions to the Association's monthly magazine *Which?*. The magazine is an invaluable source of good legal advice.

THE LOCAL PRESS

The local press are unlikely to be able to provide you with consumer advice, but what they can do is to take up a good consumer story and ask the trader for their response. If your complaint is justified, it is unlikely that many traders will risk the bad publicity by refusing to settle with you. The price, however, will be your photo in the papers and your story written up with a certain gusto by an enthusiastic reporter.

REGULATORS AND OMBUDSMEN

All the privatized industries have an official regulator who usually oversees consumer complaints. The regulator has staff who can often provide informal advice or point you to someone who can help.

Ombudsmen are rather different. The first British ombudsmen (a term which originated in Sweden in the early nineteenth century) were set up in 1967 to look into complaints about the various Government departments and the health services. These ombudsmen were, and are, funded by the State. There are now ombudsmen for legal services, banks, building societies, insurance, pensions, corporate estate agents, housing association tenants and pensions. Most of them are funded by the appropriate industry, although the ombudsman's independence is guaranteed.

Ombudsmen have often ranged wider than any court would. This is because they are not bound by the rules of evidence, so they can, and do, consider hearsay, which is the reported conversations of other people. They can also consider proper professional practice and accepted business conduct, considerations that are taken note of in a civil court, but are likely to be considered of less importance as a judge would not have the appropriate specialist knowledge.

With all these advantages, then, it is surprising that the latest research into how consumers feel about using two ombudsmen – the insurance ombudsman and the building societies ombudsman – has been more negative than positive. Certainly, the small claims court came out better.

There are plans for ombudsmen for national savings, the press, opticians and the Inland Revenue.

MEDIATION

If you have a large claim and neither you nor the other side want to risk going to court, you could consider hiring the services of a mediator. A mediator will spend time with both of you and then try and work out an agreed compromise. So, for example, if you are in dispute with your builder for £20 000, a mediator might be able to come up with a figure on which both you and the builder could agree. A day's mediation from an organization like the Centre for Dispute Resolution would cost about £400 – considerably cheaper than a day in court.

ARBITRATION

Ombudsmen are now the fashionable alternative to court action, but, 10 years ago, arbitration was seen as the future for the resolution of consumer complaints. It still exists and on some occasions, it is worth using.

Arbitration is offered by some trade organizations, some professional bodies and one or two public services, like the Post Office. It costs about the same as the small claims court, but, unlike the small claims procedure, it is based only on documents. An arbitration service is only really worth considering if it has the Office of Fair Trading's backing.

It is extremely easy to use arbitration. You simply send off your claim to the arbitrator along with your evidence. The arbitrator then sends copies to the trader. The trader replies and you then respond to the reply. All this happens by post. The arbitrator can call for independent evidence as well or go on a site visit, if necessary, before making a decision. The decision will be sent to you by post, along with the arbitrator's reasons. It is legally binding, which means that you cannot go to court if you disagree with it. However, it also means that you can use the enforcement powers of the court if an award is made in your favour.

Court or arbitration?

▷ In court, you have the chance to present your case in person and to cross-examine the trader. If you do not want to do this or you do not want to take a couple of days off work, the 'documents only' approach of arbitration is more attractive.

▷ Arbitration is likely to be cheaper than court since many of the schemes are subsidized, but note that few schemes allow you to claim expenses.

▷ You can take anyone to court, but you can only take someone to arbitration if they are a member of the professional or trade organization that administers the scheme, and then only if they agree.

▷ Arbitration is not restricted to the small claims court limit so, for a claim over this limit, it is a much less risky option than going to the County court.

The problem with arbitration schemes is that most consumers do not seem to trust them or even use them. The arbitration scheme for funeral directors, for example, has never been used and the scheme for photographic equipment only once. In a National Consumers Council survey, 60 per cent thought that the arbitration scheme offered by British Telecom was unfair, and 45 per cent of people in the same survey thought the ABTA arbitration scheme was unfair. The Glass and Glazing scheme did much better – only one in three who used it thought the scheme was unfair. In surveys, the small claims court does much better.

APPENDIX 1:
SOME THINGS
THAT MIGHT HELP

To his friends, Ronald Sydney Ayleward is a failed businessman. To his customers, he is a crook. For over 20 years, Mr Ayleward has exploited loopholes in British company law that have allowed him to continue in business after several spectacular failures. One of his first ventures was Direct Potato Supplies Ltd of Stockport. This business folded owing thousands of pounds and soon afterwards Mr Ayleward was made bankrupt for eight years. Bankrupts cannot be involved in the formation, promotion or management of a company, but this did not stop him becoming a director of a couple of companies, including the Automatic Window Cleaning Company of Torquay. This business went bust as well owing one person, a retired major, £27 000. Mr Ayleward was undeterred. He became a sales director of Sahara Products of Manchester, a central heating firm that was eventually prosecuted for the ludicrous claims made by its sales people. Mr Ayleward, the person who trained the salespeople, escaped prosecution. After Sahara Products went bust, Mr Ayleward moved on to NHC Wallcare Ltd of Knutsford, Cheshire. This company lasted three years before it, too, folded with debts of £130 000.

The story went on. Five more companies followed, including Sun Harvester (Cheshire) Ltd, which specialized in solar heating. All the Ayleward trademarks were there: national advertising, overenthusiastic claims, inferior materials and many, many complaints. The other trademark soon followed: Sun Harvester went bust in 1983, owing over £300 000.

Mr Ayleward moved on. He set up Video Jukeboxes of Leicester, which collapsed owing £15 000; Danecraft Ltd and Wessex Roof Ltd – both went bust owing over £500 000; Nationwide Indoor Carting Ltd, which folded with debts of over £100 000; State Trend Ltd of Knutsford, which owed £120 000; and ACC Standard Purpose Loans Ltd of Stockport, which owed £170 000. Finally, there was California Driveways. This firm offered the 'driveway of your dreams'. It, too, collapsed owing over £100 000.

In 20 years, Mr Ayleward has ripped off hundreds of customers for more than £3 million, yet he rarely lost any of his own money. How did he get away with it?

Over the years, he has been bankrupted twice, he has had his consumer credit licence revoked, he has given assurances about his behaviour to the Office of Fair Trading and he has been twice investigated by the Department of Trade. He has also been exposed on *Watchdog* not once but several times. In November 1992, a Manchester court banned him from being involved in the running of a business for 12 years. Whether this deters him is open to doubt. How was he able to carry on trading so unfairly for so long? (By the way, all the businesses mentioned above have long since ceased trading. They have no connection with companies of similar-sounding names.)

It is too easy to round up the usual suspects: British company law, which allows people to set up and dissolve a limited company with ease; the Insolvency and Bankruptcy service, which seems unable to keep an accurate record of banned individuals; the Department of

Trade's Companies Investigation Division, which is understaffed and badly resourced; the lack of time and resources given to trading standards officers and police to investigate small-time con men and fraudsters. All these things are true, but they are not the real reason someone like Mr Ayleward flourishes in business for so long.

The real reason is quite simple. People like him are determined con men who will get around every obstacle put in their way. There is nothing anybody can really do to stop their behaviour, short of changing the entire basis of trust and credit that shopping and trading these days relies upon.

People like Mr Ayleward spot the latest trend and then move in. They become experts on company law and on sales techniques. They know that the penalties of breaking criminal consumer law are small, the penalty of not meeting promises and commitments to their customers is a collection of unenforceable County court judgments. If the penalties are changed, they will find their way around these, too.

Fortunately, this kind of person, whose skills to duck and dive are so misdirected, are quite rare. For every Mr Ayleward, there are hundreds of other less successful con men. For every dodgy business that succeeds repeatedly in making a dishonest shilling, there are thousands of other companies that will short-change people if only they have the opportunity. These opportunities we can deny them, these con men we can do something about.

Good consumer information and advice, the kind that this book has aimed to provide, is the best deterrent. Unscrupulous trading practices often depend, if not on the gullibility of the customer, then on the lack of pointers about what else is available and at what cost. The best service to British consumers is not to introduce yet more consumer laws (Britain has one of the best systems of consumer law in the world), but to make more people aware of the rights they have. It has been over 14 years since the Sale of Goods Act 1979, yet still every week people ring the *Watchdog* hotline with only a very dim awareness of the rights that this Act gives them when they are out shopping, and this is merely one example.

However, even the most aware consumers get taken for a ride, even the most professional consumer lawyer or consumer journalist finds occasionally that they have been ripped off. There are always new scams and old loopholes that are only discovered after the event. So, here are some changes that the Government and industry could make that would make some difference to consumer life.

CONTROLS ON COMPANY DIRECTORS SHOULD BE TIGHTENED

As the examples of con men and sharp practice described in this book show, there does need to be some tightening up on the kind of people who are allowed to become directors of a limited company. Too many people are being allowed to carry on trading when a receiver has concluded that they are unfit to run a company. The Insolvency Service must be overhauled and better resourced and there should also be a procedure that enables a receiver to apply directly to a court or a tribunal to have someone banned from being a director.

REFORM OF THE SALE
OF GOODS ACT 1979

This has often been promised by the Government. The main problem is that the time limit given to people for accepting an item they buy and thus losing their right to a refund has been ruled in law to be quite short, yet it often takes time for an intrinsic fault to emerge. One solution would be to give people a reasonable time to reject an item not from when they bought it, but from when the fault becomes clear.

Another part of the law which needs to be abolished is that regarding market overt – an outdated concept that is a thieves charter (see pages 68 to 69).

Finally, two useful concepts could be incorporated into a new Sale of Goods Act: the 'lemon' (a consumer product that develops a range of small faults which cannot be fixed) and 'guarantee' (the conditions that manufacturers who offer a guarantee should meet).

Stop Press

Two new private members bills, the Sale and Supply of Goods Bill, sponsored by David Clelland MP, and the Sale of Goods (Amendment) Bill, sponsored by Lord Renton, go some way towards helping matters. Lord Renton's Bill aims to abolish market overt; Mr Clelland's bill to give a much more precise definition of 'merchantable quality'. Both Bills have full Government support but, as this book is printed, they still have not got over all the obstacles in getting a private members bill on the statute book.

REGULATION
OF THE BUILDING TRADE

In Germany, all tradesmen working in building – builders, plumbers, electricians and so on – must have a permit to work. To get a permit, they must have completed a course and passed an examination – at master level if they want to employ others. This is a very useful safeguard that if introduced into Britain could cut down the problems consumers have with dodgy builders.

CUSTOMER SERVICES OFFICERS SHOULD
HAVE MORE CLOUT

Most major companies now have specific employees who deal with complaints. Most of these do a good job, yet they have little, if any, influence on major company decisions. There is still little recognition among British companies of the importance of analyzing and understanding customer complaints.

THE SMALL CLAIMS LIMIT
SHOULD BE INCREASED

Despite its drawbacks, the small claims procedure of the County court continues to provide the most accessible form of justice in this country. The limit has gone up in England and Wales in the last few years to £1000, with the promise of a possible increase to £2500, but the limit could well be increased throughout the United Kingdom to £5000, with the safeguards of an appeal to the District Judge if one party would be at a serious disadvantage, and the proviso that the legal costs and the cost of expert reports could be allowed in cases of personal injury.

A CONTINGENCY LEGAL AID FUND

With the demise of legal aid, at least for the majority of the population, some kind of legal help is needed for complicated civil disputes where an individual is up against an organization. At the moment, many claims over £5000 that stand a good chance of success never end up in court because the cost of taking up the case is prohibitive. This is unfair. A solution that would cost very little is proposed by the organization Justice: a 'contingency legal aid fund'.

This fund would be set up with a one-off grant from the Government and it would offer risk-free litigation for people who could not afford legal costs if they lost their case. It would work like this. If a case was won, all the legal costs plus a small donation from the award would be made into the fund. If a case was lost, all the legal expenses would be taken out of the fund. As long as the criteria for accepting a case by the fund was that it stood a 70 to 80 per cent chance of succeeding, more cases would be won than lost and so the fund would never dry up. Schemes like these are running successfully in Australia and Hong Kong.

CLASS ACTIONS

A class action is when a number of people with similar claims against one company or organization put their claims and resources together and take them to court. The judge then hears all the cases at once. The advantage of a class action is that it redresses an imbalance in power, that which exists between an individual who cannot afford to risk much money, and a large company which takes risks with this kind of money every day. However, at present, under British law, class actions are not allowed. If they were, it would be another step towards a civil justice system that is really justice for all and not just for the rich.

CONTRACTS WRITTEN IN PLAIN ENGLISH

There is a proposed EC directive that may eventually be incorporated into British law that states that all contracts must be written in intelligible language. It is a useful idea, but it does not go far enough. There should be a legal requirement that all contracts be written in plain English. This would mean that anybody signing a contract would be able to understand immediately what all the clauses in the contract meant. If a contract then continued to use archaic or obscure language, it could be ruled by a court to be invalid.

APPENDIX 2:
THE ONES THAT GOT AWAY

The scene: a small, windswept town in West Wales. The time: a Friday morning. Enter stage right: a middle-aged man who emerges from one of the supermarkets in the middle of town loaded down with shopping. Enter stage left: a well-dressed young woman carrying a microphone steadfastly in front of her. The woman has an air of moral certitude, along with a slight nervousness that she attempts to control by continually pushing her hair back from her face. Action: the woman confronts the man in the centre of the street to the amusement of several passers-by. The following dialogue takes place:

> John Evans, I've come to record an interview with you now about all the people you have let down. Why have you not paid them the money you owe?

The middle-aged man keeps walking with a bemused air about him. The woman reporter sets off in pursuit.

> Mr Evans, why won't you answer our questions … ?
> I'm not John Evans.
> Yes you are.
> No I'm not.
> Prove it. Prove it. Prove you are not John Evans.
> Well I, I can't. But I'm not. My name's Williams.
> Williams?
> Yes, Williams. David Williams.

At this point, a worried look passes across the reporter's

face which she attempts, not entirely successfully, to control. She turns to her researcher, who is looking puzzled, and whispers heatedly.

> I thought you said it was Evans?
> Well, I was told it was him.

Researcher grabs one of the onlookers.

> Is this John Evans?
> No. That's David Williams. I've known him all my life
> David Williams? So where's John Evans?
> I don't know. Who's John Evans?
> John Evans. He's er been running this company er …
> that's … er … Are you sure that's not John Evans?
> Yes. Are you sure you have the right place?

It turned out they had not. They had the right street, but the wrong town – and the real John Evans got away unscathed. Mr Williams graciously accepted apologies from all concerned.

Although the names and one or two details have been changed (to avoid embarrassment), this is a true story of investigative journalists trying to track down an elusive quarry. The team was not, as it turned out, from *Watchdog,* but they could well have been.

Mistaken identity is just one of the perils of this kind of work, and it is not just making mistakes about people that is a problem. Identifying the wrong car or the wrong home or the wrong office can prove equally embarrassing, and costly.

There are other perils as well. When a complaint about an individual or company is received, the first thing any investigative journalist does is to see whether or not the complaint is an isolated one or is part of a systematic pattern. This means talking to a variety of other people who may have similar information or have received similar complaints – trading standards officers, consumer organizations and watchdogs, the police, trade associations and professional bodies.

The journalist may then check up on the individual's or company's trading record, looking at the latest annual accounts, any adverse County court judgments, any bankruptcy proceedings and so on. While none of this is exactly secret, it is done with discretion and usually without informing the individual or company concerned, although they may well find out that enquiries are being made. The reason for this is partly because the complaints may have no basis in truth or be trivial or malicious, and partly because the person who is being investigated may try to threaten complainants or just disappear.

If there does seem to be something seriously wrong, the individual or individuals responsible will eventually be contacted and given the chance to respond. If they do not respond, the journalists may try to 'doorstep' the person in charge. This means that they will turn up without permission or notice at a person's home or work and try and do an interview there and then. Despite the term, most 'doorsteps' do not actually take place on the doorstep, but in the street or in another public place. Some doorsteps work well, but some, inevitably, go wrong:

▷ *The conditions were against them:* It was just after six in the morning and inside the back of a blacked-out van sat five people. It was cold, so cold, in fact, that professional reserve was soon abandoned as everybody tried to keep warm. The researcher kept trying to cheer the team up by reassuring them all that the man they were going to 'doorstep' always left home at 8am. This morning, though, was the exception. Two and a half hours later, at 10.30, their quarry eventually came out of his house to walk the short distance to his car, a Jaguar. Out of the van jumped the team, the reporter in the lead, followed closely by the cameraman and sound recordist. Unfortunately, it had been so cold waiting in the van that the reporter's feet had gone to sleep and so he and the rest of the team did not so much run as waddle. By the time they managed to reach the car, the man had shut the door and the Jaguar sped off into the distance.

▷ *The villain hits back:* These days, most villains know better than to try and intimidate a television crew, especially when the camera is running. They reach for a lawyer rather than a lead bar, or at least most of them do. One exception was road haulier Danny Ryan.

Through a network of companies, Mr Ryan managed to ignore repeated prosecutions and fines for running dangerous, untaxed and unlicensed lorries up and down the motorways of Britain. His behaviour exemplified the ease with which cowboy operators could break traffic laws and get away with it. So, *Watchdog* paid him a visit. When Mr Ryan realized what was happening, he threw milk bottles and a cup of tea at the reporter and the cameraman, hitting the cameraman on the head. As the cameraman tried to wipe milk off the camera lens, Mr Ryan then grabbed hold of him and started thumping him and stamping on his toes.

He then tried to lock the team in a Portacabin and

rang some friends of his to come round and give him a hand. When the team got out of the cabin, two lorries were blocking the way out and another lorry tried to ram the *Watchdog* car. The team eventually managed to escape with the film that revealed to viewers what a nasty piece of work Mr Ryan was.

▷ *The quarry uses the law:* It was the consultant who blew the whistle. He had been called in by the company to give their holiday camp the necessary safety certificate, and what he saw disturbed him. He wrote a 30-page report for the company, claiming that it was a disaster waiting to happen. However, the company seemed to want to do nothing about it, so, eight months later, the consultant got in touch with *Watchdog*. The programme began the process of checking the facts by contacting people who worked at the camp. However, the company found out and applied, successfully, for an injunction banning employees and ex-employees from talking to the programme on the basis of breach of confidence. Many of the people *Watchdog* had talked to were gagged, apart from one from Derbyshire who had been forgotten about. Very early the next morning, the team sped up to Derbyshire to record an interview, only to discover on arrival a Porsche parked outside the house. The company's Managing Director had made it before them, with a new injunction naming the one person previously left out.

▷ *The perils of doorstepping abroad:* It was not the crew's fault, or at least not really. They were Belgian and had never done a doorstep before, so they could hardly be blamed for turning up in a large van with 'van hire' in Flemish plastered all over the sides. Nor could they be expected to know that it is a good idea to black out the sides of a van when attempting a doorstep. Most interviews done in this fashion, like any kind of surveillance, consist of long hours of sitting around. In a street in suburban Antwerp, six people sitting in a van with television equipment for several hours is not the most inconspicuous of sights. However, all this the team could cope with, just about. It was the door that defeated them. When the con man emerged from his house, the director shouted 'go' and the reporter tried to get out of the back of the van. She found that it would not open. She pushed and pushed, but it stayed shut.

These were just four occasions when the hazards of doorstepping worked against even the best-prepared team. Most of the time, however, doorstepping works. As a weapon of last resort, as a means of putting people who have consistently tried to evade their responsibilities to their customers on the spot, it is an extremely useful addition to a consumer journalist's armoury, even when the quarry gets away.

Although used comparatively rarely, the doorstep interview is seen, and rightly so, as the image that defines consumer journalism. It is the action which seems to sum up attempts by consumer journalists to get an answer to complaints, the icon which regular viewers and listeners to programmes like *Watchdog*, *The Cook Report*, and *Face the Facts* recognize and expect. But in the last couple of years, another technique has increasingly taken the place of the doorstep interview to become the new image of consumer broadcasting. It is secret filming.

This is partly due to developments in the technology of

film-making. Miniature camera lenses are now available that fit not just into a bag but into a buttonhole or a shirt sleeve. The picture quality is often so impressive that viewers cannot distinguish these shots from film shot openly with a conventional large camera and tripod. But if the technology makes secret filming easy and relatively straightforward, it does not explain why it has become so fashionable.

The reason for this is that the focus of consumer and investigative journalism has shifted from the dubious activities of unrespectable con men to the inequitable practices of respectable businesses. When a target is a business and not an individual, when there is no particular person to blame but rather a set of unfair rules and procedures to expose, it makes sense to show viewers how these rules operate. The most powerful way to show this kind of routine unfairness is to film it.

So at *Watchdog*, we have secretly recorded double-glazing salesmen not providing their customers with warnings about the problems of breaking their glass if there is a fire. We have taped salespeople being taught how to give the impression they are electricians. And we have secretly filmed *Watchdog* viewers finding out just how many reputable shops will give them a discount if they just ask for one.

Most secret recordings are done discreetly and with the people being filmed not realizing what is going on. But sometimes things can go wrong.

There had been many complaints about the techniques used by a particular branch of alternative medicine but little hard evidence. So two members of the *Watchdog* team enrolled in an intensive weekend course and one of them carried a small bag with a miniature camera hidden in it. It looked completely inconspicuous, unless somebody really was suspicious and then the lens could just be seen. Unfortunately that was the case. There had been a tip-off that *Watchdog* were investigating and so the people running the course were scrutinizing everybody on that weekend. In a session on the Saturday evening, the leader told the group that they were being investigated, and then pointed at the two Watchdog members of staff. There was nothing they could do apart from confess, rather sheepishly, that yes, they had been recording. It was embarrassing for everyone concerned. The cameraman handed over one of the tapes which had virtually nothing of importance recorded on it but kept the more incriminating evidence to himself. The team made their excuses and left, and the story went out.

In fact, there was no need to hand over any tape. Secret recording breaks no criminal law even if it is done on private property, at least not yet. The Government's proposed privacy bill will make it extremely difficult to do this kind of recording in the future, and it will also give people the right to sue for damages in the civil courts if their privacy has been violated. This right will almost certainly be used, in practice, not by ordinary people whose privacy has been violated but by individuals and companies who do not want their antisocial activities to be examined. The effect will be to curtail significantly secret recording of the kind that has been developed by *Watchdog* and other popular investigative programmes in the last few years, and that has resulted in all kinds of shady and disreputable practices coming to light.

But perhaps by then it will be time to move on and

develop a new technique to replace secret recording and doorstepping, a new technique that will sum up consumer journalism in the mid-1990s.

APPENDIX 3:
DON'T RING US UNLESS . . .

Every week, *Watchdog* receives some 1000 telephone calls and letters. They all tell of consumer wrongs, of laws and regulations that do not work, of traders who behave badly or wrongly. Sometimes a letter suggests not one target but two or three.

It is impossible, of course, for the programme to take up all, or even most, of these calls. Every programme reports on five or six items, most of which originate from a viewer's experience, and all the other letters that do not end up as a report on air are read, thought about and then filed away. This is all the programme can do. There is not enough money, time or resources to answer every letter or call, let alone provide advice or information about each problem. These are just some of the reasons for our having put together this book.

We are more than happy for anybody to call us about their consumer problems, and, although we feel for everyone who has suffered in some way at the hands of others, there are some stories that will interest us more because they are more likely to produce a report that will interest and inform *Watchdog* viewers. It is hard to lay down precise guidelines, but here are some of the things we look for:

▷ Is it the kind of experience that is guaranteed to make your friends listen? Or the kind of experience that other people will immediately sympathize with?
▷ Does your experience throw into question laws, regulations or trading practices?

▷ Are there likely to be other complainants as well as yourself?
▷ Does it strike you as new? A scam you have not heard about before or a dodge or rule that surprised you?
▷ Are there any obvious solutions or could it all be put down to just bad luck?

Obviously not every story featured meets all those conditions, but a surprising number do – and so they should. People expect to see interesting and important reports on national television and this applies as much to consumer reports as to the national news. Do not be put off contacting the programme if your experience does not seem to be all that remarkable, but ask yourself if you would be interested in watching a report based on what you have experienced if it had happened not to you, but to someone else. If the answer is a straightforward 'Yes', do get in touch. If you are uncertain, perhaps it might be best to contact your local paper or radio station or take action yourself. Best of luck.

ADDRESS LIST

ABTA - Association of
British Travel Agents,
55-57 Newman St,
London
W1P 4AH
Tel: 071 832 5620

Action for Victims of
Medical Accidents,
1 London Road,
Forest Hill,
London
SE23 3TP
Tel: 081 291 2793

Advertising Standards
Authority
2-16 Torrington Place,
London
WC1E 7HN
Tel: 071 580 5555

Air Transport Users
Council,
5th Floor,
Kingsway House,
103 Kingsway,
London
WC2B 6QX
Tel: 071 242 3882

ARCUK,
73 Hallam St,
London
W1N 6EE
Tel: 071 580 5861

Association of British
Insurers,
51 Gresham St,
London
EC2V 7HQ
Tel: 071 600 3333

Association of
Independent Tour
Operators (AITO)
133a St Margaret's Rd,
Twickenham,
Middlesex
TW1 1RG
Tel: 081 744 9280

Association of Personal
Injury Lawyers (APIL)
10a Byard Lane,
Nottingham
NG1 2GJ
Tel: 0602 580585

ATOL - Air Travel
Organiser's Licence,
CAA,
45-59 Kingsway,
London
WC2B 6TE
Tel: 071 832 5620

Banking Ombudsman,
70 Gray's Inn Road,
London
WC1X 8NB
Tel: 071 404 9944

Bankruptcy Search Room,
Insolvency Service HQ,
9th Floor,
Commercial Union
House,
22 Martineau Square,
Birmingham
B2 4UZ
Tel: 021 233 4808

Bar Council,
3 Bedford Row,
London
WC1R 4DB
Tel: 071 242 0082

British Association of
Removers,
3 Churchill Court,
58 Station Road,
North Harrow,
Middlesex
HA2 7SA
Tel: 081 861 3331

British Standards
Institution,
PO Box 375,
Milton Keynes,
Bucks
MK14 6LL
Tel: 0908 226888

British Veterinary
Association,
7 Mansfield St,
London
W1M OAT
Tel: 071 636 6541

Broadcasting Complaints
Commission,
35-37 Grosvenor Gardens,
London
SW1W OBS
Tel: 071 630 1966

Broadcasting Standards
Council,
5/8 The Sanctuary,
London
SW1P 3JS
Tel: 071 233 0544

Building Societies
Ombudsman,
Grosvenor Gardens
House,
35-37 Grosvenor Gardens,
London
SW1X 7AW
Tel: 071 931 0044

Central Rail Users
Committee,
8 Duncannon St,
London
WC2N 4JF

Centre for Dispute
Resolution,
100 Fetter Lane,
London
EC4A 1DD
Tel: 071 430 1852

Chartered Institute of
Arbitrators,
24 Angel Gate,
City Road,
London
EC1V 2RS
Tel: 071 837 4483

Commissioner for
Complaints (Northern
Ireland),
Freepost,
Belfast
BT1 6BR
Tel: 0232 233821

Commission for Racial
Equality,
10-12 Allington St,
London
SW1E 5EH
Tel: 071 828 7022

Companies House,
Crown Way,
Cardiff
CF4 3UZ
Tel: 0222 380801

Consumers
Association/*Which?*
magazine,
Freepost 2,
2 Marylebone Rd,
London
NW1 4DF
Tel: 071 486 5544

CORGI,
4 Elmwood,
Chineham Business Park,
Basingstoke,
Hants
RG24 8WG
Tel: 0256 708133

Criminal Injuries
Compensation Board,
Tay House,
300 Bath St,
Glasgow
G2 4GR
Tel: 041 331 2726

Data Protection Registrar,
Wycliffe House,
Water Lane,
Wilmslow
SK9 5AF

Department of the
Environment,
Drinking Water
Inspectorate,
Romney House,
43 Marsham St,
London
SW1P 3PY
Tel: 071 276 0900

Department of Transport -
Marine Safety Agency,
Spring Place,
105 Commercial Rd,
Southampton
SO1 OZD
Tel: 0703 329100

Department of Trade &
Industry,
Companies Investigation
Department,
Room 354,
123 Victoria St,
London
SW1E 6RB
Tel: 071 215 6525

Electrical Contractors
Association,
34 Palace Court,
London
W2 4HY
Tel: 071 229 1266

Equal Opportunities
Commission,
Overseas House,
Quay St,
Manchester
M3 3HN
Tel: 061 833 9244

Estate Agents
Ombudsman,
Beckett House,
4 Bridge Street,
Salisbury
SP1 2LX
Tel: 0722 333306

FIMBRA
(See Personal Investment
Authority)

Finance and Leasing
Association,
18 Upper Grosvenor St,
London
W1X 9PB
Tel: 071 491 2783

Gas Consumers Council,
15 Wilton Rd,
London
SW1V 1LT
Tel: 071 931 0977

General Consumer
Council for Northern
Ireland,
116 Hollywood Rd,
Belfast
BT4 1NY
Tel:0232 672488

General Dental Council,
37 Wimpole Street
London
W1M 8DQ
Tel: 071 486 2171

General Medical Council,
44 Hallam St,
London
W1N 6AE
Tel: 071 580 7642

Glass and Glazing
Federation,
44-48 Borough High St,
London
SE1 1XB
Tel: 071 403 7177

Health Service
Commissioner,
Church House,
Great Smith Street,
London
SW1P 3BW
Tel: 071 276 2035
Tel: 0222 394621 (Wales)
Tel: 031 225 7465
(Scotland)

HPI- Autodata,
PO Box 61,
Dolphin House,
New St,
Salisbury
SP1 2TB
Tel: 0722 422422

IATA - International Air
Transport Association,
Imperial House,
15/19 Kingsway,
London
WC2P 6UN
Tel: 071 497 1048

ICSTIS,
Freepost,
WC5468,
London
WC1V 7BR
Tel: 0800 500 212
(Freepost)

IMRO,
6 Appold St,
London
EC2A 2AA
Tel: 071 628 6022

Insurance Brokers
Registration Council,
15 St Helen's Place,
London
EC3A 6DS
Tel: 071 588 4387

Institute of Public Loss
Assessors,
14 Red Lion St,
Chesham,
Bucks
HP5 1HB
Tel: 0494 782342

Institute of Plumbing,
64 Station Lane,
Hornchurch,
Essex
RM12 6NB
Tel: 0708 472791

Institute of Structural
Engineers,
11 Upper Belgrave St,
London
SW1X 8BH
Tel: 071 235 4535

Insurance Ombudsman
Bureau,
135 Park St,
London
SE1 9EA
Tel: 071 928 7600

Investors Compensation
Scheme,
2-14 Bunhill Row,
London
EC1Y 8RA
Tel: 071 628 8820

LAUTRO
(See Personal Investment
Authority)

Law Society of England &
Wales,
113 Chancery Lane,
London
WC2A 1PL
Tel: 071 242 1222
Tel: 031 226 7411
(Scotland)
Tel: 0232 231614
(Northern Ireland)

Legal Services
Ombudsman,
22 Oxford Court
Oxford Street,
Manchester
M2 3WQ
Tel: 061 236 9532
Tel: 031 556 5574
(Scotland)

Local Government
Ombudsman,
21 Queen Anne's Gate,
London
SW1H 9BU
Tel: 071 915 3210
Tel: 031 229 4472
(Scotland)
Tel: 0656 661325 (Wales)

Mail Order Protection
Scheme (MOPS),
16 Took Court,
London
EC4A 1LB
Tel: 071 405 6806

Motor Insurers Bureau,
152 Silbury Boulevard,
Central Milton Keynes
MK9 1NB
Tel: 0908 240000

National Association of
Estate Agents,
21 Jury St,
Warwick
CV34 4EH
Tel: 0926 496800

National Inspection
Council for Electrical
Installation Contracting
(NICEC),
37 Albert Embankment,
London
SE1 7UJ
Tel: 071 735 1322

National House Building
Council (NHBC)
Buildmark House,
Chiltern Avenue
Amersham
Bucks
HP6 5AP
Tel: 0494 434477

National Rivers Authority,
Waterside Drive,
Aztec West,
Almondsbury
Bristol
BS12 4UD
Tel: 0454 624400

National Union of
Journalists,
314 Gray's Inn Rd,
London
WC1X 8VP
Tel: 071 278 7916

Occupational Pensions
Advisory Service,
11 Belgrave Rd,
London
SW1V 1RB
Tel: 071 233 8080

Occupational Pensions
Board,
Scottish Life House,
Archbold Terrace,
Jesmond,
Newcastle Upon Tyne
NE2 1ED
091 213 5000

OFFER,
Hagley House,
83-85 Hagley Road,
Edgbaston,
Birmingham
B16 8QG
Tel: 021 456 2100

Office of Fair Trading,
15-25 Bream's Buildings,
London
EC4A 1PR
Tel: 071 242 2858

OFGAS,
130 Wilton Road,
London
SW1V 1LQ
Tel: 071 828 0898

OFTEL,
50 Ludgate House,
London,
EC4M 7JJ
Tel: 071 634 8700

OFWAT,
7 Hill St,
Birmingham
B5 4UA
Tel: 021 625 1300

Optical Consumer
Complaints Service,
PO Box 2JX,
London
W1A2JX
Tel: 071 261 1017

Parliamentary
Commissioner for
Adminstration,
Church House,
Great Smith St,
London
SW1P 3BU
Tel: 071 276 3000

Patients Association,
18 Victoria Park Square,
London
E2 9PF
Tel: 071 981 5676

Pensions Ombudsman,
11 Belgrave Road,
London
SW1V 1RB
Tel: 071 834 9144

People's Dispensary for
Sick Animals,
Whitechapel Way,
Priorslee,
Telford
TF2 9PQ
Tel: 0952 290999

Personal Insurance
Arbitration Service
(PIAS),
24 Angel Gate,
City Road,
London,
EC1B 2RS
Tel: 071 837 4483

Personal Investment
Authority,
3-4 Royal Exchange
Buildings,
London
EC3V 3LL
Tel: 071 929 0072

Police Complaints
Authority,
10 Great George St,
London
SW1P 3AE
Tel: 071 273 6450

Press Complaints
Commission,
1 Salisbury Sq,
London
EC4Y 8AE
Tel: 071 353 1248

Registry of County Court
Judgments,
173-175 Cleveland St,
London
EC4Y 8AE
Tel: 071 380 0133

Royal College of
Veterinary Surgeons,
32 Belgrave St,
London
SW1X 8QP
Tel: 071 235 4971

Royal Institute of British
Architects,
66 Portland Place,
London
W1N 4AD
Tel: 071 580 5533

Royal Institute of
Chartered Surveyors,
12 Great George St,
London
SW1P 3AD
Tel: 071 222 7000

Securities and Investment
Board,
2-14 Bunhill Row,
London,
EC1Y 8RA
Tel: 071 638 1240

Solicitors Complaints
Bureau,
Victoria Court,
8 Dormer Place,
Leamington Spa,
CV32 5AE
Tel: 0926 820082

Solicitors Indemnity Fund,
100 St John St,
London
EC1M 4EH
Tel: 071 566 6000

Textile Services
Association,
7 Churchill Court,
58 Station Road,
North Harrow,
Middlesex
HA2 7SA
Tel: 081 863 7755

Timeshare Council,
23 Buckingham Gate,
London
SW1E 6LB
Tel: 071 821 8845

INDEX